# A Matter of Choice

## 25 People Who Transformed Their Lives

edited by

Joan Chatfield-Taylor

SEAL PRESS

# A Matter of Choice
25 People Who Transformed Their Lives

Published by
Seal Press
An Imprint of Avalon Publishing Group, Inc.
1400 65th Street, Suite 250
Emeryville, CA 94608

Library of Congress Cataloging-in-Publication Data
Matter of choice: 25 people who transformed their lives / [edited] by
Joan Chatfield-Taylor.
   p. cm.
ISBN 1-58005-118-9
   1. Change (Psychology)–Case studies. 2. Life change events–Psychological aspects–
Case studies. I. Chatfield-Taylor, Joan.

BF637.C4M365 2004
155.2'4–dc22
                        2004019804
9 8 7 6 5 4 3 2 1

Cover Design: Amber Pirker and Domini Dragoone
Interior Design: Susan Pinkerton
Printed in the United States of America by Malloy
Distributed by Publishers Group West

*For Luc, a most welcome change*

# Table of Contents

# Introduction

## Joan Chatfield-Taylor

When I announced to my friends and acquaintances that I was going to move to Paris for six months, their first question was, "Why?"

Inwardly, I gasped. Why would I—or anyone else, for that matter—*not* move to Paris? Outwardly, I was polite. I knew that they were expecting specific answers. "I'm going to Paris to master the subjunctive." "I'm going to Paris to eat all the cheeses that General de Gaulle referred to in his famous statement about the difficulty of governing a country with 246 *fromages*." "I'm going to Paris to spend every afternoon in the Louvre."

✦ ✦ ✦ ✦ ✦

In truth, I was going to Paris to prove that I still could. To prove that I was still flexible enough to create a new life for myself. I had discovered, after dozens of visits to the French capital, that even a stay of two months was not long enough to force me to make new friends, to live on another schedule, or to get to know the delightful cheesemonger and the crabby watch-repair lady of my chosen neighborhood. To put it in the simplest terms, in two months you can get away with not having your hair cut. However, if you stay for six, you'll have to start asking around for a skilled hand with the scissors—and then you will finally have time to feel at home with the stylish Frenchwomen, Yorkies in arm, who frequent your new salon.

In San Francisco, where I have lived most of my life, I am surrounded by friends I have known for fifty years. I have expectations of them, and they have expectations of me. We don't surprise each other very often. I do meet new people, because San Francisco is a city that attracts people from all over the world, but it's usually in the context of familiar friends and acquaintances. One of the reasons I went to Paris was to see how I measured up in the eyes of strangers, and to see if I could make the kinds of social efforts that I was too shy or too lazy to make back home.

✦ ✦ ✦ ✦ ✦

I went to Paris because I believe in change, as some people believe in yoga, vegan diets, or faith healing. I believe that change keeps people alive, keeps the synapses firing, makes us grow. Maybe, with my thirst for new experiences, I have a harmless form of Adult Attention Deficit Disorder. On the other hand, a wise therapist once said to me, "Your flexibility is what has enabled you to survive some of the things that have happened to you." So I went to Paris to reinforce my ability to bend rather than break.

In Paris, I had taken a vow to myself: Whenever someone suggested that I try something new, I would say yes. Whatever I was curious about, I would explore. When a new idea popped into my head, I would consider it. As a result, I visited a *hammam*, ate pig's ears and a dozen unfamiliar blue cheeses, went to avant-garde theatrical performances, and visited a half-sister I had met only once in my life.

When I came home I was a braver and more independent person. I felt more resilient, and I cared less about what other people thought of me. And I began to wonder whether other people had had similar experiences and had felt the same way about their life changes, which is how the idea for this book came about. As I planned the anthology, I worried a little that I would be inundated with stories of people making changes in their work life, discovering that they should be selling blodgets instead of widgets, or teaching middle schoolers rather than kindergarteners. There's no doubt that professional transformation is often difficult, and certainly emotional, but I was interested in other kinds of changes as well.

I sent out the request for submissions, mainly over the wondrous Internet, and then I fretted until the deadline approached and the mailman began arriving with envelopes from all over the world. I need not have worried that the essays would be echoes of each other. Every submission, whether from Mumbai or Memphis, was an adventure in itself, and I found myself so curious about other people's lives that I was opening the envelopes downstairs by the mailbox so that I could read them faster.

The authors ranged in age from twenty to eighty, and their stories were fantastically diverse. What they had in common was an awareness of the dramatic, transforming moments in their lives, when suddenly nothing was the same as before. In some cases, they chose change—in others, change was thrust upon them. Sometimes it seemed to come easily, the transformation taking place practically overnight. For others, change was unwelcome and at first misunderstood, requiring years of struggle and bitterness before the wisdom of the transformation finally revealed itself. In all cases, though, there was an element of choice. These writers had come to terms with their transformative experiences and used them to enrich their lives. These essays are full of inspiring examples of how to deal with life's surprises—be it a poisonous snake hissing above the sink, the loss of a job and an identity, a diagnosis of cancer, or a fall from the sky—and of the surprising rebirth that can come from such seeming tragedies. The stories are brave, candid, and often funny.

If I ever find myself on the Trans-Siberian Railway, with days between Moscow and Mongolia, I would hope to discover one of these writers, or someone like them, sharing my compartment. I suspect that these writers wouldn't whine about the luke-warm tea or the monotonous scenery. They would smile, and we would talk about life long into the night.

# Road Trip

## Claudia Rowe

I was changing my life, leaving everyone I had ever known on the East Coast and flinging myself across the country because I wanted to try something new. A road trip, solo, seemed a suitably adventurous way to get there—more mind-expanding than flying and cheaper than shipping my belongings, I told skeptical friends.

Actually, I was dazzled by the romance of a cross-country drive. I would sail into scarlet sunsets through seas of yellow prairies. I pictured myself sitting at Western bars, talking to cowboys.

I had ideas about the Great Plains and Small Town Americana, and I had spent fifteen years as a journalist, presenting other people's freakish, far-flung stories to the wider world. Nonetheless, I had virtually no experience of life beyond the Hudson River. Most recently, I'd been holed up in a cottage in the Catskills, scraping by as a freelance writer. Any excuse to shatter my quiet routine would have looked good, and after one summer afternoon spent ogling purple cowboy boots and the offerings at a women's sex shop in Seattle, I was sold.

The thought of moving west had gnawed at me for the better part of a decade, ever since a brief camping trip with a tense boyfriend on the Olympic Peninsula. Our trip had metastasized into a five-year relationship that I staggered out of at thirty-five, exhausted and worn, as though I'd been walking around dead for half a decade. But I still saw snow-capped mountains in my mind.

Two years to the day of the breakup, I was packing my Volkswagen, getting ready to leave the tight little valleys of the East. People asked what I planned to do in Seattle and I could not answer. I had no clear idea—except that everything would be new.

Before setting off, however, I had to plan my route. The South suggested Gothic oddity and ghostly deserts. Very dramatic. Very Thelma-and-Louise. But I had never spent more than four hours in one go behind the wheel, and traveling that way I would have to cover three states at a single clip to make decent time. A northern path—from New York to Chicago, into the midwestern Plains and across the Rockies—seemed the saner choice.

Only in cyberspace did I betray my misgivings.

"Are there things a woman driving alone should know?" I asked the faceless browsers at roadtripamerica.com. "Places to avoid, indispensable items to bring, reasons to turn back?"

"All you need is excitement," the webmaster replied.

"Pepper spray," said a friend. "At those truck stops, you've got to have pepper spray."

I was determined that my trip should cost as close to nothing as possible—I had minimal savings and only vague half-leads for work on the other end—so my itinerary was based largely on the locations of people who might put me up along the way. This made Pittsburgh my first stop, and I planned to set out from Saugerties, New York, early on a sunny September morning. But road trips never begin on time—not for rock bands or families, and certainly not for freelance writers—so it was three 3 P.M. by the time my tires touched the New York State Thruway.

Most travel manuals insist you leave the interstate to find what's left of American quirk, but on that first afternoon, even the superhighways seemed profound. I gazed at the green valleys lining I-80, thrilled by the limitless, gray asphalt unfurling before my windshield. In the rearview mirror I scanned my life, piled neatly in the back seat: a book-in-progress and fifty pounds of attendant notes; suede jackets for every occasion; magazines I'd loved fifteen years ago and others I still planned to read; a box of cassette tapes from the 1980s, and an address book filled with the names of ex-friends. By the time I got to Pennsylvania, the rush of freedom I felt had me laughing like a madwoman.

My greatest concern about the trip had been road hypnosis, the fear that I would be lulled into a lonely sleep at the wheel. But it never happened. People kept calling on my new cell phone, rousing me from dreamy reverie.

"Where are you now?" a former boyfriend asked from his desk in Manhattan. "What are you seeing?"

I was in Indiana at that moment, racing past a tractor-trailer filled with mangy cattle who stared at me on their way to slaughter, but I told him instead about biblical sunsets and the open road. During those first few days, I got tired after four or five hours behind the wheel and tried to chat with gas station clerks wherever I could, hoping that folksy inspiration might propel me onward. At the Ernie Pyle rest stop outside South Bend, Indiana, a freckle-faced cashier was so flummoxed by these attempts at conversation that he rang up my purchases twice.

It took three days to push through Pennsylvania, Ohio, Indiana, Illinois, and Wisconsin, and I spent much of that time pondering the tidy farmhouses dotting my route. Any of them could have starred on an "America-the-Beautiful" calendar, and I wondered what it felt like to live inside a picture postcard by the side of a superhighway. I wondered if midwesterners, so famously circumspect, had come to be that way because they felt so exposed.

Heartland uniformity shattered in Spring Green, Wisconsin, about forty-five miles west of Madison, where I stopped to see Alex Jordan's House on the Rock, the one roadside attraction I'd planned to visit. Mr. Jordan, a medical-school dropout turned compulsive hoarder, built his sprawling monstrosity of a home upon a chimney rock as a nose-thumbing to Frank Lloyd Wright, who had once snubbed him. Then he filled his grudge-fantasia with mechanical orchestras, piles of jewels, suits of armor, cuckoo clocks, sea monsters, and antique telephones. I arrived at 4:40 P.M. on a Friday to hear from the staff that it takes five hours to properly absorb "The House," so I tore through Jordan's private dream world like one chased by demons.

"All by yourself?" a guard whispered in the noisy darkness.

"You're doing very well," another voice said as I raced past an enormous calliope.

Stone hallways hung with yellow lanterns led to caverns housing miniature circuses and village street dioramas; all of it funneling me toward a huge, clanging carousel where 239 serpents, mermaids, and satyrs spun around and around. Naked, winged mannequins floated from the ceiling. Life-sized elephants mounted each other in a pyramid. It felt like wandering through a child's nightmare, or what we may find when Michael Jackson dies.

Afterward, I was starved and felt inexplicably dirty. Greenspirit Farm, a mile down the road, beckoned. I decided to buy a bag of apples for dinner and eat them all the way into Minnesota. An old man with a thick beard sat on a bench outside, whittling.

"When'd you leave New York?" he said, barely glancing up.

"Four days ago."

"Where you headed?"

"Seattle," I said. "Do you have any apples?"

"I used to live in New York!" a younger man called out, walking toward me from the vegetable barn, a blond baby attached to his hip. "Crown Heights. What street did you live on?"

Greenspirit Farm had no apples, just two farmers who wanted to talk about Woody Allen and Coney Island as the sun sank into the valley behind them. They said they'd never heard of a New Yorker leaving the city. I told them I was happy to be their first.

Dark hills framed the rest of my drive along bucolic Route 18, and in the twilight I wanted to shout out at their beauty. Then I passed a sex shop outside Rochester, Minnesota, where a fifty-foot neon sign beamed messages toward the highway— "Welcome sinners, we accept checks!"

I stayed as often as possible with friends and friends-of-friends receptive to the idea of a midlife traveler making a leap. But my presence had disquieting effects. Each morning my host or her spouse would rise early, commandeer me at the breakfast table, and whisper choked-out dreams. "All of us are living through you," said a medievalist who put me up in Chicago.

When I craved anonymity, there was Motel 6. The franchise is supposedly aimed at road-trippers who value cleanliness and hot showers, but its cement-block walls and cigarette-scented lobbies occasionally suggested the kind of place where bad things might happen to naive girls. It was always a teenage boy with sullen eyes who buzzed me in to the front office. In Minnesota, he was flinging a pink rubber ball against the wall as I pulled out my wallet.

"I've made a reservation," I said.

Throw. Thump. Catch. Somewhere, a television murmured.

"Just you, is it?" the boy said, keeping his eyes averted.

I slept poorly many nights, memories thronging my mind. Everyone I had ever known came back to haunt me in the dark—old friends who had failed me, teachers who'd inflicted childhood humiliations. But the road washes away every indignity. You speed forward into endless horizon, and the past no longer matters. By the time I hit the waving fields of South Dakota, I was free. Doing ninety across the top of Montana, I took off my shirt and drove half-naked.

My meal plan consisted of trail mix, water, and fruit; I figured I'd arrive on the West Coast cleansed and thin. But in Glasgow, Montana, a friend-of-a-friend who worked for the State Department of Fish and Wildlife pushed a shiny breast of pheasant toward me—bagged and smoked by his hunting buddy—and suggested I make a sandwich for lunch.

"Watch out for birdshot," he said, as I, a vegetarian for twenty-one years, hacked at the meat and smushed it between two slices of brown bread spread with horseradish.

Six hours later, I pulled the sandwich from my cooler, bit into it, and reeled. I could taste alder chips and wood smoke, the slow, deliberate preparation—and something else, something hard and small like a peppercorn. It ricocheted against my teeth and I spat it into my coffee cup with a tinny ping. Birdshot. Two Indians in cowboy hats stared at me as I zoomed past their pickup truck, heading for the mountains.

Several people had spoken reverently about Going-to-the-Sun highway, a fifty-mile stretch of road cutting across the high peaks of Glacier National Park. My bird-hunting hosts in Glasgow had insisted I drive it. But it was late afternoon, and I'd already had one flat. Thoughts of the previous night spent racing through darkness, haphazardly slaughtering various small animals that crossed my path, would not fade. And really, how breathtaking could a landscape be?

"On your way to college?" asked an aging trucker at the gas station in Shelby, Montana, eyeing my license plates and the clothes crammed roof-high inside my car.

I shook my head and laughed. College had been almost twenty years ago.

"Well, I graduated in 1996!" he crowed. "Graduated high school in 1959!"

In between, he'd supported a wife and four children by driving every road in the country. He reeled off several I might take from our gas station to Seattle.

"I was thinking, actually, of Going-to-the-Sun," I said. "Is it worth it?"

"Beautiful," said the trucker's wife, poking her head out from his rig.

"Go for it!'" he added, with a goofy thumbs-up.

I set out along a road lined with golden aspens and studied

the faces of every driver headed toward me. I was looking for signs of strain, but saw only beatific smiles. I crept up forty-degree inclines, passed a glittering, glacial lake, and pulled over to touch rainbow droplets from a roaring waterfall. At the summit, I sat with two leathery bikers, staring across a misty canyon at the tips of evergreens poking from impossible precipices. Above us, the dark peaks seemed to be breathing.

The last leg of my journey followed the craterous Columbia River Gorge to the Oregon Coast. I wanted one long look at the Pacific before turning north toward my new life. On that subject, my mind was still a blank, bare as the windswept rocks lining my drive. Strangely, this inspired a surge of confidence. Nine days before, I'd stood in a friend's living room, sobbing with fear at what might come. Fear of failure, of girlishness, buffoonery, fragility. Fear, in truth, of possibility. Now the unknown looked different. It seemed to be waving me on. I'd covered 3,800 zigzagging miles and I'd seen how much farther I could go.

It was pouring rain when I got to Oswald State Park in Manzanita, Oregon, but I sloshed down a muddy path that meandered to the sea and tromped across the sand. Sky and ocean blended into a silvery sheet and the sound of water was everywhere, trickling down the ravine, crashing onto the sea stacks, drumming from the sky.

In a grove of tall pines, a lone guitarist sat under a rickety shelter, strumming and eating oysters. He sang folk songs and offered to open a few Kumomotos for me. I tasted the brine, breathed the salt air, and tallied the last week and a half: I'd covered eleven states on thirteen tanks of gas and twenty-one large cups of coffee. I'd aged nine days but felt younger than I had in years. Two elderly women wandered up and I convinced them to try raw oysters for the first time.

My face was soaking wet, and I was changed.

*intrepid*

7

# Machete Lessons

## Bonnie Lee Black

Of all my Peace Corps stories, my grandson Thomas and his fourth-grade classmates liked the one about the snake in my kitchen most. Thomas has a deep appreciation and respect for snakes. Among his many pets is a five-foot-long orange-and-red corn snake named Arnold, who lives in a large covered tank in his bedroom. One day Arnold went missing. He was found a few days later, curled up like a garden hose, at the bottom of the laundry hamper, sound asleep. Harmless as a kitten.

Not so, the snake in my kitchen. That one was a green mamba, one of the most venomous snakes in sub-Saharan Africa. Coming face to face with it, alone in a faraway house on a hill, was a turning point in my life—and made me a dragon-slayer in my grandson's eyes. There I was, a newly posted, fifty-one-year-old Peace Corps volunteer, standing at the kitchen sink in my rented cement-block house in the middle of the rain forest of Gabon, in central Africa. Dripping with perspiration from the hundred-plus-degree heat and humidity, I was washing the morning's dishes as I would anywhere in the world. Then, suddenly, out of the corner of my eye, I noticed something at eye level that was long and thin and pale green, wiggling.

Without looking up, I thought, *Clothesline? No, the cord I picked up the other day in town when I bought these dishes was white, not green*. I washed and rinsed my coffee mug, set it in the dish drainer, and, at last, lifted my head. The young green mamba was no more than two feet away from my face.

*Ohmygod, ohmygod*, I said aloud to myself. Then, instinctively, I splashed the snake with dishwater—a foolish move indeed.

Whereas the snake may have been merely uncomfortable before—stuck somehow in the window's screening—now it was angry at me. I could literally see the anger in its eyes. I'd obviously forgotten the warning: Whatever you do, don't make a snake angry. Africans say that snakes don't like to feel trapped or cornered or, God forbid, attacked. They're all right as long as they're free to slither away. You go your way, they go theirs; no problem. It's when they feel threatened that you're in danger.

This snake had somehow gotten caught in an undetected tear in the newly installed screening over my kitchen window—screening designed to keep malaria-carrying mosquitoes and countless other equatorial insects out, and a sense of much-needed security in—and he was now writhing in anger. Clearly, I was in danger.

My mind raced; my body froze. My hands, dripping with soapsuds, levitated above the dishpan. Should I scream? *Why bother?* No one would hear me. In my studio apartment in New York City, neighbors could hear each other sneeze during the day and snore at night; but here in the African rain forest, my new neighbors were either too far away or out at midday. The house stood alone at the top of a hill, surrounded by thick, muffling vegetation. And besides, I'd heard that the locals considered the long-abandoned house I'd rented *maudite*—cursed, haunted. They kept their distance. I was utterly alone.

Should I run? *Where to?* This house was my home now, for the duration of my two-year service, and I had no intention of relinquishing it to deadly intruders, even if they considered themselves the rightful tenants. I stood my ground. The snake hissed at me hideously, its eyes bulging. I knew I had to do something. "It's you or me, buddy," I said, affecting my best tough-girl New York accent. I knew if the snake bit me, there'd be no Poison Control hotline to call for guidance—I didn't even have a phone. I dashed to the kitchen cupboard where I kept my machete.

Luckily, I'd invested in my two-foot-long, razor-sharp machete just a few days before. Machetes, I'd observed, are the all-purpose tool in Gabon. Men carry them when they go hunting in the forest. Women carry them into the fields when they harvest their crops. Kids carry them to school to help with the yard work there. Once I saw a crowd of schoolchildren running down the hill, alarmingly in my direction, waving their machetes in fun on their way home. I immediately realized, *I should get one of those, too.*

Having spent ten years as a caterer in New York—and having become so burnt out that I would have joined the Foreign Legion if the Peace Corps didn't exist, just to have a chance at a new life—I knew very well how to wield a twelve-inch chef's knife. But this machete was twice as long, at least twice as wide, and many times heavier than my favorite Henckels. I had to lift the machete with both hands to swing at the snake. I came down on its head like a guillotine. It must have been the adrenaline, because I kept whacking until there were pieces of snake, like chopped-up sausage, all over my kitchen floor.

When there was no more snake to chop, I stopped, bent down, and studied the bloody mess. This was the first time I'd ever killed anything bigger than a fly—something with a face—a silenced, wide-open mouth, eyes.

If Albert Schweitzer—doctor, humanitarian, and theologian, who was the first man to bring Western medicine to Gabon and believed it wrong to kill even a fly—had been in the room, I might have felt ashamed of what I'd just done. But he was not, and frankly, I felt relieved, empowered—reborn. The Peace Corps promises adventure, and I was getting it.

The next day, as I walked in the midday heat from the top of my hill to the center of town, I had to tell some locals what had happened. Africans, I had discovered even in the short time since my posting, are impressively strong and courageous human beings. They have to be, to withstand the crushing physical obstacles they encounter every day of their lives: debilitating weather, unremitting insects, ever-present bacteria, intestinal worms, unspeakable germs. Those who make it past five years of age are sturdy specimens indeed.

My job as a health volunteer—the first one sent to this small town of tiny mud-wattle houses with outdoor cook fires—involved teaching young mothers how to keep their babies alive past the age of five. I, a thin-skinned white woman, a grand-mother far from home, soon realized that they had far more to teach me.

To keep snakes away, one shopkeeper counseled me, you should cut all the grass around your house, then pour gasoline all around it. Snakes hide in grass, and they hate the smell of gasoline. I crossed the dusty main road and approached the town's only gas station to buy a *bidon* of petrol to carry up the hill to my house.

"I killed a snake yesterday," I told the burly owner in my still-feeble French. He listened silently, nodding his head, his strong black arms crossed at his massive chest.

"In my kitchen. With my machete. All by myself . . ."

The man looked me up and down. As the town's only Peace Corps volunteer, living at the socioeconomic level of the townsfolk—without a car, without a servant, without any money to speak of—I was something of a curiosity. White people are assumed to be rich, and I didn't fit the air-conditioned profile. What that gas station owner saw was a thin, middle-aged woman, short blond hair gone wild with the humidity, T-shirt stuck to her chest from perspiration, well-worn mis-sionary-style skirt modestly drooping to her ankles, sensible walking sandals (so sensible that no female French expat would be caught dead in them). I was getting used to being stared at and studied.

But when this man finally spoke to me, he said something that struck me as the kindest compliment a strange newcomer could possibly have received. *"Vraiment,"* he said, still nodding his head, "you are an African now."

Carrying the heavy *bidon* the mile up the hill, I felt tall and strong, and proud.

# Making a Soldier, Molding a Sculptor

## Ken Hruby

It was a great start to an art career. "Mustering Out," my first solo sculpture show, was described by the *Boston Globe*'s art critic as "poignant and provocative . . . neither rancorous nor therapeutic . . . far more effective than the most blaring protest art." The review was exactly the sort of response I had hoped for, and since the show was the culmination of five years of study of the visual arts, it served as a demarcation point in my transformation from soldier to sculptor. It was now official; I was an "erstwhile combat soldier, now an artist."

This transition had actually been easier than the one that had molded an officer and a gentleman out of a strapping adolescent a quarter of a century earlier. That had taken four years, with the most intense pressure applied during "Beast Barracks"—two months of basic training designed to weed out those who were not suited to "close with and destroy the enemy," the mission of the infantry soldier. We had to pass this extended physical and psychological stress test before we could get on with the academic challenges of the next four years at West Point.

They trained us in the most primal ways to kill the enemy. Kill or be killed, they told us. My own survival then as a cadet and, perhaps, later in combat depended on how well I learned my lessons, the techniques and maneuvers. The basic combat-training moves were embedded in my muscles so that the drill could be conjured up, without misstep, decades after it had been hammered home. Repetition was key. Caked with sweat and sawdust and with well-honed bayonets fixed to our rifles, we ran through the prescribed course to charge, thrust, parry, lunge, recover, slash, and lunge again at sandbag surrogates. With grunts and growls we cheered each other on, convinced that we would be invincible on the battlefield when the call came to "fix bayonets." After emotionally insulating myself from the brutality of the drill's ultimate intent, and physically transcending the pain, I found that it actually felt good to run the course and run it well; there was a real beauty to the movements when the steps and the rhythm were done right. The steps were the key to a smooth execution; done correctly, the upper body followed the feet in a gracefully coordinated flow of motion.

A quarter of a century later, I wanted to create rather than destroy.

From the moment I stepped through the double red doors of the School of the Museum of Fine Arts in Boston, I knew that I was entering the antithesis of military life. The paucity of structure, the vague program objectives, and the permissive aura were all counter to my engineering training. I was a student again, no longer a leader or a supervisor, just one of a class of curious, eager newcomers, most of them younger than my children. My classmates devoted a lot of energy to looking like artists. The olive drab fatigues and rank insignia were replaced by another uniform, of sorts—blue and purple hair and black clothing, accented by mostly visible tattoos and piercings.

I had learned to weld years earlier, while posted in central Texas, and was a competent carpenter and mechanic, so I had come to this new world of art school with journeyman skills in addition to a lot of preconceptions about art. My young classmates brought neither the skills nor the baggage to class. They

were open vessels eager to be filled. They were creative, accepting, experimental, and nonjudgmental about contemporary art. I
was not. Initially baffled, continually intrigued, and ultimately
naturalized in this new world, I would return from school trips to
New York unable to sleep for two or three nights, my head spinning with imagery I had seen in the galleries and museums of
SoHo or TriBeCa. Military and art training did have one thing
in common, at least for a mature student: a sense of urgency. So
much to learn, so little time.

My training in the Army put an emphasis on observation. I
was taught how to observe and report what I saw. The difference
between learning to observe in the Army and learning to see in
art school was that, in the field, you reported what you observed
to your superiors; in art you internalized it, stowing it in your personal bank of visual references. One of the art school axioms was
"God is in the details," and with that counsel, I began to look at
things with a new and more critical eye. I inspected everything:
sculpture, paintings, architecture, appliances, tools, furniture. I
examined how they were put together, how the transitions
between materials were handled, how things worked physically
and conceptually together; I noted what did and what did not
work visually. This was the basic training of art school.

As our technical skills developed, it became a matter of
personal choice what we chose to say in this new visual language.
Initially, I chose to speak in the dialect of abstraction—with a
heavy welded-steel accent. It was safe ground for me. What mattered in my dialogue with the viewer were formal issues: balance,
contrast, rhythm, surface texture. It was a luxury to focus on the
pure pleasure of forming, forging, cutting, and joining steel into
objects that left the viewer in wonder. I would rush each day to
the school welding shop and let the process swallow me up. On
occasion I would have a vague idea of what I wanted to create,
but normally I simply indulged my fantasies in three-dimensional
form and let the muses guide me toward visual poetry. I had
learned the visual scales well enough not only to play the tune,

but to improvise. For a long time, I worked without hidden meanings or content: It was pure escape from the news of the day and the memories of my former career. In the studio I frequently experienced a form of transcendence that lifted me away from the heat of the forge, above my tired feet and apart from my thirst and hunger, in the artist's version of a jogger's high.

✦ ✦ ✦ ✦ ✦

Then I went to see Oliver Stone's *Platoon*.

Though I later felt it was a flawed film, that first viewing had a profound effect on me. It was the first of the Vietnam War films that was remotely close to my experiences there. My tour involved many more shades of gray and little of the black and white that Stone's protagonists projected in their portrayal of the forces of good and evil, but the movie spoke to some of my emotional conflicts and served as a catharsis. Suddenly I found myself reexamining the experiences of Vietnam and Korea, my whole twenty-one-year career in the infantry and, further, the tenuous relationship between soldier and society. That reexamination gave me a voice that had been repressed for decades and was now ready to be expressed in a newfound vocabulary.

During the next eight months, the work spilled out of my studio. It covered the floors and the walls. I completed nearly two dozen pieces between the time I saw *Platoon* and the school's annual Traveling Scholar's Exhibition and Competition. In place of abstraction were strong statements about the military experience that was then, and still is, so exotic and arcane to many civilians. I transformed familiar icons of the military into ironic, unexpected statements about the military experience.

The first piece was a transformation of dog tags. We always wore them when we were at risk—in combat, during field exercises, and while flying in—or jumping from—military aircraft. My daughter would hide them from me, hoping that without them, I would not have to deploy with my airborne unit when the alert call came in the middle of the night. The tags came to represent the burden we had to carry, the personal risk, the constant disruption of family life, and the months and years of separation. They came in pairs: one hung from a long ball chain around the neck; the other hung from a smaller chain, just big enough to encircle the big toe, dangling from the same necklace. The transformation came by changing the scale from one inch in length to ten inches and fabricating them out of half-inch steel stock, etched with my personal data. They weighed six pounds each and had a commanding presence.

Ideas for work came from my memories, which remained hidden just beneath the surface of consciousness like mines laid in a rice paddy, ready to explode and echo across the decades when the right pressure was applied. Sometimes a sound tripped them, occasionally a word, usually a smell.

I began to look back at the full breadth of my military experiences with a new eye and saw in them a series of ironies that I wanted to explore in sculptural format. As I looked back at the basic training we had gone through at West Point, I remembered that, in addition to bayonet and rifle-marksmanship training, we were given ballroom dance lessons.

It's hard to believe, even now, that dance lessons were integrated into our training schedule as we struggled to shed our civilian skins and don the gray of new cadets. Imported up the Hudson River from New York City, instructors from the Arthur Murray Dance Studio came to teach us the fine art of ballroom dancing. The instructors were usually attractive young women, and my most vivid recollection is not of how fine they looked but of how good they smelled. Twenty years before the admission of women as cadets, we men had to dance with each other during these lessons, taking turns at leading. "Effective leaders must first learn to follow," we were often told, but this put a new twist on that saying. Our steps and turns, our skips and twirls, were performed under the stern stares of famous graduates and former dancers, all heroes for one reason or another, all frozen in bronze bas-reliefs hanging on every wall in Cullem Hall, the very formal setting for our lessons. When our lessons in social graces and civility were completed for the day, we marched, double time, back to the barracks to change into fatigues for bayonet drill. As a class we learned—often in the same steamy afternoon—the vertical butt-stroke series and the tango; the high-port cross-over and the cha-cha-cha. Brutality and civility. We were expected to show equal finesse in both arenas.

Interestingly enough, bayonet drill and dance lessons, the last resort in combat and the first skirmish in the battle of the sexes, use the same circular choreographic notation. The irony escaped us at the time. We new cadets were too close to the events to look back at our footprints with any objectivity. But during that sultry eight-week period of "Beast Barracks" in 1957, there were imprinted within us forever the feet of a dancer and the hands of a fighter, both more or less under control.

*Fix Bayonets, Let's Dance* was a sculpture installation that came directly out of this strange juxtaposition. I fabricated a circle of shoe and boot prints that were made of parquet squares and cement globs. In the parquet I carved the precise male dance notations of a waltz and in the muddy cement I pressed boot prints in the step notation for the vertical butt-stroke series. The steps melded into each other. Above the circle of steps I suspended two photographs, back-to-back, that had appeared in *Life* magazine just after the basic training had been completed: One showed two cadets dancing together in an exaggerated state of mock ecstasy, the other a growling classmate fiercely attacking the bayonet course. The photographs spun slowly as the viewer imagined the dancer and fighter carefully stepping through his marks in unending counterclockwise circles and continuous transformations between the two roles.

✦ ✦ ✦ ✦ ✦

My wars are behind me now—so far as I know. I now look to the muses and not to Mars for inspiration. I spent twenty-one years as an officer and have spent twenty as an artist; details of the combat experiences fade as the years pass. I never did, and do not now, hold romantic notions about going off to war; it was mostly dull and boring, with interminable periods of waiting and inactivity, accented by brief flashes of terror and frantic action. Making art has much the same cycle. It involves a lot of research, experimentation, documentation, and administration; the actual fabrication is normally brief and frantic.

✦ ✦ ✦ ✦ ✦

I have found that what lasts for a lifetime is the strong stuff of basic training. I was returned to "jump status" as a paratrooper fourteen years after I finished basic qualifying airborne training. It was not the same body that had been so finely tuned at age twenty-two, but when the "go" light flashed green at the exit door of the C123 troop-transport plane and the jump master tapped me on the butt, I leaped into the slipstream without a second thought; the body knew exactly what to do and it did it perfectly. When I attempted to translate the bizarre experience of dance lessons and bayonet drill into the *Fix Bayonets, Let's Dance* installation, the same intense training allowed me to waltz and stomp around my studio to get the steps right, with a broomstick alternating as partner and weapon. It did not take long before I had retraced the three-quarter step and twirl. The horizontal butt-stroke series took longer. Happily, I have had more occasions for dancing than for fighting since the steps were burned into my soul.

# Fighting for Breath

## Melissa Peterson

Going to South Carolina turned out to be harder than I could ever have imagined. When I explained my plan to the woman working the desk at the Mason County Corrections Office, she raised her eyebrows.

"They're not going to let you do that," she said, taking off her eyeglasses. "You're wasting your time. You are a violent criminal, you know." She smiled, clearly taking pleasure in bursting my bubble. As I faced her, I tried to think of a reason why someone would want to work at a corrections office in the first place. It wasn't a place for minor criminals; it was a place where rapists and murderers lingered and eyed me in the waiting room. I knew that I didn't look like a good person on paper. I had been caught stealing and had hit a security guard while trying to escape. But I knew I was better than that; I just had to prove it.

I made an appointment with my corrections officer. He was a young man who had formerly been a cop and had a deep and chilling voice. The first time I went in to see him, I caught him checking out my breasts. The next time I wore a short skirt and knee-high black leather boots, and attempted to use my blue eyes and shapely hips to my advantage. I explained to him that I had been accepted to participate in a ten-month national service program. I would travel around the southern United States with a group of kids my age cutting trails in state parks and volunteering with Habitat for Humanity. If I was allowed to go to South Carolina, I would receive money for college—and a way out of the trap of my hometown. The problem was, I was still on probation in Washington State, and I wasn't allowed to leave.

"I looked into transferring your records to South Carolina," he said, leaning back heavily in his chair. "Since you'll be traveling a lot, and you will not always know what state you are going to be in, I don't think that's going to work." He offered instead to petition the courts to cancel my probation at the end of September. "Just get your community service hours done," he ordered.

That short sentence had a long stream of consequences for me. It meant that I had to complete a year's worth of community service in less than three months. I went home and took out the shirt I had been arrested in. I smelled the perfume I had been wearing and fingered the dried blood. I thought of how crazy the air had felt that night. I arose with scarred confidence and shaking hands.

I did my community service time at Gwinwood, a Christian Bible camp that was run by a couple. Named after Gwin Hicks, a man who used to own Hicks Lake and all the land surrounding it, the camp was later turned into a male retreat where rich white men could smoke cigars and remember what it was like to be manly. My work wasn't stressful, mostly involving dirty toilets and overflowing garbage cans. I soon stopped taking a CD player and headphones there because I enjoyed the quiet time for reflection, as my life otherwise stormed with stressful events. In addition to my community service, I was going to school full-time and working part-time. My weekends and evenings disappeared as I got used to ten- and twelve-hour days.

To keep myself going, I thought of the warm southern breezes and peaceful traveling that would be my reward. I wanted to set myself free. I was finished with 8 P.M. curfews and random drug tests. I didn't want to meet with my corrections officer and watch him take notes about me in his little book. I didn't want to have to remember that I had lost my full-time job for something stupid I did when I was drunk or that I had given my lawyer all the money I had saved up for college. I didn't want to watch my friends trafficking stolen AK-47s for drug money, or not sleeping due to methamphetamine-induced paranoia and bloodshed. I wanted to meet people who didn't know what track marks and meth burns looked like. I whispered hopeful words after I brushed my teeth every morning. I didn't reply to the messages on my answering machine from old friends. I no longer had time to drink beer.

One Saturday afternoon while scrubbing floors at Gwinwood, I was overwhelmed with a sense of failure. To compose myself, I smoked a cheap cigarette and watched the sun glistening on the lake. People who had more money than I ever would were water-skiing behind brightly colored boats. The wakes made small ripples at my feet. I became abruptly aware of myself. I felt ashamed that my eyes were bloodshot, my clothing tattered and dirty. The happy, unruffled voices floating over the water reminded me of fishing poles, nice trucks, and houses in the suburbs. The gentle rewards of people who had worked hard and stayed out of trouble all of their lives. They filled their worldly space with material possessions and found pleasure in them. It was so simple and natural for free people. I realized that I didn't own anything of consequence, and might never do so.

My hometown, Shelton, Washington, was an ugly place with a high unemployment rate, an excessive number of teen pregnancies, and a nasty drug problem. I remembered the poem I had written on the wall of my childhood home when I moved out:

> I leave this place of questions
> I leave for unanswered pain
> I leave on winds of anger
> I leave with limbs of rain

I blamed that town for the limits I felt it placed on me. Yet, I gradually realized that I couldn't blame it for everything. I realized that if I really wanted to forgive my hometown, I would first have to forgive myself. *I* had wasted time selling and consuming drugs and alcohol, *I* had dropped out of school, and it was *me* who had lost sight of what I really wanted.

The program I wanted to join was designed for respectable college kids. I'd been accepted before my arrest; I wasn't exactly a "respectable college kid" anymore. I wrote to the program to see if it was still possible for me to go now that I was a convicted felon. No response came, so I called the national offices in Washington, D.C. The woman who answered the phone told me that I wouldn't be able to do the program with a felony on my record. I called back and asked to speak with someone at a higher level. The admissions director said that it showed honesty and openness to have called and explained my situation; she would read my letter and think about it. Even if the program accepted me, I still had to be released by the court system. I went in to speak with my corrections officer once more to tell him when I would be finished with my community-service time. The same woman who'd told me that I was a violent criminal told me that my corrections officer had moved, and that I now had a new one. My new CO was new to the profession; he had been working at the prison outside of town, and this was his first day.

"This office doesn't recommend people to end their probation early until they have finished at *least* half of their time. You won't be halfway done until October," he told me.

I don't know what my face looked like, but I remember that I spoke like a child. "But Dave was going to," I replied.

"Well, I'm not Dave," he said, "and I'm not signing anything," he said with finality. He swiveled in his chair. I was glad they had given him the shitty office.

I decided that if my new CO wasn't going to help me, I would have to help myself. If I asked the judge to end the state's hold on me early, it wouldn't matter what my CO said. I called my lawyer. He told me he would petition the courts for me, and that I wouldn't have to pay him. He was a good man. I thanked him, and sighed after I hung up the receiver. The words of the rap artist Tupac Shakur crossed my mind. He said that he was being punished for things another person had done in another life. I understood this so well; I felt like another person had been living my life for years. I felt I was finally seeing clearly. My head was emptying of pot smoke and alcohol and filling with passion and direction.

The office for the service program in Charleston, South Carolina, sent me my plane ticket. I was booked on a red-eye flight that left at ten o'clock Tuesday night. My court date was the Friday before, which cut things very close. I registered at my community college for the next quarter—desperately hoping that I wouldn't have to go there that fall. I tore my bottom lip to pieces with my teeth and barely slept at night. And even though I was done with my community service, it wouldn't show up as complete on my record for weeks due to the slow system. I got copies of my completed paperwork from Gwinwood and verified them myself through the corrections office in Lacey, Washington. I hadn't been allowed to do community service in my hometown because there was no place that offered community service for *violent criminals*. Lacey was a twenty-minute drive from Shelton every morning but I didn't mind, because it was part of the process of getting out of there for good.

When I dressed for court Friday morning, I was too exhausted to be nervous. I wasn't surprised when the judge didn't recognize me as I stood before him in pressed black pants and a sheer top. The last time he had seen me, I was wearing an orange jail suit and bruised face, and my hair reached toward the ceiling. The prosecutor explained my situation and the judge removed his eyeglasses.

"Well, I don't see any reason why your probation shouldn't be ended so that you can do Job Corps," he said while readying my paperwork.

I corrected him before I could stop myself. *I wasn't doing Job*

*Corps; I was participating in a domestic Peace Corps.* The judge raised his eyebrows and nodded his head.

As I walked out the door, the heaviness drained slowly from my heart. Love for my mother washed over me in waves as I watched her gentle face through my triumphant cigarette smoke. I leaned over the railing, gazed at glistening Capitol Lake, and said nothing. Even the waves seemed to move more serenely than I had thought possible when I was a girl trapped inside state lines.

I now had a mere weekend to ready myself for a move across the country. After frenzied days of packing, I sat bolt upright in my mother's Jeep Cherokee as she sped north on Interstate 5.

The airport was like a dream. One week before, I wasn't even allowed to cross the mountains. Now I was flying to a place of sunshine and palmettos. South Carolina was almost as far away from Washington as I could get and still be in the country.

On the jet heading east, I couldn't close my eyes. I felt my accomplishment with the pure joy of a child. I was afraid to breathe or sleep, lest I awake and discover that the last three days had been a dream. I felt truth flow through me as I flew high above the farmlands of the Midwest. I sucked oxygen from the steamy air of Washington, D.C., as I changed planes and talked to a stranger from Long Island. When I stepped off a small plane at the tiny airport in Charleston and felt the humidity that reminded me of sex, I told myself that I had made it.

I felt fulfilled as I was fitted for boots and khaki uniform pants on the base where I was to go through training before I began my service. I was filled with pride as I recited our pledge the first morning we had physical training. Every day was full of movement, and I felt buoyed by a sense of unity every time I worked with my new team of ten college students who had traveled from all over the country to volunteer. Slowly, I would get to know these people. Eventually, I would learn their stories, heartaches, and hardships, just as they would learn mine.

I walked under a row of happy-looking palmettos and touched each one in turn. A lot of old things inside me were transforming—churning and crashing just like the waves on the cream-colored sand of Folly Beach. As a twenty-year-old who wanted better things in life, I was changing, and not just on the inside. I no longer needed my mantle of defensiveness nor my tough way of talking. I no longer needed my shifting gaze nor the thought patterns that wouldn't stop calculating against people.

I felt a warm breeze tinged with Atlantic salt water as I walked the south Battery and read a recipe for She Crab Stew in a Southern cookbook. The breathtaking houses made me want to cry, and I wished I could share my eyes with my mother for one moment. I remembered her reading to me from *Gone with the Wind* when I was a little girl. I knew that she would love Charleston. I stepped across the slave auction grounds and thought of how far people had come since the times when those cobblestone streets were filled with living human flesh ready to be sold. I walked the streets of a very old ghetto in north Charleston and thought of how much there was to see. I penned messages in a federally supplied green notebook as I sat along the streets of Rainbow Row and recalled the smooth coolness of my skin against an old lover.

I bought a postcard, but I didn't know exactly what to write on it. "It's not like they can send it back to you if you write the wrong number," a girl said when she found me staring blankly at the card. She must have sensed my hesitation, and assumed that I was trying to remember an address. *What could I really write home about?*

I wanted to express things. I wanted to describe the cracked concrete beneath my feet and the sweat of a city day. I wanted to talk about the dirt that jail and crack houses had left on my skin. I wished to let them know that I had washed it off but that I would never forget how it looked over fine blond hair and tan skin. Just like how I would never forget what a line of meth tasted like in my throat, the long-lasting numbness of ignoring my depression with drugs, throwing up alone, or my stomach burning dully.

I wanted to talk about these things because they were all over now.

In Charleston I saw through warm mists and watched the sun as it first touched America. I was lulled into smiling by the soft accents of the islanders from Seabrook and Kiawah. The days passed, and I wondered when I would fall again. The difference was, this time I knew I would be able to get back up.

I started jogging, running along the banks of the Ashley River. One hot night I had to stop and rest my hands on my knees. I fought for breath as my chest heaved and screamed from years of abusive cigarette, pot, and meth smoke. The humid breeze slowly dried the sweat from my forehead and played with the tendrils of blond hair that had fallen in front of my face. I stayed bent over even after the physical pain was gone. I lowered myself to a sitting position on the ground facing the water. I listened to the fiddler crabs that were hiding in the marsh grass.

I'd barely said good-bye to my friends and family before leaving. Tears welled up in my eyes; my hard heart was finally breaking. I had gotten out of town, but some people never would. I thought about the still-blank postcard under the lamp in my room. Leaving home was never a clean break. My heart will always ache for the ones I left behind. While I fought for breath, searching and struggling to redeem myself in South Carolina, they were slowly asphyxiating on their own vomit in crack houses and cheap hotel rooms. While I was trying to suck enough air into my lungs to explain myself to my new teammates, they were taking shallow breaths of apathy on borrowed couches inside rotting trailers. I realized then that I was actually trying to prove myself not to the judge in Thurston County or the woman at the corrections office, but to me and to my old friends. I wanted to prove that it was possible to get out of Shelton. They were choking on smoke that was slowly killing them; they were fighting for breath, too, on another coast, in another life, for completely different reasons.

# Slipping the Noose

## Elizabeth Simpson

It was a glorious spring morning in Victoria when my husband, our dog, and I set out to do what we always do. Our standard poodle lopes along the ocean path, and I speed-walk to keep up with my lanky husband, who strolls along. Acquaintances who greet us know my husband as the man who never wanted a dog until he read that puppies help cancer patients survive, and then fell in love with the one we bought.

Seven years before, when I was fifty-three, the odds had been stacked against me when a persistent cough turned out to be lung cancer. Even before I had grown accustomed to my terminal diagnosis, a team of doctors gave me a flicker of hope by opting to remove the cancerous lobe. A surgeon cleaved open my chest, pushing aside the breasts that had been my pride and joy since puberty, and I woke up from the anesthetic to a second diagnosis. The cancer had metastasized, slithering outside its lung of origin to wrap itself around my heart. I was terminal, inoperable, and scarred from neck to belly.

I was also lucky. A trial run of radical chemotherapy and radiation, a supportive partner, and nurturing friends helped me regain my health. Survival gave me time to do the unthinkable in my small life: to marry the man I love, to win a teaching award from the college where I still work, to publish two nonfiction books about survival, and to finish a three-year draft of my first novel. Without worrying that I will tempt the gods of health to strike me down again, I can now buy a dress, order season tickets to the theater, get a swimming pass, and plan vacations six months in advance.

On this particular morning of blue sky and bright sun, I am fretting about my husband's cheerful accusation that I can never leave home without having to return for something I've forgotten. Today my sunglasses are missing from my fanny pack, and my dog and husband lope on without me while I go back for them. The sun is so bright on the dewy meadow and along the ocean path that I squint even behind the dark lenses.

When I reach the ocean, my husband and dog are waiting for me, and we follow the same hour-long path we always do, varied only by the dog's meandering and our stopping to greet friends. Everyone talks about the impact of spring flowers on the spirit. Each spring, daffodils and narcissus carpet Victoria, surprising us when they appear hot on the heels of February's cream and purple crocuses. My husband and I are impressed. We are both prairie-born, and spent our childhoods in places where March makes powerful statements about winter's bone-chilling wind.

At a point where the dog runs down the cliff and into the ocean, we circle toward home. By this time the sun has teased off our protective clothing—first a scarf, then gloves and toques, and finally even jackets. We walk now on the far side of a grove of trees that divides us from the beach, passing the quaint public restroom and then a man-made pond and a famous sign that marks Mile Zero, the western tip of the Trans-Canada Highway. We try to guess whether there will be another busload of Japanese tourists scrambling to take digital pictures of our dog.

We are almost to the duck pond when I realize I need to use the restroom. My husband is expecting a conference call, and I tell him to carry on with the dog and leave me to mosey home alone, but he insists on waiting. I look back to see him leashing our dog, who wants to chase the ducks. The two of them stand under the big weeping willow tree that drapes green lace into the pond in summer. We have joked that this tree has no cause to weep, since it overhangs a pool where mother ducks teach their ducklings to swim and grown men race toy boats across shallow waters.

A concrete wall divides the restroom into a women's and a men's room, their doors on opposite sides, invisible to each other. When I push open the women's door, I feel its weight and realize that it is not usually closed. I can still see the blue sky and two eagles that have just soared so close overhead I thought I might reach up and touch their feathers. As my eyes adjust to the dark, the glint of cream-colored boots emerges through the murk. They are six inches off the floor.

Time slows as my eyes register the chic-casual cream trousers and red jacket, the head tilting above me, the thick brown hair brushed to perfection, the anguished face. My stomach grasps what my brain cannot acknowledge: While daffodils and narcissus open up to this first Tuesday in March of 2002, a woman hangs by the neck from the doorframe of a metal toilet cubicle. I open my mouth to scream, but I cannot make a sound. In a flash I am outside, running, adrenaline pushing me toward the familiar face of my husband. I reach the willow just as my scream breaks through the barrier of my throat.

"I think there's a woman hanging," I cry, gasping for breath.

"In the washroom?" my husband asks, running toward the open door as he speaks. When he returns, I see by the odd line of his mouth that it is true. "I've never seen a dead person before," he breathes.

"I'll cut her down, we have to save her," I say, running back.

"She's dead," my husband says, catching my arm.

"I'll cut her down anyway," I say, hoping he might be wrong, pulling a knife from my fanny pack.

"You can't cut electrical wire with a paring knife," he says, his voice strange now.

"I can stand under her, hold her up," I say, as he tightens his arms around me. He says we need to call the police. "Will you stay with her, make sure no one looks at her, while I find a phone?" I ask, thinking privacy is a gift we can offer her.

It is shortly after eight-thirty in the morning, and people are either sleeping or already at work. Houses are rare along this main road dotted with apartments, but suddenly a father and young daughter turn the corner as they come home from jogging. The man promises to call emergency.

When I return to my husband, the minutes drag on, wasting what seems to me precious drops of life. "I should go inside and stay with her; she's all alone and it's been half an hour," I say.

"It's been seven minutes, and she's beyond help." My husband's voice is firm now, but the unfamiliar twist to his bottom lip confirms that he shares my horror. "For a minute I thought she was a wax effigy from last week's protest against the new government," he says, taking my hand and looping my arm through his.

After what seems like hours, paramedics arrive in two ambulances and confirm the woman's death, a photographer records the scene, a detective asks us if the woman was alone. When I tell him yes, he says, "That's all for now."

"We can't do anything more," my husband tells me gently.

"Take the dog, I'll come home soon," I promise.

"Why don't you cut her down?" I ask the detective, but he doesn't answer me. "If the sun hadn't been so bright and I hadn't returned home for my sunglasses, I would have been in time," I say. A stranger interrupts to describe how he saw a woman get out of a black sports car around eight-thirty A.M. He says she peered over her shoulder as though fearful of being followed.

"Are you all right?" the detective asks when we're alone again and I am following him as he circles her car, peering in the windows, noting how she has vacuumed and polished it for the occasion.

"I should have held her up so she could breathe," I say.

"Probably too late," he says. "Takes only seconds to cut air from the brain. You wouldn't want to save a brain-damaged victim," he assures me. "She knew how to make a slipknot that held."

It occurs to me as I walk home that the woman had planned her death with meticulous care—the noose, the wardrobe, the shiny car, a place where she could have privacy and yet be found. In the late afternoon, a counselor from the police department calls to ask how I am and to tell me that the victim was in her early forties and of sound mind, but that no further information will be given out. In my mind's eye, the woman still hangs in the bathroom, and I am wondering how "a sound mind" endures the long moment from leap to gasp.

After dark, I step onto my deck to listen to the rustle of the trees and feel my hair blow in the wind. I look into the gardens around me and see that no other trees are moving but mine. I feel certain that the woman's spirit has come to touch mine before it settles wherever spirits settle. In that moment, she and I exchange something akin to love. It is like no other feeling I have ever shared, not even with my mother and sister, who each died inch by inch and whose loss is still too great for me to ponder alone.

I go to bed with the woman's face looming in front of me. When I wake up, I remember the detective telling me that suicide is a selfish act. Later in the morning, a doctor tells me suicides are so common they barely cause a ripple in the medical world. I cannot accept the idea that this woman was either selfish or common. I think of her as troubled, as breaking free from some immeasurable weight of loneliness and despair.

After washing her car and polishing her boots, she had jumped into public scrutiny, and I wonder if she had a husband or a child. I wonder if a daughter or female friend could have tempered her desperation. I can't help wishing someone had commiserated with her over the cause of her despair, and I think of the difficulty women have in expressing their fears to men without being made to feel foolish. I cannot help but think, too, how others might have used the years this stranger shucked off—my two girlfriends who died young of cancer, or my god-child who was killed on Whistler Mountain just days after his seventeenth birthday.

The next night I try to comfort myself by thinking that a child or an old woman adjusting to widowhood might have come upon the suicide instead of me. The thought of having borne a weight that protected someone vulnerable eases my mind.

The phone rings, and a friend who works as a poet by night and a private eye by day tells me that the woman was a married mother of four sons, a hockey mom, an employee much loved by her colleagues, a woman devoted to bringing light into the darkness of those who are blind. She tells me that neither her family nor her neighbors nor her colleagues understand why the woman chose to die. When I hear the word "chose," a memory pushes its way through years of resistance in my mind.

✦ ✦ ✦ ✦ ✦

It is 1986 and I have just landed in Singapore. I am slim and smiling. I wear an orchid in my hair. The receptionists at the Sheraton Hotel would probably say that my husband and I make an attractive couple. We are on the youthful side of middle age and brim with energy. Our passports tell them we are from Canada, land of innocence and abundant space. No one would guess from our speech or manner that my husband's golden curls hide a brain fueled by alcohol and illicit sex or that my smile hides my desperation over having a dozen years before mistaken his charm for affection. Minutes later he would disappear into the folds of this vast and foreign city, abandoning me to the equatorial heat and silence.

I look down from my eighth-story window to see guests swimming in a large pool surrounded by flowering trees. Putting on my bathing suit and going to join them, I discover they are all families, insular and preoccupied. My vision becomes milky and my heart pounds as though it would like to escape my chest. I believe that children are the only cure for loneliness, but I have mystified doctors for more than a decade with my inability to get pregnant. The sounds of splashing arms and legs grow more distant, and I wonder if I am suffering from heatstroke.

Back in my room, I sit alone on the edge of the bed, and I take a bottle of blue pills from my purse. They appear small and innocent. My doctor insisted I carry them in case my heart fibrillates, as it did once when my spirit proved too rigorous for my body. Rolling the bottle between my palms, I remember a famous author telling me after his wife had left him that a broken leg gets more attention than a broken heart. Long ago I realized that heartbreak is not merely a terrible force; it is an emptiness worse than pain.

Outside, darkness falls, and the night encloses me in its net. I watch as my right hand pours the contents of the vial into my left hand and I put my head back and open my mouth as I have seen students do when they toss in handfuls of raisins and nuts. The pills taste like dusty orange pits. I lie down on the bed and pull my summer dress down over my knees, tidy its creases, stroke my hair, straighten my legs, and place my hands alongside my thighs. I lie at attention and wait to die.

"Want to check out the town?" my husband says, bouncing through the door, cheered by alcohol and his day's adventures.

"I swallowed some pills," I say, my voice muffled as though coming through flannel. "Will you come and sit beside me?"

When he refuses, I close my eyes, and another face comes to mind. My father's smile is so real that I want to lift my hand and touch his cheek. His hazel eyes and thick white hair comfort me until I remember that he is far away, a widower who wonders why he couldn't save my mother from her recent death.

I remember being fourteen and afraid to ask why he thought he could save his parents, who had died within two years of each other and left him orphaned at thirteen. Then I recall being seventeen and choosing the wrong career. It was my father who gave me a second chance, and with it a better future.

Still lucid, remembering, I see where I inherited my exaggerated sense of responsibility for others, for the world. I also feel a flash of gratitude for that second chance that gave me a chance for humanity. Lying there, I realize that my husband will feel nothing about my death beyond its giving him a story to tell his buddies after the inconvenience of shipping my body home in a box. But I also know that my death will take away the last shred of my father's faith in himself.

I have no memory of leaving the room, but I can still see the elevator button in my memory's eye, feel myself spinning through a revolving door, climbing into a taxi.

"Take me to the hospital," I say.

"Which one?" the taxi driver asks.

"The nearest one," I tell him, and the world disappears.

"We almost lost you," a woman in white is saying as I open my eyes. She stands in sensible shoes near the foot of my bed and waits for me to respond.

"Can I see the doctor?" I ask.

"I am the doctor," she says, her voice soft and confident. "You will have to become more spiritual if you want to survive middle age." I am not sure what she means by this, and I look around the room to see that all the other beds are empty. I wonder if I am dreaming and will wake up on the Canadian prairies, a child living with a family that loves her.

"I'm going home now," I tell the doctor.

"It's two o'clock in the morning," she says, "and your husband has returned to your hotel."

"He might come for me if I phone him," I say, realizing he must have followed me but not stayed to see if I recovered.

The next day he and I take an overnight bus to Thailand. I watch enchanted as we pass one Malaysian rubber tree plantation after another, under a full moon. Their haunting beauty surrounds me. As the bus moves north, I am unable to bring up a picture of the previous day. Nothing seems different, yet everything has changed.

In Koh Samui, my husband flirts with a fragile Asian waitress who would like to move to America, but knows only a few words of English. In the evening he and I chat with two doctors. After we arrive back in Canada, the younger of the two sends a letter and a photo of us. In the picture, I am sitting on my husband's knee, and we are smiling. On the card, the doctor has written that we are the happiest couple he has ever met, and that he would like to visit us in Canada.

Months later when I am grading students' drama papers, I wonder if actors lose their souls to the roles they play before they shed old dramas for new ones. This thought astounds me, and with it comes an awareness of how misguided the notion is that unhappy couples should remain in the bed they have made for themselves, denying themselves future delights.

My divorce brings with it confusion, anger, and renewal, but once it's over, I never look back with feelings of loss. Even the frightening cancer that follows seems gentle compared to years of torment in a soulless marriage and the shame of my attempted suicide. Cancer is blameless. It brings out human kindness and concern. For me it also brought out the nurturing of friends, the courage of my lover, and the joy of survival.

The image of a woman stopped at the end of her rope comes unbidden now, when I least expect it. Her face hangs between my college students and me, between the food on the grocery shelf and my reach, between the end of a sentence and its beginning. It comes with the knowledge that I was saved by love and have returned to its blessing. The sources may differ—an old father now dead, a new husband to share my future—but the message is the same: the arrival of love is never too early or too late. It makes us feel lucky, like I do when I think back on the serendipitous arrival of a taxi driver who spoke English, of the compassion of a female doctor who refused to give up on a tourist's anguish.

❖ ❖ ❖ ❖ ❖

A sudden snowfall covers the spring flowers this morning, three days after the woman's suicide. I walk through damp snow to return to the restroom with my husband and dog, hoping to change a living moment into a memory. They wait outside while my nausea and exhaustion merge with terror, and I push open the door. I see nothing except my own haunted face in the bathroom mirror. With my reflection comes the realization that the stranger I found hanging here is not so different from me. We are sisters in a moment of despair, divided by a second chance.

# Rookie Restaurateur
## Marie Campagna Franklin

People everywhere fantasize about running a restaurant—dreaming of a funky bistro, a white-linen café, or a beachside bar and grill. What is it about the thought of owning such a place that tugs at so many men and women? Power? The allure, perhaps, of watching Bogart and Bergman as they light up cigarettes in *Casablanca*? The chance to open one's own Rick's Café? Or is it the recognition that comes with presiding over a public dining room and offering "a drink on the house"?

For me, it was all of these.

When I reached my forties, I found myself in a period of intense introspection. I questioned my priorities and tried to come to terms with unfulfilled dreams. My fantasy took form in the forty-two-seat Andiamo Café in South Chatham, Massachusetts.

The idea to open Andiamo actually came to me in a dream back in 1995. After more than twenty years of superior evaluations and dedication to my various jobs as teacher and journalist, I had a midcareer, I've-hit-the-wall crisis that felt like a ton of bricks sitting on my head. Denied two promotions, I'd come to realize I was dispensable at work. The only things that saved me were a smart and sensitive female therapist who happened to be Italian-American, as I am, and the night I met Granny in my dreams.

"What did Granny say to you?" Dr. Cantorini asked when I confided my reverie.

"She said people want to give love and receive love and that if I owned a restaurant, I could create more of both, with food. She told me to call it Andiamo," I declared.

Days later, on a snowy afternoon in January 1996, I was standing inside the Irish Family Restaurant in a run-down building around the corner from my summer home, just to look around once more. Bill, my husband of two decades, and Emily and Anna Kate, my nine- and eleven-year-old daughters, were with me. "We're serious," the owner said, brushing snow off her boots as she led us inside. "We're ready to listen to offers."

We proposed a price lower than what they thought the pancake place was worth. It had been on and off the market for years, and no one else seemed interested in buying an old building in a small fishing village with a tourist trade that lasted only two months a year. No one but me, that is.

We raided our savings account for the down payment. All I needed was a mortgage, a line of credit, and someone to believe in me, fast. "We'll give you the loan," the Cape Cod banker said when I phoned him in early March, "but we'll want both of your homes as collateral." I am crazy, I know, but I am also exuberant. Reluctantly but lovingly, Bill agreed to my plan.

London has its pubs. Rome has its trattorias. Paris has its cafés. And now, Cape Cod would have Andiamo.

✦ ✦ ✦ ✦ ✦

In mid-May, the honeymoon ended. It didn't look like we were going to make the scheduled opening on May 31. The dining room, draped top to bottom in dropcloths, smelled like turpentine. To complicate matters, I was commuting back and forth from our primary residence near Boston to Cape Cod to care for my family and work part-time at the *Boston Globe*.

Hale, my cousin's husband and my newly hired chef, arrived in New England after a winter in Key West. To say that Hale cooks food is like saying Leonardo da Vinci came up with some new ideas. Hale *creates* food. He has cooked for Elizabeth Taylor, who was so impressed with his dishes that she invited him to her table at a Santa Fe café. He was Katharine Hepburn's private chef at her home on the Connecticut shore. By now, dear reader, you will understand the magnitude of my mistake when I say I asked Hale if he would help me paint the dining-room walls.

"I am a chef," he responded, his tall frame expanding by the second. "You pay me because I am a master with food. You pay me because I make the best demi-glace on the planet. You pay me for my reputation. But you do not pay me to paint."

It was the first of many lessons he and other chefs would teach me: I did the painting, he did the food. I ran the front of the house, he was the boss out back. The chef spent the money. The owner paid the bills. The owner toiled all day preparing the dining room and taking reservations. At night, the chef got most of the compliments. The chef/owner relationship is a seesaw: up and down, unbalanced, a marriage of convenience more than a shared passion or an approach to life.

✦ ✦ ✦ ✦ ✦

Hoping for miracles, we opened at five P.M. on May 31, as planned. There were no TV cameras present, but there was enough melodrama to fill a book. And lessons galore. For example: Success comes from ignoring the bookie's odds and betting on yourself instead. If you believe strongly in something, there is power in your convictions. Running a restaurant is decidedly *not* like throwing a dinner party.

As we threw open the front door and placed our menu board on the sidewalk in front of the yellow café, I ran across the street to get a better look. Hale was standing proudly, immaculately dressed in starched chef whites, two servers by his side. Just then a car pulled up.

"Welcome to Andiamo," I said, a bit out of breath.

"A table for two," the man replied.

I snatched two menus from the hostess table and led my first guests inside.

We served twelve people our first evening—five of them friends. Bill, Emily, and Anna Kate were not there for opening night. It was Anna Kate's tenth birthday and back in Newton, there was a party, complete with DJ and prizes. As a mother, I felt guilty that I was not able to be there. But I had a new baby to bear.

✦ ✦ ✦ ✦ ✦

By late June, Andiamo had a reputation as the cool new kid on the block and I was known as the storytelling rookie restaurateur. "Food is life," I would say. "And life is a story." At first, I was the one telling the tales. Soon, my customers were also sharing theirs. "My *nonna* made the best pasta *e fagioli* in Brooklyn," a relaxed diner bragged to me one night.

In July, we participated in Taste of Chatham, a local charity event that draws five hundred foodies to sample delicacies from the town's thirty-five eateries. Hale whipped up our offering—grilled focaccia with roasted-eggplant tapenade, crab-filled tarts, and lobster ravioli in a sage cream sauce. That evening, standing at the edge of the massive white tent watching patrons in summer seersucker sampling our treats, I said to myself: *I am here, feeling powerful, alive, and strong.*

In the weeks ahead, lobster ravioli became our signature dish as more and more customers found their way to South Chatham to have dinner.

✦ ✦ ✦ ✦ ✦

There's an old joke about the restaurant business that goes like this: How do you make one million dollars? Start out with two million and buy a restaurant. Ha! A restaurant can be an easy place to lose money. It's also a great place to make money. It all depends on how you manage the cash flow.

One lesson I learned fast is that a restaurant's cash flow is as deceptive as a snake going after its prey. In the day-to-day operation, the money that comes in and out of the cash register, even in a small café, is staggering. Some nights we're awash in cash, and I'm tempted to run off to Italy and spend it all on leather and limoncello. And then—whack! I'm hit on the side of the head. There's a statement from Chatham Fish & Lobster. There's a bill for produce and vegetables. A tab for espresso beans and a five-page statement for wine and beer. And let's not forget the mortgage, the insurance, the payroll.

Industry statistics are daunting. Odds are that nine out of ten restaurants that open in a given year won't be in business in three. The majority of those will fail within the first year. For the restaurant that does manage to keep its doors open, there's only a one-in-five chance the restaurateur will ever earn a return on her investment.

Despite its successful launch, I almost lost Andiamo that second year.

✦ ✦ ✦ ✦ ✦

It began the night my new chef (unlucky for me, Hale and my cousin divorced and he didn't return the second year) demanded a raise. The twenty-six-year-old graduate of the Culinary Institute of America wanted an extra two hundred dollars a week on top of his already generous salary. This culinary stud was already causing me trouble, making expensive ordering mistakes with the purveyors and showing uneven performance under pressure. It was June 1997, ten days before the Fourth of July and the annual Cape Cod tourist stampede.

The hotshot told me he didn't mean to break our commitment, but either I paid him more or he'd look for another job. "Bastard," I said. "You're taking advantage of me." I held back my tears. There was no way I was going to give away my power to someone twenty years my junior. I was already paying him $850 a week, more than my fledgling business could afford.

A few nights later, after a particularly stressful shift, the situation came to a head. Midway through the chef's tirade, after the guests were gone, I threw a wineglass against the wall, purposely missing him but making no mistake about my point. It shattered, along with my dream that the people I hired to work for me would care as much about Andiamo as I did. Like a pot of simmering marinara sauce, our altercation—which led to his walking out— left me with a great big mess to clean up in the morning.

✦ ✦ ✦ ✦ ✦

Two days passed, Andiamo was dark, but my SWAT team was on the way. My brothers, niece, husband, and daughters agreed to help me reopen the restaurant that weekend. Bill conceded to wash dishes. My brothers, Paul and Tom, stepped up to cook. Our girls were ready to take reservations and bus tables, and we could feel Granny's energy pulsating through the restaurant. I was empowered by my family's love.

We served thirty-seven diners the night my brothers got their baptism by fire in restaurant cooking. The second night, we turned the tables one and a half times. At the end of the weekend, with a promise from a new chef to begin Tuesday, I closed the cash register, turned off the lights, and moved toward the door. Then I noticed a note on the counter with my name on it. It read: "The dishwasher has a crush on the owner. Please deliver my check in person. Love, Bill."

Angels, oh angels. Come out, come out wherever you are. I swear: Granny is directing this play. The only thing missing was the trained actors.

✦ ✦ ✦ ✦ ✦

At first I worried I'd made a mistake in naming my restaurant Andiamo. Aside from a few familiar words and phrases, Italian is not widely understood in the States, and a cute name won't work if people can't remember it. Sheryl Julian, the *Boston Globe*'s food editor, whom I greatly respect, advised me to choose a name people would remember three days after hearing it. "Hmm," she said when I told her I'd decided on Andiamo. "It means 'Let's go' in Italian," I said. "Hmm," she said again. "Check back with me in three days."

I never did.

*Andiamo* is not my favorite Italian word, but it's certainly in the top ten, along with *mangia* (eat), *ciao* (hello or good-bye), *buona sera* (good evening), *nonna* (grandmother), *mercato* (market), *amore* (love), *va bene* (okay), *passaggiata* (stroll), and *sopratutto* (especially; above all). But *andiamo* is the word that reminds me of growing up in my extended Italian-American family. I still hear Granny's voice calling me to the kitchen to help her make stuffed artichokes or deep-dish pizza. "*Andiamo, andiamo*," she would say, and my siblings and I would go.

Having this story to tell gave me confidence when I visited with my customers at their tables. As a rookie restaurateur, I was nervous when I worked the room. The dining public has high expectations and standards. It expects McDonald's to be McDonald's and a cozy bistro to be a fine dining experience, so I knew I'd better not have stage fright when the shift began. Storytelling was my grounding force. Once I started talking about Granny's kitchen, I was at home with my guests.

✦ ✦ ✦ ✦ ✦

When I used to imagine owning a restaurant, I would see myself as a cross between a Food Network chef and my grandmother. The chef wore a tall white hat, a coat monogrammed with his name, and a neckerchief printed with red peppers on a green background. Granny wore a waisted cotton dress and an apron, nylon stockings with a seam running up the back of her legs, and tightly laced black shoes like the nuns used to wear. The chef was trained at the Culinary Institute of America in Hyde Park, New York, or somewhere in Italy or France. Granny learned to cook by observing and helping her mother in my great-grandmother's Sicilian kitchen. The chef cooked in a commercially equipped kitchen with eight-burner stoves and convection ovens and all sorts of culinary gadgets, like whisks and mandolines. Granny cooked in a farmhouse kitchen with an old gas stove, a two-bay porcelain sink, a pantry stocked with pickled vegetables, and a few sharp knives. The celebrity chef guarded his recipes unless someone paid big bucks to buy his cookbook. Granny handed down her recipes to her daughters and daughters-in-law as part of her legacy. To the chef, cooking was the day's work. To Granny, cooking dinner was part of the day's work of raising nine children. There was a world of difference in the way Granny and the chef thought about food, but they shared the need to love others by cooking for them.

✦ ✦ ✦ ✦ ✦

Few diners pay any attention to what goes on behind the scenes in a restaurant, as long as the final product turns out well. Why should they? If the food is good, the mood right, and the wait staff efficient and friendly, the diner simply enjoys the experience. The whole point of eating out is to leave the work to someone else.

Owning a restaurant gave me an entirely different insight into the food world, a behind-the-scenes picture most patrons—thankfully—never see.

In the calm dining room, patrons sip their wine and wait; in the kitchen, the cook grunts as he throws scalding pots and pans at the dishwasher. In the dining room, the bartender uncorks the wine with a sommelier's finesse; in the kitchen, the grill cook brings the neck of the bottle to his mouth and yanks the cork out with his teeth. The dining room is refined. The kitchen is raw. It's black and white, with nothing but a sheer curtain—or maybe swinging doors—separating the calm from the storm.

And, in the dining room, everyone is usually speaking English. In the kitchen, it's restaurant speak. Try translating this.

Chef (screaming): "Whose dupe is this?"
Dishwasher: "One of the floor whores."
Chef: "Got that, pearl diver, but which one?"
Dishwasher: "The one who skates."
Chef: "Shut up, sudbuster!"
Server (to chef): "Fire table two."
Chef: "Only if you pick up your deuces."
Server: "Is table eight up yet?"
Chef: "Go easy. My balls are to the wall."
Server: "Yeah, well, I'm in the weeds since you eighty-sixed the veal."
Owner: "Excuse me, what did you say?"

✦ ✦ ✦ ✦ ✦

By August, the customers aren't as friendly as in May. The regulars are in retreat until the tourists disappear, and we miss our local diners. Andiamo is a sea of vacationers—some deliriously happy, others downright miserable, because it's raining, or because their vacations aren't going as planned.

"What kind of Italian restaurant are you if you don't serve chicken parm?" one scolds. *A good one*, I think to myself. "What, no children's menu?" another asks. "I'm allergic to garlic and my mother can't eat anything made from wheat."

*Then stay home!* I want to shout, but don't.

✦ ✦ ✦ ✦ ✦

One night I'm chatting up table nine. The woman sitting between the two men is speaking Italian.

"*Signora*," I say, "You speak beautiful Italian." One of the men responds, "Her father is Perry Como." Yeah, right. "Well, Frank Sinatra is my uncle," I joke. "No, really, Perry Como is my father," the woman says demurely, "and I traveled to Italy often as a child."

When I was growing up in the sixties, my mother loved to listen to Perry Como on the radio. And now, thirty years later, I own Andiamo and Perry Como's daughter is sitting in my restaurant. Suddenly I understand what Alison Arnett, the *Globe*'s restaurant critic, meant when she likened owning a restaurant to giving a dinner party every night and never being sure who is going to come.

✦ ✦ ✦ ✦ ✦

I admit that sometimes the restaurant business brings out the worst in me. I already mentioned the night I threw the glass at the chef. Another night, I clumsily tripped over my own feet while serving wine at a table and stood shocked and motionless as dark red wine poured all over my guests. There was the evening I came down really hard on one of the servers, simply because I disliked her. And there was the time I insulted the professor from the Harvard Business School when, on a particularly busy night, he asked, "What is the problem in your kitchen and why in God's name is it taking so long for my meal to come out?" I replied: "The only thing wrong in my kitchen tonight is that my husband, who is a vice president of a major Wall Street firm, has the unfortunate job of cleaning your dirty dishes."

✦ ✦ ✦ ✦ ✦

Then there are those late nights when the customers are gone, the dining room is clean, the tables have been set for tomorrow, and I'm counting the tip money one more time to make sure I haven't made a mistake.

It's August 1999, and Andiamo is having its best season yet. "Timing was perfect tonight," says Douglas, the waiter. "The food was great and everyone was happy. It's the kind of night I love to work."

Dawson is the chef this Thursday evening and he wants to serve the staff a meal.

"Make some Bolognese," another server yells. "And a plate of grilled calamari," says a third. "Go easy on my wallet, no lobsters or filet mignons, please," I yell into the crowd.

Soon, Dawson is ringing his bell and we all help carry our feast to the dining room. "What was it with the guy at table ten and the zucchini allergy?" Dawson asks. I ask a server about the couple at table three. "Oh, they loved the place and left me a 32 percent tip," she says, as if she has just received her annual bonus.

And so it continues, our after-shift meal. We eat and we talk, laugh, and drink wine together. Adam tells a few jokes. Beth changes the hard rock to soft. Dawson begs the staff one more time, "No substitutes until after Labor Day." Three servers make plans to go to a bar, Squires, after we close. For me, moving toward my twenty-fifth college reunion and my forty-seventh birthday, the camaraderie feels like the good old days, breaking bread with friends in the cafeteria.

✦ ✦ ✦ ✦ ✦

Building Andiamo from the ground up was an incredible experience for my family. Together, we envisioned, created, and took chances in a high-risk game. But eventually the reality of keeping a restaurant going became impossible to ignore. Our automobiles were showing wear and tear as we commuted, city to shore, for five happy yet stressful years. The summer house was no longer a sacred space to unwind, but a messy place where we took refuge when the heat in the kitchen got to be too much.

People often ask me, "What's it like to own a restaurant?" I usually answer: "We eat out of take-out containers a lot."

✦ ✦ ✦ ✦ ✦

In September 2000, I invited a real estate broker to appraise Andiamo. I was tripping toward the end of my fifth year as a restaurateur, still working at the newspaper job that more than once paid a chef. Most nights, the restaurant was full, but I was still not making enough money to pay myself a salary. The future became crystal clear when I realized that the only way to prosper would be to expand: Andiamo had value only if I kept it open year-round, or sold it. The decision was gut-wrenching.

There was another problem, too. When school started each fall and my husband and daughters returned to the city, I was lonely, running a restaurant in Chatham while they lived their lives in Newton. Someday Bill and I planned to move full-time to the beach, but with Emily starting her senior year in high school, and Anna Kate just beginning tenth grade, this was not to be our season in the sun.

I was betwixt and between—and then the Realtor gave me a number. Suddenly I was dizzy with the payoff on my original investment, relieved I might have a future that didn't include working seven days a week. A few weeks later, an attractive offer came from a female chef from the city yearning to open her own place.

✦ ✦ ✦ ✦ ✦

The day I sold my restaurant, in April 2001, I was filled with both sadness and relief. Some of the sadness came from knowing I might never see my customers again. The relief came from knowing I'd never have to hire another chef or dishwasher again. As Bill and I drove home from the closing, I giggled more than usual and clutched his hand tightly while we talked about how the sale of Andiamo would make it easier to send Emily and Anna Kate to college.

In the following weeks, I refused to dwell on what could have been. I tried not to listen to the inner voice that jabbered, "Another career failure, out of business after five years." I laughed at the voice this time and demanded it to shut up. Soon I was able to hear my real voice, the voice that knows exactly why I did what I did. I had a midlife dream to open a restaurant. I followed my heart and I did it. And my decision to sell would make our family's life easier, logistically and financially.

"Don't be too hard on yourself, Marie," I talked back. "Remember, Andiamo was a huge success."

Would I do it all over again? Would I buy the little breakfast place around the corner from my summer home and turn it into an Italian restaurant, knowing what I know now? Absolutely. How many people dream of starting a restaurant and never do? How many people know they need to do something bold to save their souls, and don't? Most people have regrets. I have none.

# Why Did the Attorney Cross the Road?

## Geoff Griffin

What does it take to change course and go from a highly paid job you hate to a poorly paid job you love?

All it takes is surrendering everything you ever thought you were. All it takes is throwing away what you've spent years working for. All it takes is becoming a complete disappointment to those you care about. All it takes is sleepless nights. All it takes is admitting all of the goals you ever had were things you never really wanted. All it takes is having people not take you seriously when you tell them what you are proposing to do. All it takes is leaving yourself completely, hopelessly vulnerable.

Once you've got all that taken care of, it's a piece of cake.

Maybe I should also say that if you actually make it to the other side, you might learn some good things along the way. You might learn that life is too short to worry about what everybody expects of you, that the person you were trying to be wasn't who you were intended to be, and that you have more of a chance to pursue your dreams than you realized.

That was my experience, going from being a very well-paid attorney in the city to becoming a very poorly paid sportswriter and househusband in the country. I made the change after turning thirty with a wife, two kids, and a stack of student loans from law school. The end result was worth it, but don't try this at home if you're not willing to give up everything. It's easy to throw out the stuff you hate, like long hours and pressure. It's much harder to throw out a lot of the things you like, such as money and prestige.

How do you know if you've got what it takes to trash everything and start over? First, you need to figure out just how unhappy you feel about having to do the work you currently do for the rest of your life. In my case, I couldn't stop thinking about these things, and I had fallen into a serious depression. If you are depressed, unless you get help, you won't have the energy to make a change. However, once you get enough medication and therapy to start feeling somewhat stable again, everyone will try to convince you that it was just a phase you were going through, or bad brain chemistry—anything but the fact that you have good reason to hate your life.

Then there's the process of letting those around you know you are serious about wanting to make a change. Who can blame them for doubting you? You are about to do something that makes no sense. You are giving up something they watched you spend years striving for. People are going to think you are crazy. You have to show them that your current lifestyle is making you even crazier.

People still can't resist asking me why I spent three years of my life going to law school to prepare myself for a job that would make me so miserable. My reasons were probably the same as those of the 66 percent of lawyers who tell surveys they wish they could do something else but they're locked into the lifestyle their salary has purchased, in spite of the insane hours, intense pressure, and constant battling with people. Like a lot of people who end up in law school, I couldn't really think of anything better to do at the time, and I had heard you could make a lot of money as a lawyer. The only problem was, I later discovered that all that money couldn't seem to keep me off Prozac. I also found something else I really wanted to do.

My first step in getting out of law and into sportswriting was to work a few hours a week as a sportswriter while still working as a full-time lawyer. It doesn't hurt to dip your toe in the water of your dream life before chucking your old life. In my case, this involved working as a stringer for a weekly newspaper with a circulation small enough that lawyers I worked with wouldn't notice my night job. As an independent contractor paid on a per-article basis, I would cover a couple of high school athletic events every week. It was good to be exposed to the realities of the job I'd been coveting in my daydreams, and I recommend it. You may find that the new job isn't everything you thought it was going to be. You may even find that your present job doesn't look so bad after all.

I found I loved sportswriting. I like to watch sports. I like to write. Somebody, maybe even a sportswriter, reputedly said that the closest thing to being a bum while claiming to have a job is being a sportswriter. Sportswriting became the part of my week I looked forward to rather than dreaded, even as I learned things about the field that might have driven others away.

People tell me all the time that they would love to be a sportswriter, and then proceed to ask me which professional teams I cover. They imagine themselves covering their favorite pro team at events attended by thousands and watched by millions on TV. They imagine an endless parade of interviews with big stars. Being a sportswriter, they think, will make them the coolest person around and the envy of all their friends.

There are some sportswriters who lead such lives, but they are few and far between. There are probably more people playing in the NBA than there are covering it full-time for a daily newspaper. There is a track you need to get on to be one of those people, and as someone entering the field past thirty and without a journalism degree, I wasn't one of them. Furthermore, I came to realize that while law is a meritocracy, where one can get to the top simply by working harder than everybody else, success in sportswriting is more of a timing-and-connections type of thing. Many lazy and unimaginative people have found their way to the top of the field and stayed put for years.

It didn't take me long to figure out that I would be one of the vast majority of sportswriters who cover high school, junior college, and small college teams at events attended by hundreds and televised to no one. If you jump into sportswriting you are more likely to find yourself covering a girls' high-school basketball game than the NBA.

I was fine with this. First, my worst day of sportswriting was still better than my best day of lawyering. Second, I was getting out of law partly because I was sick of working eighty-hour workweeks and not seeing my kids. The last thing I wanted was a job where I would be on the road for weeks at a time following a professional team around the country. Furthermore, I didn't want to waste my time talking to spoiled pro athletes who didn't want to talk to sportswriters anyway. If I wanted to listen to rich people whine that they didn't get the money they deserved, I could easily have stuck with corporate law.

I quickly realized that with my new career I wasn't just going down a couple of rungs on the money ladder. I was sliding all the way to the bottom.

I know people who left journalism to work at a grocery store because they could make more money that way. I know people who earn nearly as much money delivering the newspaper they work for as they do writing for it. At one paper where I worked, there was a very good "news assistant," a term that basically means a secretary-receptionist. The editor was impressed with this young man and offered him a crack at a reporting job when one opened up. The young man said he was flattered, but he couldn't give up his secretary-receptionist salary to take the noticeably lower reporter's salary. It took me eight years of raises as a sportswriter to finally make a full-time salary that was half of what I made in my first year out of law school.

When I was a lawyer, I worked with people who left their mansions in the morning and drove their kids to private school in a Mercedes before arriving at a job they hated and would probably be at until 8 or 9 P.M. As a journalist, I've worked with people who love their job but arrive at work in a fifteen-year-old car after leaving their low-rent apartment next door to drug dealers.

Which scenario would you rather live with? The decision is much tougher if you have kids. I was thinking of entering into financial ruin while I had two young children. If you don't have kids and are reading this, what are you waiting for? Get out there and do whatever you want and live in a hole-in-the-wall. If you've got kids, you may have already quit reading this a couple of pages ago because you just can't bear to think of dragging them down with you.

People like to say that you don't need a lot of money to raise kids, just a lot of time and love. They insist that it is better to raise kids without all of the material obsessions of our commercial culture. Of course, these same people seldom want their kids to go to school with the kids who are being raised on love without materialistic hang-ups.

If you were raised at a middle-class standard or higher, you may genuinely not care about the size of your house or car, but you will still want your kids to have the same "opportunities" you had while growing up. Opportunities like going to science camp, being on the dance squad, taking music lessons, playing on a club soccer team, or attending a private school or at least a good public school. In America, giving your kids "opportunities" can end up costing a lot of money.

The toughest problem may be dealing with the guilt of putting your personal happiness ahead of the opportunities available to your children. So how did I come to be selfish enough to do this? Well, I rationalized that if I didn't make a change I wouldn't be around much longer for my kids anyway, given how my depression was progressing. I figured Poor Dad was better than Hospitalized Dad.

Before you go thinking that I entered into a noble vow of poverty, I must confess that my secret weapon was that I was married to someone willing to support the family while I changed course. I know this is like telling somebody that the best thing to do to be a good basketball player is to be seven feet tall, but it is the truth.

I didn't work one more day as a lawyer once my wife was admitted to a program to become a physician's assistant. We moved back to Southern California, where I had obtained the law degree I was now turning my back on, while she pursued her own degree in an intense two-year program. I found an entry-level sportswriting job with a group of weekly newspapers that paid me a grand total of $8.50 per hour.

The first place we lived, for the longest eight months of my life, was with my in-laws. I can't even begin to tell you how low it made me feel to have to move in with them while their daughter was studying so she could take care of me. After my wife's student loans came through and we saved up some money, we were finally able to get a decent apartment—in a dicey neighborhood. When my daughter started kindergarten, she was supposed to go to a very poor school in the district, but we were able to get her into a somewhat less-poor school in a much nicer district by saying that we needed her to be able to be near her day-care provider. We were allowed into the better district, but we also got a snooty letter from them letting us know that they were doing us a favor by taking in our child, so it would be nice if we could pony up some cash to help offset the trouble we had caused them.

My daughter qualified for free school lunch, since our only income at the time was the grand total of $16,000 per year that I was pulling in from my job. That meager total also let us qualify for low-income breaks on our electric and phone bills. I often wondered during those two years if there was anybody in the country who had a greater education-to-poverty ratio than I did. Perhaps Ted Kaczynski, but probably not many others.

When my wife completed her two exhausting years of training, we decided to try living in a small town so isolated that it was two hours from the nearest Wal-Mart. She worked in a rural health care clinic while I wrote for the town newspaper. We lived in that town for four years before moving to an even smaller town. Once you've become used to the pace of life in a small town, it seems downright strange to be someplace where you don't know everybody and you have to wait at stoplights. Of course, the greatest benefit to living in a small town is that you don't need a lot of money. Property values are low and nobody is trying to impress anybody else, since you all shop at the same store and eat at the same drive-in. You don't have to worry about buying a house in a good school district, because there is just one school in the entire town.

People ask me all the time if I ever intend to go back to practicing law. I usually jokingly tell them that the only way I would practice law again is if I am so financially desperate I find myself walking along the street carrying a cardboard sign that reads, "Will litigate for food." What I don't tell them is that every July when it comes time either to pay my bar dues or give up my license to practice law, I pay the money—just in case.

If I had stayed in private practice and slogged my way through what would now be fourteen years of eighty-hour work-weeks fighting with people over money, I would now be a partner in a law firm making at least ten times as much money as I currently do.

There's just one problem with that scenario. If I hadn't changed course, I'd probably be dead.

# The Novice

## Alice Steinbach

For weeks I had imagined my first day in Paris: I could see myself sipping a *citron pressé* at the Flore, a famous Saint-Germain café that was once the haunt of Picasso, Sartre, de Beauvoir, and Camus; then darting in and out of the shops on the rue du Bac or browsing the bookstores in the historic rue Jacob. Always in this fantasy I saw myself responding with curiosity and excitement to the pulsing street life of Paris.

I had night dreams, too, along with the daydreams. In one particularly appealing dream, I bumped into Scott and Zelda Fitzgerald, who once lived on the Left Bank in a hotel just blocks from where I would be staying. I accepted their invitation to Sunday breakfast at their favorite café, Les Deux Magots. Waking from this dream, I scribbled a note to myself: *Must have Sunday brunch at Deux Magots.*

In another dream I entered an unnamed passageway on the Left Bank and, after a short walk, emerged on the Right Bank in the Marais district. Both during the dream and after, I felt quite pleased with myself at having made this historic discovery, one that eliminated the need to cross the Seine by bridge.

I liked these dreams, both the day and night versions. They seemed to signal a willingness on my part to go where the moment took me and to trust it would take me to an interesting place. They also reminded me of how it felt to approach every day as I once had, guided less by expectations than by curiosity.

On the day I left for Paris, I drank champagne with a friend in the Air Force lounge at Dulles airport. "Here's to a successful trip," said my friend, raising her glass. I raised mine in reply, saying, "And to an interesting one."

What I didn't say was that "success" was not something I was seeking from this venture. In fact, I was determined *not* to judge this trip, or its outcome, in terms of success or failure. Too much of life—my life, anyway—seemed to be aimed at achieving success and avoiding failure. I was determined not to carry that baggage with me on this trip.

"You must be excited," my friend said. "I know I would be."

I laughed. "That's an understatement. I'm probably the most excited person in this airport." It was true. I felt the way I did at twenty when, on the spur of the moment, I threw some clothes into a suitcase, bought a ticket at the airport, and left for Turkey.

But later, while waiting to board the plane, another feeling crept in, one I couldn't quite identify. Was it apprehension? Or just too much champagne? Such thoughts were swept aside, however, once I felt the plane lift off the runway, headed for Paris. *This is it*, I thought, tightening my seat belt, *the beginning of the next part of my life*.

✦ ✦ ✦ ✦ ✦

To my dismay, I arrived in Paris not an excited woman but an anxious one. Without warning, halfway through the flight, my sense of excitement deserted me and a new, less welcome companion arrived: a complete failure of nerve. *What am I doing on this plane?* I asked myself. Panic was lurking beneath the question. What had seemed a wonderful idea—*une grande aventure*, as my friends put it—began to feel like an ill-conceived fantasy that should have provided fifteen minutes of amusement before being discarded.

By the time my plane landed in Paris I had considered every bad outcome—from loss of livelihood to loss of life—that was likely to result from my incredible mistake in judgment. It was a little before eight in the morning and the air terminal was chilly and deserted. A tiring wait to get through customs was followed by a longer and more tiring vigil at the luggage carousel. By the time I had retrieved my bags and made the long trek to the public transportation area, my mood was dangerously low. I decided to cheer myself up by taking a taxi to my hotel instead of the bus that dropped passengers off at some central location.

"Rue de l'Université," I told the driver, directing him to my hotel. He'd never heard of it. "On the Left Bank," I said. "Rue de l'Université. Off the quai Voltaire." He shook his head and sighed wearily, as if to say, *It's no use trying to understand these Americans.* Then suddenly he lurched into gear and abruptly hurled his taxi into the traffic headed for Paris.

It is a long drive from the airport into the city, one that offers little in the way of scenic diversion. The truth is, there is no difference between the morning rush-hour traffic in Paris and that of any big American city: bumper-to-bumper cars and lots of ugly industrial parks separated by the occasional cluster of sterile high-rise buildings. The hour-long trip did nothing to bolster my morale.

Just as I was wondering whether it was madness or stupidity that had landed me in the back of this taxi, something happened: We entered the city of Paris and the Seine came into view. Silvery and serpentine, it moved like mercury through the center of the city, a mesmerizing force. From the taxi window I could see the tree-lined quays along the river. A few more minutes and we were on the quai Voltaire, driving past ancient buildings, their stone facades tinted a rosy pink by the morning sun.

Here it was that Voltaire had lived and died, I thought, looking at the silent buildings, each one with a story to tell. As I allowed myself to be drawn into the net of beauty and history that hangs like a bridal veil over Paris, my excitement grew.

We drove along the Seine, turning finally into the heart of the Left Bank, into the narrow, picturesque streets lined with bookshops and galleries and cafés. Ernest Hemingway once lived in this neighborhood, and so did Edna St. Vincent Millay. The thought buoyed my mood even more.

By this time the sun had burned through the early mist, leaving the air fresh and damp, as fragrant as the ocean. I felt elated; it was the same feeling I'd had as a child when, headed for the beach with my parents, the first whiff of sea and salt air would blow through the open windows of our trusty green Plymouth.

The taxi made another turn and then stopped in front of a small old building that from the outside bore little resemblance to a hotel. I was more or less dumped out into the middle of the narrow street, and with the traffic piling up behind us, horns blaring, I counted out seventy dollars' worth of francs. The driver pocketed the money, unloaded my belongings, and immediately drove off, leaving me and my suitcase—a large black number about the size of a baby hippopotamus—at the curb in front of the hotel.

I peered through the glass door, looking for someone to assist me. The place appeared deserted. Draping my raincoat around my neck, I slung my tote-sized handbag over one shoulder, a small duffel bag over the other, propped open the door with my left foot, and proceeded into the lobby, dragging my suitcase behind me.

It was my first look at the small hotel, once a private residence dating back to the seventeenth century. I'd decided to stay here on the advice of friends who knew and liked it. Immediately upon entering, something about the small reception area put me at ease. The furniture, under the original vaulted ceilings, was old and beautiful; the winding wooden staircase was polished and gleaming; and in one corner a young woman was arranging long-stemmed, fresh-cut flowers in large Chinese porcelain vases. There was a sense of history here. And, just as important to me, a sense of order.

It was also, I might add, the hotel's first look at me—at the rumpled, tired, luggage-intensive figure sloughing toward the small reception desk. But those who work in hotels are not unused to seeing people at their worst. After all, the word "travel" comes from the Latin "trepalium," which, loosely translated, means "instrument of torture." So whatever judgmental thoughts may have passed through the mind of the receptionist, she tactfully kept them from appearing on her face.

It was still early, a little before nine, and my room, she informed me, would not be ready until twelve-thirty. She suggested I take a walk.

Outside, the shopkeepers were washing down the narrow sidewalks. In the air I could smell bread baking. I headed for a café I'd seen on the rue Bonaparte. I stopped on the way to buy a *Herald-Tribune* at a newsstand where a large gray cat sat grooming himself on a stack of *Le Monde* newspapers. Timidly, I touched the cat's head. "His name is Jacques," said the elderly proprietor proudly, "and he is very friendly." I scratched Jacques under the chin; he immediately began drooling. After that, my first stop every morning was to see Jacques and, as I came to call his owner, "Monsieur Jacques."

By ten-thirty I was seated in a neighborhood café near the rue Saint-Benoît, reading the paper, sipping café au lait and wondering, *Is this really happening? Am I really in Paris? Do I really not have to go to the office or write a column or go to the supermarket?*

As if to answer my questions, a tall man wearing a tuxedo and a beret walked by, pushing before him a perambulator. In it I could see an accordion, and behind that a puppy and a cat. I turned to my waiter, who answered my question before I asked it. "*Madame*, he is on his way to the place Saint-Germain-des-Prés to perform for the tourists."

*Yes*, I thought, *I really am in Paris*.

✦ ✦ ✦ ✦ ✦

I left the café and walked along the rue Bonaparte, scanning the numbers above the doors. When I came to number 36, I stopped. The sign outside said HÔTEL SAINT-GERMAIN-DÉS-PRES. It was the small hotel where Janet Flanner lived in her early days in Paris, and I had come to pay my respects to her. Of course, she was no longer around—she died in 1978—but it's my belief that you can be as close in feeling to the dead as you can to the living. Sometimes even closer.

I entered the lobby, an elegant, refined space that in all probability bore no resemblance to the modest surroundings in which Flanner lived in the 1920s. At that time it was a hotel where young American expatriates with talent but little money rented rooms. Still, it was from this hotel that Flanner began filing her fortnightly articles, signed with her *nom de correspondence*, Genêt.

"May I help you, *madame?*" asked the receptionist.

"No, I am here to meet a friend," I said, walking the few steps to the breakfast room at the rear of the lobby. Breakfast was over and the room was empty. It seemed as good a place as any to deliver my respects to Madame Flanner:

*Well, I finally made it here to thank you,* my thinking voice said. *So thanks for sharing with me your fifty years in Paris. I couldn't have asked for a better guide.*

✦ ✦ ✦ ✦ ✦

After leaving the hotel I walked along the tiny rue Jacob, a charming street that seems to surface suddenly at a little garden near the rue de Seine and then, several blocks later, disappear into the rue de l'Université. *Now this is more like it,* I thought happily, as I popped in and out of the bookshops and antiques galleries along the street. It was at this point that, high on a combination of strong coffee, excitement, and jet lag, I found myself actually skipping.

Later, of course, when the first exhilaration lost its edge, another question would present itself: How does one structure a

life that has no responsibilities or set routines? Such an existence, I came to see, had the potential to deteriorate into idle
wandering.

But on this particular day I was open to wandering, to idle-
ness, to losing myself in the glorious ether of Paris. I wandered
through the narrow streets, my mind spinning, going over all the
things I wanted from this trip.

A list began forming itself in my head: I wanted to take
chances. To have adventures. To learn the art of talking less and
listening more. To see if I could still hack it on my own, away
from the security of work, friends, and an established identity.

Of course, I also wanted to lose ten pounds, find the perfect
haircut, pick up an Armani suit at 70 percent off, and meet Yves
Montand's twin—who would fall deeply, madly in love with me.

My first chance to get my self-improvement plan rolling
presented itself in the form of a cosmetics shop I passed on the rue
de Beaune. I stepped inside. It was an elegant shop, staffed by
beautiful young Parisiennes with perfect skin, perfect hair, and
perfect bodies. Dressed like doctors in crisp white jackets with
name tags, they moved like models through the aisles of glass
shelves piled high with eye balm, corrective facial masques, and
salmon mousse hair balm. I was approached by Françoise, who, in
addition to her lab coat, wore a Hermès scarf and Chanel earrings.

Françoise asked if I would like an analysis of my skin. It
struck me as a wonderful idea. "What are your problem areas,
*madame?*" Françoise asked, her concerned voice suggesting there
might be many of them.

Within minutes I was like an analysand on the couch,
blurting out my long list of problems to Françoise. She listened,
jotting down notes on a white pad with a Mont Blanc pen.
Undaunted by the challenge I presented, she proceeded to fill a
white wicker basket with items from various parts of the shop.
She then explained the purpose of each product and the miracles
that would result from using it. Always, she ended with "I myself
use this product, *madame.*"

That was good enough for me. In less than twenty minutes I blew almost half a week's food budget on creams, balms, and restoratives. What better way to celebrate the New Me than by sprucing up the facade of the Old Me? Besides, I told myself, I'd make up for it by eating in cheaper places. Still, I worried a bit. Between the taxi from the airport and my foray into the world of French cosmetics, I'd already spent a lot more than I'd planned.

But what the heck, I thought, heading for the hotel and my first look at the room where I would spend at least the next month. I was excited, but also a little nervous about seeing it. Although I know many travelers think of a hotel as "just a place to sleep," it was important to me to feel at home in this room.

A young chambermaid preceded me up the winding staircase, stopping in the middle of it. Pulling out a key, she opened a door I hadn't noticed, one situated between the reception area and the second floor. It was the door to my room. I stepped inside. What I saw disappointed me.

After passing through a narrow entry hall, I entered a long narrow room. It seemed to tilt to one side, the side occupied by a huge, dark armoire. At the far end of the room was the bed; or, to be precise, two twin beds that had been pushed together. In the middle of the room was a round table covered with a fresh linen cloth and flanked by two straight-backed chairs; it served as both desk and dining space. Opposite the bed, near the small entry hall, was a slightly worn love seat, its wine-colored velvet arms and back rising and falling in classic Art Deco fashion. All in all, it was not what I had hoped for.

But the room had two big, beautiful French windows that opened out over a small green courtyard. There was one in the large, well-appointed bathroom, too, situated in such a way that it could be left open without any lack of privacy. Brushing my teeth in the morning while looking out over the courtyard became one of my real pleasures.

Still, at first glance, I couldn't imagine living in this room for several weeks. Later, when the room became home to me—

when I had learned to appreciate how comfortable the bed was and how elegant the linens that covered it, how spotlessly clean the room was kept and how well it actually functioned—I realized that first impressions about hotel rooms are like first loves: Neither is based on the concept of how, over time, one can come to appreciate the pleasures of durability over infatuation.

✦ ✦ ✦ ✦ ✦

At a little before five in the afternoon I left the hotel and headed for the Café de Flore. It was early, but I was quite hungry and, in fact, almost ready to retire. The Flore, which was only a short distance from my hotel, was a great place to sit and take in Paris while eating the perfect omelette.

It was a mild evening, so I chose a seat on the terrace and ordered wine. This was the best time to come to the Flore, I thought, looking around. Lunchtime here always seemed hectic, a time when people came to see and be seen, to make deals and use their cellular phones. Late afternoon at the Flore, on the other hand, had a relaxed ambience; people laughed a lot and gossiped and seemed not to be in a hurry to go somewhere else.

It was a lesson I hoped to learn in the months ahead: how to stop rushing from place to place, always looking ahead to the next thing while the moment in front of me slipped away unnoticed.

I knew it once, of course—the feeling of connection that comes from seizing the actual world. When I was a child, very little that happened in the real world escaped my attention. Not the brightly colored ice in small paper boats we bought at Mr. Dawson's snowball stand; or the orange-and-white pattern that formed a map of Africa on my cat's back; or the way Mother sat at her dressing table, powdering her beautiful face to a pale ivory color. It used to surprise me, the intensity with which I still remembered these distant memories. But when I entered my fifties—the Age of Enlightenment, as I came to call it—I understood their enduring clarity. By then I'd knocked around enough to know that, in the end, what adds up to a life is nothing more than the accumulation of small daily moments.

A waiter appeared with my omelette and salad. *"Bon appétit,"* he said, placing my meal on the small round table. He reminded me of someone. Belmondo? No. Louis Jourdan? No. I studied his face, a very Gallic one; a little gaunt but handsome in a bony way. It crossed my mind to flirt with him. This was Paris, after all, where women of a certain age are thought quite desirable. But before I could act on my thoughts, the waiter moved to the next table.

After polishing off the salad, omelette, and a bowl of vanilla ice cream, I ordered a *café noir.* Then I settled into one of the great pleasures of café-sitting: surveying the scene. At the next table, a young, shy-looking couple spoke softly in Japanese, trying not to call attention to themselves. Across the way, a darkly handsome man dressed in black sat sketching in a large notebook.

Outside on the terrace, catching the last bit of sun, were the deeply tanned Italians: beautiful women wearing gold jewelry, and sculpted, model-perfect men in Armani suits. And then, of course, there were the Americans—either overdressed or under-dressed but always friendly—and the French, who rule the Flore, rightfully so, and were elegant no matter their attire.

I sat sipping my second *café,* imagining the time when Sartre and Simone de Beauvoir practically lived at the Flore: writing, eating, and even seeing people by appointment here. It was not difficult to imagine. I could imagine doing it myself. Of course, at that moment, I could see myself doing just about any-thing, including ringing up friends to set up appointments: *"Bonjour, mon ami, it's Alice. Look, I'll be at the Flore most of the afternoon and I've decided to have some friends over. Why don't you come by sometime after one? Dress casual. See you then."*

At about eight I noticed a subtle change in the light. As the sun moved lower in the western skies, it washed the ancient Paris buildings with pale-pink patterns. The faces of those gathered at the Flore were tinted rosy by the softening light; everyone looked years younger. By now my eyes were growing heavy from jet lag. It was bedtime for me.

As I strolled back to the hotel, I stopped to watch a young couple near the tiny, romantic place Furstenberg. From a radio they'd set on the ground, the voice of Frank Sinatra rose like smoke, filling the air with words about a small hotel and the longing of lovers to be there together. I watched as they began to dance slowly to the music, arms wrapped around each other. The square was deserted except for the young dancers beneath the fragrant paulownia trees. Of course, even had the square been bursting with tourists, the dancers would not have noticed; they existed only for one another.

I knew that feeling. As I stood in the shadows, it all came back: the feel of Dick Reavey's arms around me at the high school prom, swaying to the last slow dance of the night, the swish of my silk dress, the sharp edge of his white collar against my face. Swaying back and forth to the music, our cheeks touching, inhaling the scent of his aftershave, nothing else existed. Time stopped, and we hung there, dancing, not looking back, not looking forward. After the music ended, we'd walked off the dance floor hand in hand, dazed with longing. Some part of me still felt I would never feel that alive again.

Does anyone ever forget such moments? I wondered, watching the two dancers in the place Furstenberg. What if more of life could be like that? Like the last slow dance, where, to echo T. S. Eliot, a lifetime burns in every moment?

✦ ✦ ✦ ✦ ✦

By eight-thirty I was back at the hotel. The bed had been turned down and there were fresh flowers in the room—a bouquet sent by a friend living in Paris. The food had revived me, so I decided to try one of Françoise's miracle beauty products. But which one? The mask, I thought, the one that Françoise promised would "tighten the skin and circulate the blood."

With the bathroom window open, I stood in front of the mirror and spread the green cream on my face. I watched as the mask stiffened and small fissures appeared on the surface. For some reason, I thought of my thrifty Scottish grandmother. How she would have laughed at the idea of spending money on cosmetics! Her own beauty habits consisted of going into the garden early in the morning to splash her face with drops of dew.

"Aye, it's nature's own free moisturizer," she would tell me on those Saturday-morning forays into the garden. If I closed my eyes now, I could still see it: a stocky, plain-looking woman in her sixties and a curious, plain-looking child of eight, both dressed in bathrobes and slippers, kneeling in the misty light of dawn and with cupped hands splashing dewdrops onto their faces. Afterward, I would fall back into the warmth of my bed, to doze and dream of the scones I smelled baking in the kitchen.

So strong was the image of that woman and child—one dead now for over thirty years, the other grown—that when I peeled off the stiff green mask, I half expected to see my grandmother's face emerge.

Perhaps tonight I will dream of my grandmother, dream we are back in that garden, together again, I thought, climbing into bed.

But I didn't. Instead I fell into a deep sleep. When I awakened the next morning, the Paris sun had entered my room, falling in slanted golden rays across the floor. I walked to the window and inhaled the golden air. The breeze carried with it the sound of children's voices from a nearby playground; happy, laughing voices that called to one another in high, excited shrieks of irrepressible energy. The language of pleasure, I thought, is the same everywhere.

The sounds floated into my room, swirling around the dark armoire and the red velvet love seat before drifting out the window into the skies of Saint-Germain-des-Prés. As I listened to the high, childish voices, I imagined them moving like laughing birds along the narrow street outside; I imagined them turning

right at the rue de Beaune, a tiny street that ended at the Seine;
I imagined them landing on the water, wings tucked back, play-
fully joining the river's glorious rush through all of Paris, sending
small cries of contagious joy throughout the city.

A gentle tapping on the door reminded me I had left a
request for breakfast in my room. *"Bonjour, madame,"* said a
cheerful young woman carrying a large tray with white china
plates and silver pots. She placed it on the table, just between
the two open windows. *"Bon appétit."*

I sat down and studied the tray's contents. Carefully laid
out on a white linen cloth were fresh orange juice, croissants and
brioche, strawberry jam, cheese, and a tall silver pot of coffee,
accompanied by a smaller server filled with hot milk. I thought
of my usual breakfast at home—coffee and a slice of whole-wheat
toast dabbed with peanut butter, served from the top of my television set. Usually I ate this repast while making phone calls and
watching Katie Couric on the *Today* show. In my former life, the
one that existed until yesterday, it was my habit always to do at
least two things at once; three, if possible.

But there would be no hurried phone calls or Katie Couric
watching this morning. In a leisurely manner, I draped the linen
napkin on my lap and took a sip of orange juice. Into my large
china coffee cup I poured a combination of the strong black coffee and hot milk. I added two small cubes of brown sugar from
the sugar bowl and stirred the mixture with a small silver spoon.

This is heaven, I thought, sipping the coffee.

I picked up a croissant, broke it open, and covered it in a
painterly way with strokes of red jam. Then, just before taking the
first bite, I raised the croissant and, in a celebratory mood, issued
a toast to myself: *Welcome to Paris, Madame S. And bon appétit.*

# The Fall

## Maria Antonieta Osornio Ramirez

### translated by Joan Chatfield-Taylor

My old friends tell me now how arrogant and haughty I was when I was a parachutist in the Mexican army. I felt I could do anything. There was no obstacle I couldn't conquer, no discipline that I could not master. I had everything a woman could want. I was very pretty; my long, curly hair shone, and my body was strong and svelte, thanks to the intense exercise of my job. My family was healthy and I had two little children, Mariela and Paco. I had gone from being a runaway child who had married to break family ties to being a woman who was both intrepid and in love with her husband. In a short time I had reached some important goals, and life was smiling at me at every step—or, I should say, at every jump.

As a soldier, I would participate in parades and official celebrations. On February 24, 1984, we were assigned to perform a jump in the Flag Day celebration in Iguala, in the state of Guerrero. Three of us—my husband Serafín, another sergeant, and I—would be the ones to form the national colors in the air with our green, white, and red parachutes. We had practiced the jump without any problem. Even the fact that the president of the republic, Miguel de la Madrid, would be there, didn't intimidate me. In fact, that day my greatest interest was not the jump itself but attending the Pan-American Parachuting Championship in Uruapan, Michoacán. For this reason I had an airplane ready in Iguala so that I could leave as soon as the exhibition was over.

The night before the celebration, my husband, our son, and I stayed in a hotel in Iguala. The following morning we woke up very early and got ready to make the jump. It was rare that I didn't feel up to it, but that morning I didn't want to jump and I had an indescribably strange sensation. I put on my equipment reluctantly and didn't adjust the leg straps very well. Until we were flying in the helicopter from which we would jump, I didn't dare tell Serafín that I didn't want to do it. By then, it was too late. We were practically at the target. I, the most reserved of women, asked Serafín to give me a kiss.

✦ ✦ ✦ ✦ ✦

Green, white, and red . . . the three of us jumped, making the formation. The parachutes opened and I, the green, who was above, hooked myself to the legs of the white, who in turn had wrapped his legs around the red. From the ground, they saw the tricolor flag; in the sky, I was taking the weight of the other two parachutists on my legs. We heard applause from afar. And then the trouble started. I was supposed to be the last to land, but crosswinds began to push me farther from the mark where I was supposed to touch down. Suddenly I realized that I was going too fast, and that I was going to land on the people below. I braked too hard . . . the parachute collapsed. I had taken off my leg straps in the middle of the jump, so the emergency parachute flew up to my neck.

In a matter of seconds I was on the ground. *Craaack!* . . . I heard my bones breaking inside of me. I had made a perfect jump, I had landed exactly on the mark a few steps from the president and the secretary of defense, but I couldn't move. Where was my head? Where was my body? I tried to sit up and had a terrifying sensation: I felt only my head; no part of the rest of my body had any feeling.

What had happened? In a few seconds, everything began to move in slow motion; I heard nothing. A dazzling light filled me completely and I had a sensation of divine pleasure, but it was only for an instant. An intense pain in my neck jerked me back into the present. I would have screamed with all my strength, but I couldn't. I was hardly breathing. Serafín, terrified, leaned close to me.

"I'm dying . . . I can't move."

I hadn't lost consciousness, and I observed the rescue activity as if I were watching a film.

"A stretcher! A stretcher!"

"Don't move her, leave her alone, don't touch her," Serafín screamed desperately. He removed my helmet with great care, but the commander called him to take part in the formation. In a moment I found myself in the hands of the paramedics in the ambulance. I saw them cut my uniform with a pair of scissors and remove my jewelry.

"What are they doing?" I thought.

The president gave orders that I be taken in the helicopter to the military hospital in Mexico City. They permitted Serafín and my son, Paco, to accompany me. Paco, horrified, was holding my hand. "What's going on?" his expression seemed to ask. I winked at him to cheer him up, but the pain was so intense that for several seconds I thought I would faint.

In an instant my life took a 180-degree turn and was never the same again.

I had suffered a fracture of the cervical bones. But those few words don't remotely describe the implications the fracture in my neck had. The result was a spastic quadriplegia. To put it simply, it means that I lost movement in the four extremities. The only things that I could move were my eyes and my mouth. From the neck down, I was completely immobile.

I lived the next three years in a whirlwind that shook every aspect of my existence. My life, which had appeared so stable, so successful, changed completely. I was given blunt lessons in the relativity of time.

As soon as I entered the military hospital, they put me into physical therapy and waited two weeks to operate on me. It seems that the presidential referral weighed on the doctors, and instead of speeding up their actions, they delayed them. I saw people going in and out of my room: my inconsolable family. Serafín torn to pieces. Sometimes, as if in a dream, I heard voices I knew; at other times I saw someone move their lips but could not hear what they were saying.

Finally, after two weeks, the doctors decided to operate on my shattered neck, which looked like a naked chicken. The comparison is grotesque, but I can find no other as exact. When they opened my neck, the doctor told me later, it seemed to vomit liquid through the incision: It was the spinal medulla that was spilling out. They took out a piece of my hip bone to rebuild the spinal column and put in a bone transplant that would fix my neck in place permanently. Theoretically, after the operation I would not be able to move it . . . or any other part of my body.

After the surgery, my survival hopes depended on a traction of forty pounds. They attached four screws to my skull, which in turn were attached to a kind of crown. From the center of the crown hung the weight that pulled my neck. Without giving me any anesthesia, they drilled four holes in my cranium. It had to be this way because I had to tell them how far they could drill. Two days later, the screws that held the crown came out, and they had to drill three more holes to fix it in place.

I felt that they literally were ripping apart my head and my brain. I fainted from the intensity of the pain.

In this first stage in the hospital, the most critical, I was near death several times. I remember occasions when the medical personnel were running from one side of my room to the other, saying that I didn't have a pulse and trying to resuscitate me. I couldn't speak or move, my eyes were closed, but I listened to everything and I was filled with terror imagining the possibility that they would declare me dead and bury me alive. I heard every type of commentary around me—some of which, I am sure, would not have been said if the doctors had known that I could hear what they were saying.

Sometimes I was in contact with that brilliant and beautiful light that I had seen during the accident and, for a few seconds, I bathed in a delightful feeling. I saw my father, stretching out his arms and calling me to him. Then the old sharp pain would clobber me, and the image of my mother appeared. She was holding the hands of my children and saying severely, "You will never see your father or your children again."

Sometimes I saw myself surrounded by parachutes of all colors, with me in the middle, flying freely with the wind caressing my body and holding me up like an invisible mattress.

Pain, agony, suffering, medications, needles and tubes, despairing faces, my children with fearful expressions, my husband broken down with grief, tears shed in my bed of pain, words of encouragement, doctors and nurses who came and went, morphine to dull the pain. These were the things—real or unreal, I couldn't tell the difference—that suffocated me. Day and night were no longer distinct because there was never a moment of relief, there were never changes in the pain. There was only fighting it, second after second. The hours and the days had no meaning, because my life without movement had lost it, too.

The sky, the clouds, the freedom of flight, the pure pleasure of a parachute jump had been replaced by immobility, traction, respirator, catheter, my begging them to give me another injection to dull the pain . . . the pain.

There is so much to say about pain, and at the same time there is nothing at all to say. Pain is what it is. I don't think that there is anyone who can endure it. It is a tyrant that bends the strongest and the most determined. Pain breaks through all the boundaries of human dignity and forces a person to grovel and roll around in his own unconscious. Pain doesn't offer a truce, doesn't know the meaning of pity, doesn't respond to tears. Once it goes, it has transformed the soul as iron becomes tempered steel when put to great heat.

The lack of movement atrophied my vital functions, and I had to submit to a large quantity of medications that, on the one hand, were supposed to help my recovery but, on the other hand, changed the normal functioning of my body. Normal? What did the word mean in my condition? Physically I was a deformed being, every orifice connected to tubes and hoses, with needles that in large part represented my survival. Due to the drugs I was swollen, hair had grown on my face, and I was covered with acne.

I hadn't seen myself in a mirror until the day a friend came to visit me for the first time. The shock was so great that she had to run to the bathroom to throw up. I asked for a mirror. I think that if I could have, I also would have run to the bathroom to vomit, because I was a true monster. How much my life had changed! I had been the champion—admired, envied, decorated, and honored—and now I was a wreck whose future was confined to a bed, without any movement below the neck.

Each day was an endless struggle. Sometimes I assumed that I would soon escape from it all. Other days I thought that I would simply die and that then it would all be over. Sometimes I went into a panic at the possibility that I would be like that forever. The one thing that was certain was that time was passing and that, through sheer willpower, I was still alive. But still I could not move.

Several months after the accident, I began to recover some feeling. Though this meant that I was improving, at the same time it meant I had to feel more pain. Because I had lain in the same position, motionless, for so long, I was covered with bedsores that I hadn't been able to feel. When I began to recover some feeling, I screamed as pain burned my whole body. Nevertheless, this new sensation gave me hope that I might walk again.

Weeks went by, and my morale dipped. My will to live seemed to evaporate, replaced by the pain of my reality, which was so difficult to comprehend that I would talk to God. "Why did this happen to me?" I'd ask. "Jesus Christ was crucified and tortured, but I've been waiting here for months. Who did I kill? Why do I keep on living? Did I hurt someone to deserve this punishment?

God doesn't exist, because he can't exist and let me suffer this way." I spent a lot of time crying, to the point that the cleaning woman had to mop up the puddles that formed on the floor. Serafín came often and cried by my side. He put photographs of my children on the ceiling. They were my only consolation.

Choosing to keep living under these conditions was a daily exercise of my will. The decision to live may last only a few minutes, or maybe even a whole day—and then the next day you have to start all over again. At times I thought that it would be better to die, because my life in that state was so useless. I felt that I was giving more suffering and pain than good to my loved ones and that I was becoming a burden to them.

One day when the desire to live was greater than the wish to die, I said to the doctor that I had to sit up—at any cost. I had spent more than six months lying down, prohibited from changing position because of the danger of making the lesions worse.

"Doctor," I said to my orthopedist, "if you don't do something so that I can sit up, I'm going to kill myself. Either I sit up tomorrow or I kill myself tomorrow. I can't be like this another day."

The doctor had the compassion to believe me. I suppose he felt that because I asked him for this, it meant I wanted to keep on living. So he came up with a kind of plaster cast to place around my torso, attached to my head by means of some rods so that it served as traction. And the next day they sat me up. The doctor didn't dare leave, since he was expecting the worst, but I got through the first hour . . . the second . . . the third, and I felt as if I was reborn. I had regained part of my world simply by seeing it again from a vertical position. The plaster cast in some ways intensified the pain, but it was so beautiful to be sitting that it didn't matter. Three days passed, and I stayed sitting up until I fainted from the effort. It didn't matter. It was worth the pain. I had made a giant step that fed my hopes that one day I would leave—walking.

In losing my mobility, other aspects of my perception had

been sharpened. My room was about twenty meters from the stair-case, but I could recognize the steps of whoever was coming up. I could detect the steps of the cleaning woman, of each doctor, each nurse, each daily visitor. I began to observe carefully each person who came to see me. I perceived their movements, their attitudes, their gestures with a clarity that I had never known before. Not only could I see the exterior of each person, but I also felt their inner selves, their state of mind, their character.

During those first months, many people filed past my bed. I received visits from generals and other important people with whom I had worked. Colleagues and friends came. But the pass-ing of time meant that my condition was no longer a novelty. Little by little they stopped coming, and after several months I was almost totally alone. My former friends were replaced by the patients in wheelchairs who populated the hospital, by the cleaning women, by the different shifts of guards, by the doctors and by nurses in every mood. I was part of a new family, but I missed terribly the people and the world outside. In my worst moments I felt that everyone had abandoned me.

A few extraordinary friends stayed with me. In particular I remember Guadalupe and Pilar, two beautiful sisters who had become my best friends. They never tired of visiting me, to cheer me up, to pray with and for me.

One day, more than two years after my accident, Guadalupe and Pilar got special permission to take me out. They told the doc-tors that we were going on vacation, but they took me to Ciudad Juarez for cell therapy. We did it in secret, because otherwise the doctors would never have let me leave the hospital. Guadalupe and Pilar had realized that I was severely drugged by so much med-ication, and had decided to help me. In Ciudad Juarez I endured a terrible detox treatment, as though I were a drug addict. And I was one, living as I did on strong painkillers and other drugs.

The treatment helped me a great deal, and I returned to the hospital on minimal doses of medication. I regained control of my sphincter muscles, and could dedicate myself with greater awareness to my exercises. If it hadn't been for Pilar and Guadalupe, I don't know how much time I would have spent in the hospital, and I don't know what condition I would have ended up in. They removed an obstacle that I was not capable of removing on my own.

✦ ✦ ✦ ✦ ✦

The part of my life that I'm about to recount is one that I most hesitate to speak of. It is so easy to make judgments lightly and to cast a person as "good" or "bad." It is so easy to point an accusatory finger and so difficult to have the love and the compassion to understand that we are fallible human beings, each of whom in this life has his or her own way of maturing and evolving, his or her own difficulties, his or her own limitations of character. It is the easiest thing in the world to judge others as inhuman or unfeeling, without comprehending that one day, perhaps, we will be judged in the same way.

Because of this, to whoever reads my story, I ask that they not judge those I write about as good or bad. I myself, through this process, saw the blackest part of my soul; I felt hatred, destructiveness, jealousy, anger, and the inability to forgive. Who hasn't? Who has not been selfish, vicious, jealous? Who has felt free of hatred, of the wish to kill someone, of the impulse to wish the worst for someone close to us, of the refusal to forgive?

What I am going to relate now was part of the process. From the pain that these events brought me, I gathered the strength and the impetus to move. Thus, my greatest suffering was converted into the greatest strength of my recuperation.

Notwithstanding the impact of the accident, the physical suffering that followed it, and not being able to move, it was the disintegration of my family that ripped my soul apart. The first six months after the accident, Serafín was in intense pain. He would come to see me, and his weeping was constant. Nothing consoled him. Later my friends told me how much he had suffered to see me as an invalid, and that he had changed profoundly. He became quiet and sullen, and little by little distanced himself from everyone.

Due to my physical handicaps, I understood that the relationship between us had changed. I spoke to him, saying that I was giving him his freedom but that the most important thing was that he would not stop caring for our children.

A little while later, I found out that he was going out with another woman and my heart broke like crystal that shatters and can never be repaired. I knew that it would happen, but I couldn't understand that it would happen right in the hospital, that he would not maintain a discreet distance so as not to hurt me.

"Why, when Mexico is so big, didn't you choose another place?" I reproached him.

He was furious at me. He began to complain about situations in our past life. We began to fight violently.

"It's your fault that no one speaks to me and that I'm left without friends," he said bitterly. "They don't know the kind of person you are. You get attention from everyone, and they don't know that you were the cause of everything that's happened."

I don't know what was more painful, feeling the drill in my skull when they adjusted the traction or seeing him in the company of another woman. My blood boiled and I wished every bad thing possible for him. My heart filled with hatred and resentment, and, with the strength of my rage, I decided that I would move one day if only to get hold of a pistol and kill him.

From then on I asked each person who visited me to move my hands, my feet, my legs. They helped me do abdominal exercises, squeeze sponges to close and open my hands, and pass buttons and marbles from one side to the other. I exercised my arms and legs with the help of whoever was there. In the beginning, everything was impossible. But I kept repeating over and over again, "By moving, I have to move." With anger lodged in my soul, I kept going.

Blessed be that anger, I say now, for it was my greatest strength. Seeing Serafín distancing himself from my life, my children muddling along as best they could with me immobile, gave me torrents of courage to do what the doctors had said I would never be able to do. The very pain that I found impossible to believe, that I couldn't bear, aroused me.

So I returned to my obsession. I spent hours and hours trying to move a toe by myself. Many times I convinced myself that I was succeeding.

"I moved it!" I shouted at the nurse. But she didn't believe me. It wasn't true, she said. It was my imagination.

One morning, around three, I clearly felt the toe on my left foot move.

"I'm moving it!" I shouted at the nurse. Skeptical, she came closer and saw that it was true. She ran to call the doctors.

"Tony moved a toe! Tony moved a toe!"

How relative are our successes. What for one person is the most insignificant, unconscious, and superficial thing, for another represents months—and even years—of effort. That movement of my toe required all my will, strength, courage, perseverance, and months of obsessive repetition. For people who can count on all their faculties, it's difficult to imagine what it means to be without movement. If one were tied up for a few hours, one would understand better that handicapped people don't need pity. We only need others to be aware that we have some limitations, which, in return, make us see and experience ourselves and our lives from a different point of view.

It's not easy to give up walking, running, dancing, holding a spoon, and serving oneself food—all the natural movements of a human being. It's not easy to accept the permanent necessity of help and, even more, asking for it constantly to do our activities. It's very difficult to rise above shame and pride to ask for assistance with tasks as elemental as urinating and defecating.

At that moment, a big toe in motion meant everything to me, so much so that I wrote to my brother Jose Luis, also a soldier. He had supported me a great deal, writing to me every day and telephoning to raise my morale. When he learned that I was beginning to move, he made a special trip to see me. I will never forget his face when he came into my room. His disappointment was so striking that I finally understood that my life would never be the same again.

One day, I got up my courage to ask the doctor what my prognosis was. Nervously, he began to walk around the room, without knowing what to say to me.

"The fact that you are alive and can speak is already a miracle in itself," he said, without knowing how to continue.

"Doctor, you believe that I am not going to be able to move. But I am going to prove the contrary. Even if I crawl, you will see how I'm going to succeed."

"How wonderful that you are so optimistic, Tony. This will help you a lot. Certainly you are going to succeed."

"No, doctor, you don't believe what you're saying to me," I interrupted. "You are saying it so as not to discourage me, but, you know what, I believe it and you're going to see, I'm going to prove it."

With my answer, coming spontaneously from my soul, I realized that I had decided to live. After months and months plunged in a tunnel of suffering and desperation, I glimpsed a tiny point of light, far in the distance but, in any case, light. It was the first time since my accident that I heard a different tone in my voice, and I truly found hope in myself.

## Epilogue

At one of the lowest points of her recuperation, Tony Ramirez began to work with two therapists, Dr. Martha Babb and Dr. Marcela Musi. After intense therapy, both physical and psychological, Tony was able to leave the hospital three years after her accident, having recuperated much of her ability to move. Although she never recovered the ability to walk more than a few steps with crutches, she eventually raised her two children, began to support herself, and designed herself a wheelchair-friendly house.

# Boar Hunters, Mushrooms, and Wine-Dark Seas

## Dorothee Danzmann

Rounding the bend, I almost bumped into a hunter standing motionless on the narrow footpath, and nearly jumped with fright. He gasped, and for a moment we stared at each other. Then my dog emerged from the fog surrounding us, followed by one cat, then another. All three animals passed us, cautiously giving the stranger with the gun a wide berth, and disappeared into the fog again. By now the hunter was laughing.

"Going for a walk?" he asked.

I nodded.

"And the cats as well?"

I shrugged my shoulders and said, "What can you do?" I looked at his gun. "Going to shoot wild pigs?"

Now it was his turn to shrug. "Remains to be seen."

"Please don't shoot us!" I replied, only half-joking. We wished each other a good evening and I hastily followed my little convoy uphill, vowing never to take the cats on a walk again in the fog during hunting season. As if I had a say in it!

Three years ago, when we moved two thousand miles across Europe from our home in Hamburg, Germany, to the Pelion peninsula on the east coast of mainland Greece, we were right from the start presented with a fait accompli: Mimi, a compact black-and-white cat, only partially domesticated and with a quite domineering personality. What Mimi wants, she usually gets; she does not take no for an answer. When a puppy moved in with us soon after we had unpacked our trunks, Mimi made the dog her slave, ultimately persuading it to look after the kittens she eventually produced. Now, two and a half years later, the dog, a black-and-white sheepdog who acts as our dangerous-looking watchdog, and one of the kittens she cared for, a bigger and friendlier version of her mother, are still great friends. If the cats so desire, we all go out for a walk in the evening—to the great joy and amusement of any neighbor who happens to meet us.

Following my gang farther up the mountain, I paused to enjoy a sight of great autumnal beauty: fog rising and descending, as if ordered about by a magician; mountain peaks, now seen, now hidden again; and, from behind our highest mountain, the moon, rising majestically and quite fast. It was utterly quiet and somewhat eerie, like being on stage in a dramatic theater show, waiting for the action to begin.

Occasionally I caught a glimpse of the sea, some eight hundred meters below. This proximity of mountains and sea makes the Pelion unique. On fine days the Sporadic Islands, Skiathos and Skopelos, seem to be just a stone's throw away. It is a view I will never tire of: the mountains, so green in summer, so colorful in autumn, so white in winter; the bay of Volos on one side, the Aegean, Homer's wine-dark sea, on the other.

The cats were getting restless and started chasing each other up and down trees. I whistled and soon Rita came running, ears flapping, a broad grin on her face. We trotted home, where I would sit down at my computer to finish the work I had promised myself I would do. The walk with the animals had cleared my head and filled my lungs with clean air. In spite of our encounter with the hunter—I don't like these men in camouflage who pop up everywhere in the mountains as regularly as mushrooms each fall and who do not always really know what they are doing—the walk had put me in a tremendously good mood.

Back in Hamburg, I used to ride my bicycle to clear my head. A half hour going to work in the morning, a half hour coming back, thinking about the store on my way to work, thinking about dinner on the way back—I loved those rides. Like my walks here in Greece, they presented me with colors and light and pictures; but in Hamburg, unlike here, I could never completely relax and just think my own thoughts. Traffic in Hamburg is heavy at all times of the day, and not paying attention to it can be deadly. One of the things I cherish in my new life is this ability to really let my thoughts drift as I walk the footpaths of the mountains around our house. I can pursue ideas to my heart's content, spend as long as I want with a sentence I know I have not translated right, think about stories I want to write.

Until three years ago, my partner, Petra, and I were booksellers in Hamburg, a harbor city of roughly two million inhabitants that is almost as flat as a pancake. Now we live, at a height of seven hundred meters, in a cottage on the very edge of a tiny Greek village up on mythical Mount Pelion. I can't tell you exactly how many people reside in Agios Georgios in the summer, but during the winter no more than twenty houses are lived in. Petra and I live here year-round.

Moving to the south of Europe after having been northerners for almost fifty years has transformed our lives. We no longer rent a flat; we own a house and have a garden we must look after. We are no longer surrounded by the noise and pollution of Hamburg; there is not even a road leading to our cottage, only a footpath. It's so quiet up here, you can hear yourself think. In Hamburg, there was no room for animals. Now a dog and two cats share our house, and we share the garden with the vole, the walnuts with the badger, the mushrooms with the wild boar. The changes in our daily life are considerable, but some things have remained the same.

Buchhandlung Seitenweise, the bookstore Petra and I owned in Hamburg, was miniature—only thirty-five square meters full of printed matter. We catered to the needs of the neighborhood, but we were also determined to help keep a wide-ranging literary and political culture alive and visible, to show the interested public that there are more books in this world than on the average list of best-sellers. The store made enough money for the two of us to live on; we never had much, but we had enough. More important than money was the satisfaction we got from our work and the independence we enjoyed. Our move to Greece didn't change that. The money we make now, we earn as translators. It's not much, but it's enough to get by on, at the low level we are accustomed to, and the work is highly satisfying. Here, though, we do many other things that are just as important to our lifestyle and well-being and just as rewarding as our translation jobs. We tend a vegetable garden that supplies us almost year-round with the vegetables we need. As we hardly eat any meat, that accounts for a lot. Although our own plot of land is quite small, many edible things are growing wild all around us. There are herbs and mushrooms on the hillsides; deserted apple and cherry orchards where we can pick as much unsprayed fruit as we can possibly eat, store, or preserve; chestnut trees, blackberry bushes, wild roses. The wood we use in winter we collect ourselves. We own a small olive grove farther down the mountain, so we are able to make our own oil and pickle our own eating olives. We have made our first wine and it turned out well—slightly pink, dry, and fruity table wine. Friends gave us the grapes to make it, but next year we hope to have enough of our own.

Petra was born and raised on a small farm, and I am the daughter of a passionate amateur handicraftsman who loved to pass on his skills. Both of us learned a lot of practical things at home and kept on learning while tending tiny independent bookstores run on a shoestring. There is little we are reluctant to tackle. That came in handy and saved a lot of money back in Hamburg, but it's a prerequisite for living up here like we do.

Seitenweise had been, from the bookshelves to the lighting, the work of our own hands. Now we have learned to deal with plastering as well; we construct stone walls and terraces, fix roofs, and build sheds, and I am no longer mortally afraid of a chain saw.

People here often ask us why we have come. In the past, when Greece was one of Europe's poorhouses, a lot of people had to leave this country in search of a better life, and quite a few of them went to Germany. Now things are changing. Young people can stay and find work and some families are even returning from abroad, but northern Europe is still seen by many people as the better place to live. The Albanians who come to our village each year in search of work do not understand us at all. Every one of them would rather be in Germany, earning better money than they do here.

We try to explain that, for us and right now, the Pelion is perfect. We explain about Hamburg being such a big city, where the noise and the constant onslaught of pictures and impressions can wreck your nerves if you live there too long. We explain how the gray, wet cloud that descends on Hamburg each November and sometimes stays until the end of April can send you into a deep depression. We explain how it became more difficult each year to joyfully keep on struggling in a small, independent bookstore when the big publishing houses and gigantic bookstores have transformed our trade from one concerned with culture and the hearts and minds of people to one mainly concerned with making big money.

Nobody understands, of course. Our complaints are on such a cerebral level that we are sometimes ashamed to mention them. A lot of the people asking did not leave their country, their villages, their families for philosophical reasons. They left because they or their loved ones were suffering.

The only real suffering we can name is Petra's allergies and chronic sinusitis, which, her doctor had explained, would only worsen in the damp, polluted air of Hamburg. Her doctor had strongly advised her to take her poor head to a drier and warmer place if at all possible. Wanting to be healthy is something all our questioners understand.

As I had, eventually. It had taken me quite a bit of time and hard thinking to decide to leave a town where there were roads my bicycle and I knew every crack in, where almost all my close friends, my sister, my brother-in-law, and my nephew live. The noise, the grayness, the pollution of Hamburg had not been affecting me the way it had Petra. My family owns a small piece of land and a little house on the outskirts of Hamburg, so I thought I had enough exposure to clean air and nature. I had no pressing need to change my life. But what could I say about the allergies, the sinusitis? Surely nobody should be made to live with chronic illnesses, if they have the choice?

When we were making the decision three years ago, Petra and I had been together nineteen years. If she felt she had to move from one end of Europe to the other in order to regain health and happiness, I was prepared to at least contemplate following her there.

We can't tell our fellow villagers that, of course. This is rural Greece, not alternative Hamburg. The neighbors don't know we are a couple. When we first came, some of the women offered to find good-looking Greek husbands for us, but now they have accepted the fact that we are far too old to start families. Therefore, they say, it is a good thing that we can keep each other company. People in the village are friendly to us.

When I started to think seriously about exchanging life in a German city for one in a Greek village, my thoughts and worries were centered around two issues. The first was financial security— how would we earn money?—and the second was homesickness— would I be able to live without my friends and family? Fortunately, the question of where we would go had already been settled.

For many years Petra and I had spent at least two weeks each year in Greece, sometimes much longer. We felt the Greek way of life suited us, the slightly anarchistic manner in which things seemed to be done, the spirit of improvisation so different from our sometimes-too-orderly Germany. We had started to learn the language, we had started to read modern Greek literature—and on one of our journeys we had both fallen in love with the Pelion.

The Pelion peninsula, halfway between Thessaloniki and Athens, is a green and magical place. A narrow strip of land with impressively high mountains, the peninsula has its own microclimate. When the snow melts in spring, there are streams and waterfalls everywhere. Homer already praised the lushness of the Pelion, its wealth of herbs and flowers. Here the Greek gods came when they wanted to have a really good party. The centaurs, mythical creatures, half man and half beast, are said to have lived here, too. Here, Petra, having inherited a bit of money after the death of her favorite aunt, managed to find the perfect house in the perfect village on the perfect mountain. Both of us had vacationed here, friends and family had seen it. We had already made some friends in the area.

But how were we going to earn money? The idea of giving up all we had so carefully created made me quite dizzy at first. After all, both of us were in our late forties, we had never made enough money to put anything aside, and our health insurance was connected to our status as employees of the bookstore. Bookselling is not a trade you can take abroad like tiling or carpentry; it is very much related to language, culture, history, politics, and society. Our Greek was not nearly good enough for any in-depth exposure to the educated public and, besides, there are no bookstores in Agios Georgios. Living off the land was out of the question; many *Greek* farmers find it hard to live off the land. Our income, I felt, had to come from abroad—from "home," that is. Before bookselling became my profession, I had been a translator. I would become one again, and Petra would help with the proofreading. We would buy a computer, get an Internet connection, and be able to communicate with the world and work from home.

Now I sit surrounded by modern technology: a state-of-the-art computer, flat screen, laser printer, scanner—the works. But on my desk I keep a pair of binoculars and a book on the birds of Europe. I want to know what's going on in my front yard.

When we tell people here how we make our money—working in Greece, that is, but as part of the German economy—they can relate to it. They understand that we have found a way to make the best out of two worlds. The other day I bought a pair of jeans from a young Romani at a stall near the harbor and had to tell once more what brought me to the Pelion of all places and how I supported myself here. While I explained, the woman's face lit up. "That's brilliant!" she said. "I could do that! I speak more languages than you do!" She probably does. She wasn't Greek, but her Greek was excellent. Petra and I still just get by; at our age it is not so easy anymore to learn another foreign language. And way too many of our friends speak English.

I had decided back in Hamburg that I would face the problem of homesickness when and if it arose. As my sister pointed out, Hamburg would not run away, and modern technology would connect us all via cheap phone calls, emails, and faxes. And there would be visits, of course, holidays we would all spend together, sharing quality time instead of the occasional exhausted drink after work.

Petra and I still feel very much part of the old gang at home and have made new friends in Greece. All our friends from Hamburg have been to see us at least once. The first year we had visitors from February on until late October, and for Christmas as well. Sometimes there was not enough space and time to shape our new life, but it was still reassuring to have our friends around.

Three years later, things have calmed down a bit. We send and receive a lot of emails, we know what is going on in our friends' lives, they can relate to stories we tell about Agios Georgios. I get the blues a bit, sometimes, when someone has a birthday and we are missing the great food, the fun, the companionship of everyone getting together. But there are birthday parties here as well, where our new friends come together and we can listen to their stories and get to know them better. And a lot of people have been extremely kind to us over here— Greeks and expatriates alike.

In the nearby town of Volos, an international women's group has been in existence for more than twenty years. We met some of the women even before we moved here, and the meetings, every second Sunday at someone's house, have become quite important to us. Some of our new friends—women from all over the world, but mainly from Western Europe—have been living in Greece for a long time. They are married to Greek men, and they have raised their children in two cultures and languages. A few months ago the son of an English mother and a Greek father brought home a wife from Poland, enhancing again our own, miniature, united Europe.

◆ ◆ ◆ ◆ ◆

On the whole, things have pretty much turned out as we planned, and I marvel at how lucky we have been. We did find work, Hamburg did not run away, we do not get too homesick too often. All the difficulties we encountered—there were quite a few, and fortunately we did not see them coming, because otherwise I just might have stayed home—were overcome and in the end provided us with many good stories to tell. Especially the ones concerning the winters.

When Petra bought the house—actually two tiny, one-room houses, partly connected by a roof—we meant it to be a holiday home. The farmer who owned it before the German lady who eventually sold it to us had lived here only from June to November. The whole village of Agios Georgios is a traditional summer village. People live here in the summer to tend to their cherries, apples, and chestnuts and to put their sheep onto the summer meadows. As soon as the olive harvest starts, they pack up and go down to the winter villages.

Even though few families now live on farming alone, this

cycle has not changed. When we proclaimed that we meant to stay up in Agios Georgios year-round, the women in the village told us it could not be done. There would be too much snow, it would be too cold and way too lonely. But if we insisted on trying the impossible, they said, we would need a lot of wood, noodles, rice, dried beans, and zwieback. We dutifully stocked up on all that and then had a very mild winter. That was a blessing, because we were not prepared at all for the real thing. When I think of our tiny woodpile that year, covered by a thin plastic sheet that the first decent snowstorm would have spirited off to Alaska, it still makes me shudder. That winter we had snow for Christmas; on Boxing Day it was gone. How we laughed at the Greeks then: If this was winter, we definitely had seen worse!

Whoever is responsible for snow among the gods up on Mount Olympus must have heard us laugh. Winter the following year meant business and pointed out all the weaknesses of our summer house and our somewhat naive approach to mountain life. The first snow fell on December 7. By the tenth we were effectively snowed in and it was still snowing. We had to work hard every day to keep our doors and windows open. The fences were buried, so the dog had a great time, coming and going as she pleased. The car was parked down in the village. Keeping the path to the village square open was another daily task. Carrying provisions up to the house could take up to one and a half hours, instead of the usual ten minutes. When friends from Germany came to spend Christmas, it took the four of us a whole day to unload their car. They were quite impressed. We weren't—not anymore. We were just happy to have survived so far, without more dramatic mishaps than nearly burning the house down because we had neglected to sweep the chimney properly.

After the friends had left in January, we were without running water for two weeks. I had to go to a nearby well to get water every day—an easy distance normally, but quite exhausting in a snowstorm. Our wood supply was running low, and whenever I found branches of dead trees that had not been buried completely, I carried them to the house, through meters of snow, on my own. Petra had hurt her back while picking olives. And we had a lot of translating to do, some of it urgent. The roof of the house I worked in had no insulation to speak of. It was rather cold rather often. The snow stayed till the end of February.

Last winter the snow came in February and stayed till April. Again it was no picnic, again the house disappeared beneath meters of snow; but this time we coped much better, both psychologically and physically, since we had done a lot of work on the houses. We were able to enjoy the winter landscape; we went for walks and looked at tracks in the snow, ventured out to join the other year-round people in the village pub and once even had an impromptu afternoon party in the snow with Swiss friends from across the valley.

"They"—neighbors, television, and other assorted experts—say there is going to be a mild winter this year.

✦ ✦ ✦ ✦ ✦

We paid attention to the seasons in Hamburg as well, of course, receiving new books in spring and autumn, taking time to dust all the shelves in summer, and glad for Christmas business in winter. In Greece, though, we feel the seasons more, because they affect us more directly.

Spring is the time to take stock of the damage winter has done, to repair things, to paint the windows and doors, to collect and cut wood for the coming winter. It is also the season for planting the garden and watching excitedly as the plants we will live on all year start to grow. These are the months when we prune the olive trees, go for walks, marvel at the waterfalls, and look for the tiny orchids that can be found in great quantity and variety on our mountains. Spring is when we start going out again, to see people, to go to town for pleasure. The dirt road leading up to our house dries out and we don't have to park the car down in the village any longer.

In summer, we try not to work too hard, because this is the time for visitors. Life slows down in the heat. We drive down to the sea daily and are glad that our house stays nice and cool not only in winter. The garden, of course, does not sleep, and there always seems to be too much of everything: cherries and apricots and plums and all the summer vegetables. Neighbors come visiting with bags of cucumbers, we go visiting with bags of tomatoes. Everyone is exchanging recipes, everyone is pickling and canning, longing to preserve at least some of the colors and tastes of summer to enjoy during the long winter.

Autumn means olives and the harvest of all the delicacies in and around our garden.

We celebrate the seasons. On May 1 we meet with friends for a picnic and pick wildflowers for a wreath for our front doors. We wish everyone a good summer, and in September, we wish everyone a good winter. In spring we inquire of each other how our winter has been. Did we have sufficient wood? Did anybody get ill?

✦ ✦ ✦ ✦ ✦

The last three years have been filled with adventures, new experiences, and much learning. Both Petra and I have discovered talents in the other and in ourselves that we did not think we possessed. We feel a new respect for each other and for the things we have accomplished. Not only has our relationship survived two winters in close confinement, it has thrived. I am glad we came here and glad we came when we did, when we were young and strong enough to enjoy this new life that is physically much harder than the one we led in the city, but also old enough to appreciate clean air and water, a garden, the company of pets, the chance to lead a more contemplative life. I feel I have been granted the space my mind needed after so many years of dealing with the public. I have started to write, and an English friend and I are composing a screenplay. I cherish the fact that much of my time is spent not talking to people, sometimes quite alone. I would not have felt the same way thirty years ago, when I first moved to Hamburg as a young woman searching for the kind of adventure only a city could provide.

Now a trip to nearby Volos is all the outward excitement I need. Volos, with its 100,000 inhabitants the fourth-largest city in Greece, is big enough to be lively and buzzing, small enough for a newcomer to get acquainted fast. Like Hamburg, Volos is a harbor town; like Hamburg it has a university and a rich cultural life. In the beginning I went to Volos often to feel urban again, to hear and smell the traffic. Now once a week is utterly sufficient. The other day I drove back from town to find the place where I normally park my car occupied by a mule. Going down the footpath to our house, I met a flock of turkeys and one of my cats, and I was totally satisfied to be home again.

# The Promise of Fruit

## Susanne Holly Brent

A few days after my father-in-law moved to Arizona, he decided to plant a peach tree in his backyard.

"It will die," I said with certainty. "I've never seen peach trees grow in Arizona."

"Is that a fact?" said Bernard, tipping back his stained cowboy hat. It was the same hat he'd worn while feeding cattle, hauling hay, and fixing fence on his Nebraska ranch. The old hat looked as out of place as Bernard did in his new surroundings—a retirement community in southern Arizona where people wear shorts year-round, drive golf carts instead of pickup trucks, and keep animals as pets, not as future food sources.

"That peach tree will never survive the summer," I said, nudging my husband, Ed, to agree.

Ed nodded. "She's right. This is November, Dad, but wait until August comes."

After all, we were the ones who'd survived thirteen brutal summers in the desert. Bernard had spent the last seventy in Nebraska.

That day, sparring with my father-in-law about his peach tree, I wondered if he would regret moving to a place where the only green he would ever see was on a golf course.

Bernard and Sharon's new home, like every other house on

their block, had a front yard made of stones. If it weren't for the assortment of cactus, drought-tolerant plants, and trees planted by a previous owner, their house would have looked as if it were sitting in a parking lot.

Bernard had been in Arizona less than a week and he wanted to plant a tree. I suppose it was his way—literally—of establishing roots, of making a connection with his new home.

I couldn't believe Bernard was able to make such a fast transition to a new place. Didn't he regret trading Nebraska's undulating green hills, twisting creeks, and golden wheat fields for miles and miles of sagebrush and cactus? Ed and I had lived in the desert for more than a decade, and we had never planted a tree or bought a home. We didn't even want to. I was still homesick for Colorado's gentle summers, leafy trees, icy lakes, and snowcapped mountains.

After graduating with a journalism degree, I had accepted a job at a small-town newspaper in central Arizona. At that time, we were weary of Colorado's endless winters, blizzards, icy streets, and snow shovels. Ed and I wanted sunshine and heat. We were about to experience firsthand that old saying: Be careful what you wish for.

We hauled all our stuff in a small U-Haul rigged to the back of my ancient Camaro and rented a house surrounded by cotton fields. My journalism professor had warned that new reporters had to start small, and I proved him right. The *Coolidge Examiner* served a town of about twelve thousand, not counting the migrant workers who arrived each fall to work in the corn, cantaloupe, and cotton fields outside of town. Coolidge had a main street dominated by one small building that housed the city hall, the police station, and the library.

Though we lived only fifty miles south of Phoenix, I felt as if we had traveled a hundred years back in time to a place where men still roped cattle, women cooked meals from scratch, and kids showed their lambs at the county fair.

After midnight, packs of coyotes, not people leaving

nightclubs, howled at the moon. The most excitement you could expect on a Friday night was the all-you-can-eat salad bar at Pizza Hut.

Most nights, Ed and I sat in our little house in the middle of the cotton field and watched for the occasional headlights of a car traveling on the gravel road in the distance. With no buildings, trees, or city lights to disrupt our view, we could see every star in the heavens. Sound romantic? For about a minute. A young couple can spend just so many hours counting stars and listening to coyotes. We missed movies and concerts, but unfortunately, the nearest nightlife was an hour's drive away. If our car hadn't been so old, or if we hadn't been so broke, we might have admitted that we'd made a mistake and driven up that dusty gravel road right out of Arizona and back to Denver.

My reporting job paid less than I had been making as a waitress, and Ed had trouble finding steady work. There weren't many job opportunities in the country. He worked at a fruit farm where the only benefit was free corn and watermelons, then at a dairy, and finally at a factory spraying computer frames silver. Every night he came home looking like the Tin Man from *The Wizard of Oz*.

And so continued our like/hate relationship with Arizona. We liked not shoveling snow or wearing layers of bulky winter clothing, but we hated the five months of one-hundred-plus temperatures. Actually, hate is not a strong enough word. Despised. Loathed. I'm not sure exactly what we had expected our life to be like in Arizona. Perhaps easier in a warm climate, as if troubles and disappointments can't happen where palm trees grow.

I loved being a reporter, but the claustrophobic feeling of small-town life and the intense summer heat deepened my regret at having accepted the newspaper job. What had I done, dragging us here to live in a place with cowboys and farmers, where the sun felt ominously closer to the earth? No writing career was that important.

I soon learned that journalism was not the glamorous job I'd expected, either. Instead, being a small-town reporter meant shooting photos of cotton-harvesting machines, struggling to stay awake at school board meetings, and eating fattening casseroles at women's club luncheons.

The newspaper job did require me to get out of the office and meet people, which I enjoyed. But while newcomers like my husband and I were treated kindly, the tight circle of family and longtime friendships that flourish in small towns didn't widen to include us. I missed my Colorado buddies, those kindred spirits who worked late-night hours at restaurants and clubs, who went to rock concerts and art galleries, who thought nothing of going to bed as the sun was rising. People in Coolidge went to school plays and were tucked in by the time the evening news ended at ten-thirty P.M. And so was I, now that I had a day job that required me to awaken at the hour I'd once crawled into bed.

Some of our isolation was self-inflicted. Both Ed and I were so busy looking backward that we didn't always see the offers of friendship right in front of us.

I thought often of our old neighborhood, where I could see the city's skyline out my kitchen window, walk to the grocery store, romp with my dogs in the nearby park, and sit on my porch and swap stories with neighbors. I missed our old brick bungalow, snow at Christmas, friends, restaurants that served sushi.

After two years, we abandoned our small town to move to Phoenix so that Ed could attend refrigeration school. He figured knowing how to fix air conditioners in Arizona was guaranteed job security. Like two tumbleweeds, we rolled out of town with nothing to stop us.

We brought our complaints with us. Even though we were happy to be in the city, we still dreaded the summer. Only gluttons for punishment would want to live in a place where you could request how you'd like your eggs cooked on the sidewalk. Fried? No problem. Sure you wouldn't like those scrambled with a little ham? Coming right up. Just don't mind the ants or pebbles.

We were angry at Arizona for not being exactly what we'd

expected (whatever that might have been). For not granting us perfect jobs and perfect lives. Our favorite saying was "We're not going to die in Arizona." Afraid we just might, we looked west, to the golden state of California. Southern or Northern, we didn't care. Jobs paid more there, summers were gorgeous, and so were the people. We yearned for cool, wet ocean breezes to wash the desert dust from our skin. For life to really begin for us.

As years passed, we failed again and again in our attempts to move to California. With each failure, we grew more bitter. We felt as if Arizona's soil was sticky paper, keeping us glued in place when we wanted to fly away to the happiness we were certain awaited us elsewhere.

Ed spent two years sending out résumés to California, and went on several interviews. Either potential employers rejected him or he rejected the job offer, usually because the salary wasn't adequate to rent even a studio apartment there. I was accepted into graduate school, but we had no savings to finance our move. The timing never seemed right to make our California dream come true.

We were stuck in our rented town house, telling each other over and over that as soon as we could find a way to escape this desert hellhole called Arizona, we would. Our negativity was like a repellent that kept people and opportunities from coming our way. I found work teaching English to refugees and Ed gained more experience repairing refrigeration equipment, but we still felt as if it wasn't enough. Nothing would be enough until we reached California. Even when people warned us about California's high cost of living, crowds, and earthquakes, we wouldn't listen.

When my in-laws announced they were retiring and moving to Arizona, my husband and I couldn't wait to tell them why they should hate the desert, too.

That afternoon in his new backyard, Bernard, who'd raised six children and countless head of cattle, and endured a lot of disappointment in the process, appeared unconcerned with my attempts at dashing his peach tree dreams.

"I've seen grapefruit, lemon, orange trees, but never peach trees in Arizona," I repeated. "I know what can live in the desert and what will die."

"Make you a bet I can grow one," he said.

"Okay, but you're going to lose. How about five dollars?"

"You're on," he grinned.

My husband and I spent the rest of the afternoon warning my in-laws about the dangers of the Arizona summer, including dust storms, flash floods, and sunstroke. Though it was a typical winter day, seventy degrees and sunny, we told them to make sure they had adequate air-conditioning in their car and house because the desert was a place where even the devil would sweat.

They nodded politely as my husband and I made Arizona sound hospitable only to snakes and scorpions. Nothing worthwhile could live in the desert. That's why we were moving to California, we said.

Our Arizona glass was half-empty and we weren't going to let any starry-eyed newcomers fill it.

To our dismay, my in-laws didn't appear worried about their future. They actually sounded enthusiastic about their new life. "We love the dry air. Every night we sit on the patio and watch the sun set. I expect the angels will sing at any moment," said Sharon with a happy sigh.

Bernard agreed. "My bones feel better here," he said.

"Yeah, sure," said my husband and I, thinking that these senior citizens were as naive as children. One summer of living in a blast furnace would burn their love for Arizona right out of them.

The following spring Bernard showed us his peach tree. I laughed. It looked anorexic. The few peaches dangling from its five or six spindly branches were as hard as golf balls.

"Peaches are small, but next year I expect they'll be bigger," he said, ignoring my chuckles. "It's a fine tree," he concluded.

He gently plucked a peach off the thin branch, took a knife from his pocket, and gave us each a slice. It was like biting into a rock. The peach tasted more bitter than sweet.

I grudgingly paid the five dollars when my husband pronounced his father the winner. Secretly, I believed Bernard had lost the bet.

✦ ✦ ✦ ✦ ✦

Shortly after that visit to the sorry-looking peach tree, my husband and I finally bought our first home, after years of renting apartments. We faced the fact that we would never be able to afford a similar place in California. The cost of living there was just too high for us, and it was only a six-hour drive if we wanted to put our toes in the ocean.

We'd become thin-skinned, shivering when the temperature dipped below sixty degrees, so Denver was out of the question. Besides, we had given away all our heavy coats, boots, and gloves, and didn't want to return to scraping ice off our car windows or buying snow tires. We'd lost touch with friends who had started families and were spending their money on diapers instead of nightclub cover charges.

Neither of us admitted we'd given up on California, but we both stopped talking about moving. Even so, the roots we were putting down in Arizona still felt tentative, as if one good yank would pull them from the earth and send us tumbling in another direction.

Nevertheless, our endless complaining about the heat began to bore us as much as it surely had others. We stopped yapping so much about what we hated and focused more on what we liked about Phoenix. Our new home was spacious and affordable, and there was even a sushi restaurant and a movie theater right down the block.

Now and then we go back to Coolidge and, though we prefer city life, we can appreciate the open space, lack of traffic, and the peace and quiet there. The fields lush with white cotton look like clouds fallen from the vast blue sky.

I discovered hiking in the mountains around Phoenix. I

spent hours on secluded trails, marveling at fuchsia-colored flowers on cactus, listening to the howl of elusive coyotes, and admiring the dramatic vistas of Phoenix from the mountain peaks. I walked alone or with my husband, but I also walked with new friends. I hiked all year, especially enjoying the summer, when the trails were empty except for the occasional rabbit, quail, or coyote.

Step by step, I began to appreciate the solitude afforded by all that space. I found myself standing alone on a trail and saying thank you out loud.

Lo and behold, my husband found a job he really liked and was earning more than he ever had. I established a freelance-writing career. We met neighbors who became close friends. Our Arizona life began to flourish like a plant that has just the right balance of sunshine and shade. We still disliked the summer, but nowhere is perfect. Not even California.

✦ ✦ ✦ ✦ ✦

On a hot spring afternoon, sixteen years after we moved to Arizona, I walked in a peach tree orchard on a farm outside Phoenix, not far from Coolidge. The trees, about eight to ten feet tall, were laden with fuzzy pink and yellow globes. The air was filled with a scent as sweet as any perfume.

My friends and I shouted at each other, pointing out the trees with the ripest fruit. Soon my bag became heavy with peaches. I bit into a warm, sweet peach and recalled the five-dollar bet I had had with my father in-law. Unlike me, he had believed something was possible before seeing proof of it.

I stood in the orchard a moment and listened to my friends talk and laugh as they plucked fruit from the trees. Though the temperature was inching close to a hundred, I became aware of how at peace, even happy, I felt in that moment, with those people, in that place. In Arizona.

I called out to my friends, pointing at the yellow butterflies dancing around them.

# Border Crossings

## Liz Seymour

It's not difficult to identify the low point. That would be midnight at a nearly deserted Burger King off the highway near Drummondville, Quebec, eating a dank veggie burger, my back aching and my eyes burning under the bright, shadowless lights. The night before, I had slept on a futon in a borrowed apartment in Quebec City; the night before that on a floor under a skylight in Montreal; the night before that on a couch in a punk house in Baltimore. This night I wouldn't be sleeping at all. I had at least two more hours of driving ahead of me under a moonlit Canadian sky. When I got to the tiny town near the border that was my destination, I was supposed to park behind a particular hotel bar with my car pointed out front first so my American license plate wouldn't show. Instructions after that were hazy.

All that week I carried a little spiral-bound notebook in the pocket of my overalls; my notes from Drummondville read: "How have I drifted so far away from everything familiar? What happens next? And what on earth am I doing here?" I was fifty-two years old, a freelance writer, the mother of two daughters, aged twenty-two and eighteen, graduate of a Seven Sisters college, wife of a high school English teacher. Most of my professional career had been spent writing and lecturing about other people's beautiful homes. I am white, middle class, unexceptional—the default setting of contemporary American life. I drove my children to play practices and swim meets, sat on the boards of charitable organizations, recycled my newspapers and milk bottles, went to the dentist twice a year. I was not the person you would expect to find parked in the dark on a chilly April night waiting for a group of anarchists less than half my age to emerge from the woods after crossing into Canada illegally on foot by starlight, but that is somehow exactly what I had become.

I had come to Quebec along with some thirty thousand other people to protest something called the Free Trade Area of the Americas, or FTAA. The issue was corporate globalization; the tactic was full-on resistance, whatever that was going to turn out to mean. The protestors were of many stripes, from union members to pagans, but I had thrown my fortunes in with the anarchists, mostly because they were already my friends but also because I was slowly falling in love with their vision of a world without borders, a world in which people had control over their own lives. Now, I was learning, the borders were more than metaphorical: With their combined arrest records from earlier protests, four of our group of six could not get past the official checkpoints.

Allan and I, two-sixths of our affinity group, had driven up to Canada two days before. We had offered to travel separately from the others because, as the only two who had never been arrested, we had the best chance of making it across the border. Even so, we were nervous. We chose a crossing far away from Quebec City, traveling through New York's Finger Lakes district under bright skies and scudding clouds, listening to Nina Simone on the CD player and watching the landscape turn from early spring back into late winter. We sailed through the border with no questions asked and stopped at the first pay phone we could find, a windy roadside phone booth in a shuttered lakeside village. We received the first of what was to be a three-day-long string of discouraging messages—our friends, like hundreds of others trying to get to Quebec City, had been turned back. There was nothing for us to do but leave a message saying that we had made it through and were driving east.

Now, a day later, I was waiting for the other four to arrive. I was bone-tired sitting there all by myself in my winter coat in that lonely Burger King, but I was also bone-weary, which is a very different thing. I had traveled a long way very fast in the last couple of years, had done things I had never known were possible, had discovered new kinds of longings, had found a new vocabulary. Step by step I had strayed off the path, off the map, off the book, and into new territory, but I was still a middle-aged woman still driving people around, still alone. I rubbed my eyes and pressed my cold fingertips against the veins in my temples. At that moment there was nothing I wanted more than my old life, but as I looked at my pale, tired reflection in the darkened window beside me I realized that that version of life was gone for good.

After I left the Burger King, the roads grew narrower and more rural under a high night sky as I headed south toward the U.S. border. After miles of still and frozen farmland, I missed a turn and found myself on an icy dirt road cutting through a forest of dense black trees, the road lit only by the moon and stars through the bare branches, my only company the glowing green digital clock on the dashboard and the speedometer that trembled lower and lower as I threaded my way through the ruts.

Someone had set up a voice-mail number so we could leave messages for each other about our plans. For three days we had been getting strange and worrisome messages: The border crossing at the Mohawk reservation didn't work, the attempt to get through at Burlington didn't work, the only option left was to cross through the woods and meet on the other side of the border at a town I could barely find in my road atlas. That's where I was headed. The last message, picked up at a pay phone in the freezing cold outside the Burger King, said I should only wait until two A.M.; if they weren't there by then I should assume that the plan hadn't worked. In all of our discussions none of us had articulated the various ways the plan could go wrong, but they haunted my mind on that quiet night. I was starkly aware that we were collaborating on a crime. I didn't feel like a criminal, but I desperately, numbly didn't want to discover that I had put myself or anyone else in danger.

It was already close to two o'clock as I made my way slowly along the endless dirt road. I was too tired and too frightened to do anything but keep moving forward in hopes of finding the road I had lost, so that I could begin looking for the hotel bar. Finally, gratefully, I felt my tires smooth out on asphalt and I took a turn back onto my road. I had it all to myself, fields and distant trees on either side, occasionally a wire fence and wooden fence posts standing up suddenly in the headlights, a leaning barn at a curve in the road, a pair of animal eyes that shone for an instant and then were gone.

The town turned out to be just a few miles up the road, just a couple of bends north of the place where I had rejoined the asphalt. My destination—marked with a big sign, now extinguished, that read HOTEL BAR in curly letters—was in the center of the straggly little town. I cautiously pulled into the dirt parking lot and turned the car around. The front of the bar was dark, but lights were still on in the back, although I couldn't see any movement. I rehearsed in my mind the thin cover story we had worked out—that I was driving north and had grown too sleepy to go on, that I had just stopped for a nap.

In fact I felt anything but tired—I was too jacked up to sleep, too nervous to stay in the car. I finally got out, quietly swinging the door shut. I walked up and down the street, a block or so in either direction. House, gas station, combination post office and grocery store. Dirty mounds of snow, bare trees, and somewhere in the distance the sound of running water, crisp and musical in the dark. It was the kind of town you would only be in if you had a reason to be there; the explicable motives for me to be there after midnight had dwindled to somewhat below none. I looked for a pay phone to check the voice-mail number again, but there were none to be found. I walked back to the car and climbed in as noiselessly as I could, listening to the wind and the ceaseless tinkling of water in the trees behind me. I pushed the driver's seat back and pulled my coat a little closer around me. The last lights in the building went out and a door at the back of the bar opened; a man and a woman came out, their feet crunching on the frozen ground. The woman looked in the direction of my car and hesitated; I slid lower so that I could just see over the top of the steering wheel, willing myself to be invisible; then she moved on. The two of them got into a car and drove away, leaving me alone with the stars, the shadows of the trees, and the silence.

Oddly enough, this was going to be my first protest. In the sixties when my college classmates were out protesting the war, I was mostly in my dorm room writing gloomy poetry. Outside of a little mild sign carrying and petition signing, I had never attended a demonstration, never taken part in any civil disobedience, never given way to political passions.

All that changed abruptly, though I didn't know it at the time, on August 5, 2000, when the phone rang in my kitchen. The young woman on the other end of the line asked my name and then said: "I'm calling about your daughter but I don't want to say her name. She asked me to tell you that she is in jail but she's okay and she'll probably be there for a while."

Isabell! In jail! The sunlight on the kitchen floor, the coffee mugs on the shelf, the afternoon mail on the kitchen table, the Vivaldi on the radio were all the same as they had been a minute before, but everything was different. The anonymous woman had left us a number to call and a code word to use to get more information. I called my husband, Bill, into the kitchen and together we made the phone call.

We discovered that Isabell had been in jail for four days. We had known she was in Philadelphia protesting at the Republican National Convention, but we weren't surprised when we didn't hear from her; she had explained to us that she wouldn't necessarily be near a phone or a computer and might not have time to call or email, so we should not worry. Now she was in jail along with more than four hundred other people. She hadn't even had a chance to protest: She had been arrested while standing on a sidewalk with a walkie-talkie in her hand, charged with obstructing a highway, a misdemeanor. Her bail had been set at $10,000.

Isabell could have gotten out of jail anytime she wanted to, we learned, but she and her fellow detainees were practicing something they called "jail solidarity." At first it seemed foolish; it was hard to explain to our friends. When I told them that Isabell was in jail and why, they would offer indignant sympathy and say, "Can't you bail her out? Don't you have a lawyer?" I would explain that she didn't want us to bail her out, that she and her fellow prisoners were being represented by a group of lawyers who were volunteering their time, that Isabell was in jail as one of hundreds of Jane and John Does who had left their driver's licenses and picture IDs at home so that if they were arrested they would have to be processed as a group and no one would be left hanging out alone.

A week after we got the news—a long and terrible week of mounting worry—we got a letter from Isabell, return address Jane Doe #3498, Philadelphia Prison System. She described her first few days in the Roundhouse, Philadelphia's central booking jail. "Conditions there were awful," she wrote. "We were six to ten people in cells meant for one. Most of the guards were cruel, punishing people arbitrarily. We got a cheese sandwich and carton of tea once every ten to twelve hours. Sleeping was really hard and it was really cold. One night the five other women in the cell and I were cuffed right hand to left ankle and left overnight. The shift the next morning took us out."

Isabell was there for three nights before she was moved to the county women's prison; finally she was transferred to a minimum-security unit. ("If we're so minimum security," she asked in her letter, "why are our bails set at between ten thousand

and a million dollars?") The day after we got the letter, eleven days after she was arrested, Isabell called from a pay phone to say that she was out.

Once the world begins to fray, it doesn't take many tugs on the loose threads for the whole fabric to unravel. It's happening all the time: Right this minute as you read this, a woman is lying in bed looking at the afternoon light on the window shade, making up her mind to leave her husband. A man is dropping the keys to the company truck on his supervisor's desk and walking out into the bright parking lot. A man and a woman are holding hands in a doctor's office trying to understand the cautious uninflected words of a bad prognosis. People who have been through an earthquake say that once you have felt the ground ripple under your feet, all the old sureties and verities are never quite the same again.

I had always known that other mothers' children were in jail; I had always known that jail is a terrible place. It's a shame that it took my own child in jail to wake me from what, looking back, was a kind of moral torpor, but it worked. In the weeks after Isabell's arrest I found myself growing angrier and angrier at the casual injustice of both her arrest and her treatment. I began to feel threatening and oddly powerful in my anger, although outwardly my life was exactly what it had been before: I went to the grocery store, hung new rolls of toilet paper on the toilet paper holder, did the laundry, worked in the yard, had dinner with friends, wrote more articles about other people's beautiful homes. But inside, over and over again, almost like a prayer, I was saying: "They shouldn't have brought it to my house. They shouldn't have brought it to my house. Now I'm really angry, now they're in trouble. They never should have brought it to my house."

Who were "they"? I didn't even know. It wasn't as simple as the Philadelphia police department or the Republican Party. It would have been easier if it had been. No, the "they" who haunted my waking and sleeping moments, the "them" I would have liked to have taken by the shoulders and shaken, were the invisible ranks that surround us always, the ones we can ignore when things are going well but who move in stiflingly close when we stray toward the boundaries. They had made the first move and had made a terrible mistake. Thinking was almost a physical ache as I tried to hold on to the old world while I made room for the new world. "I expect this will turn out to have been a life-changing experience for Isabell but not one that derails her completely," I wrote in my journal. "It has certainly changed my life—I don't even entirely know how yet, except that I feel as though I've turned inside out and made my inner life into my outer life—that's what has the weight these days. I can't shake the feeling that the odometer has just turned over a whole lot of zeroes and that something huge and fully engaging is about to happen."

I had never before used the word "anarchist" when I spoke to my family about Isabell, mostly because I couldn't trust myself to keep the invisible quotation marks out of my voice, with their implication that somehow anarchism wasn't serious. I wasn't so much bothered by anarchism's violent history as I was by what seemed then like its utter futility. Of all the ideologies Isabell could have chosen to pledge her allegiance, intelligence, and passion to, anarchism seemed like the all-around worst bet. But with Isabell in prison I couldn't keep her beliefs a secret anymore. I explained as well as I could, loyally defending her ideas as I understood them, trying on her behalf to suppress my own bafflement and ambivalence. When she was finally released from prison, my sister-in-law Katie sent Isabell an email congratulating her on getting out and asking her to explain her anarchist beliefs. All that fall, between school assignments and political actions, Isabell worked on what became an eleven-page essay about her political beliefs. By the time I got to read it, several months after her arrest, the ideas no longer seemed foreign to me. I had been struggling with discontent for some time, and Isabell and her fellow anarchists, with their vision of a world in which "power to" is stronger than "power over," were offering a way to put that discontent to use.

✦ ✦ ✦ ✦ ✦

I woke up from a light doze to the sound of someone tapping on my car window. They had arrived, and a scout had been sent out to find me where I was waiting, scrunched down in my seat behind the steering wheel. The little town was asleep and the moon had set, but the light from the stars threw deep papery shadows across the dirty early spring snow. My companion slipped into the car and we drove quietly and cautiously down the road. No one. We turned and drove slowly back, the car wheels sounding terrifyingly loud on the loose pebbles of the road. And then there they were, running out of the shadows of the trees, lumpy ungainly silhouettes in boots and heavy coats and scarves and mittens scattering onto the dark deserted road with their hands upraised and waving. They tugged at the doors, piled in on top of each other, interrupting each other in loud urgent whispers—"Drive, drive!" "Shut the door!" "Shhh! Cut the lights! Cut the lights!" The windshield misted and I wiped it down with my coat sleeve; the air in the car was suddenly tropically warm, thick with humidity and the smell of sweat. I felt a profound gratitude, a quickening of excitement, an electric sense that suddenly, finally, everything mattered. "Oh my God," someone said into the close and intimate night. "Oh my God. We fucking goddamn fucking made it!"

It was full morning by the time we got back to Quebec City. I had picked up four people: Peter, tall, energetic, and forgetful, taking a week off from his last semester in college; Mike, an environmental activist from Maine, tirelessly talkative, acidly opinionated, with a round face and a sudden enchanting smile; Geoff, quiet and sweet-natured, with close-cropped blond hair and incongruous tortoiseshell glasses; and Johnny, blond dreadlocks and sleepy eyes, a traveler who spent his time hopping trains and hitchhiking from town to town. The four of them, still bundled in their winter coats and scarves, slept as I drove, sprawled over each other like puppies. In the dark, before we got to the highway, I gently braked to let a mother deer and a fragile-looking fawn pass across the road in our headlights. As we turned into the parking lot of an all-night diner, another car pulled up behind us and four men in identical dark blue jump suits leapt out—I could taste old pennies in my mouth as I saw the rest of my life as a parade of trials and depositions and humiliating newspaper exposés and eventual prison sentences—but it was just four guys from a local plumbing company stopping for a cup of coffee. At last, just before noon, I pulled into the underground parking garage at Laval University. There were only a few minutes before the march down to the old city was to begin.

The day before, when Allan and I had first arrived, the old town section of Quebec City felt like a coastal town under a hurricane watch. The meetings and the protests were scheduled to begin the next day. The assembled FTAA delegates would be meeting at a conference center; the protestors—estimates of the expected numbers were veering wildly from ten thousand to sixty thousand—would be massed beyond a twelve-foot-high chainlink fence anchored to a heavy concrete base. As I walked around the old city in the chilly April sunshine, I watched sections of fence being maneuvered into place; here and there you could hear the universal "beep beep beep" of heavy equipment backing up as men in white hard hats and heavy winter jackets expertly slipped the tines of forklifts under fence sections, closing the last gaps in the fence. The wind stirred crepe-paper flowers attached to sections of fence with pipe cleaners; some of the concrete bases were already spray-painted with anti-FTAA messages.

I climbed the narrow streets up to the Place Quebec, soon to be inaccessible without a pass, where news reporters stood talking into TV cameras and the chief of the city police was giving a sidewalk press conference, promising again that the protestors would be contained outside the fence and the summit would go on undisturbed. Apparently not everyone was so confident: Many of the businesses along the Avenue Dufferin had already covered their windows with plywood and as I walked I could hear the sound of hammers and circular saws. The city was full of police: It was reported that more than six thousand had been brought in from across Canada. I saw an old man stop a policeman in a blue uniform with brass buttons and ask him a question in French. The policeman, about my age, short and a little rounded in the stomach, his face pink with wind, apologized and said he only spoke English.

"I'm from Manitoba," he explained.

"Ah, Manitoba!" the old man said. "Got much spring there yet?"

"Not much," said the policeman, "still pretty cold when I left. Hasn't been too bad a winter though."

"Well, we're seeing some spring today," said the old man.

"Feels good," said the policeman, and they smiled and walked on in different directions.

By the same time the next day, after things fell apart, after the tear gas, after the water cannons, after the broken bank windows, I would be standing in front of a double row of riot police dressed in heavy olive drab body suits and black boots and helmets. Behind their heavy Plexiglas shields and face masks it was impossible to distinguish one person from another or even tell the men from the women. Some of the police held shiny black truncheons in their gloved hands; others held rifles and wore low-slung cartridge belts filled with plastic bullets. I knew that somewhere in there was the cheerful policeman from Manitoba but there was no longer any way to tell. I had come up to the boundary and crossed over.

# Before and After Mexico

## Gina Hyams

January 1997. My husband, Dave, and I were deliriously happy—giddy with the reality that we were officially unemployed, homeless, and about to blow our life savings by boarding Taesa flight 572 (Oakland-Zacatecas-Morelia) with one-way tickets, one two-year-old, three suitcases, a bag of books, a laptop, a pink teddy bear, a diaper bag, and three saxophones. The only plan for our new life in Mexico was that Dave would play jazz, I'd finally have a go at writing, and our daughter Annalena would chase lizards.

We sold nearly everything we owned to finance this escape. Our Tahitian-green Honda Civic named Uma, Macintosh computers, Navajo rugs, a fifties reclining beauty-parlor chair, Bang & Olufsen stereo system, reading lamps made of twigs, goose-down comforter, garlic peeler, and Weber grill: all sold to the highest bidder. People described our liquidation as "the flea market of the gods." Estranged friends descended like vultures to paw through our belongings.

Everything was gone. Dave's beloved collection of obscure R&B Christmas albums: gone. The books of French literary criticism I never actually read in college: gone. Annalena's primary-colored plastic educational toys: gone. The five bottles of extra-fancy grade A pure Vermont maple syrup, four of which I bought because I never could remember if we had any, and brunch with friends was an ideal I perennially aspired to mid-supermarket-aisle: gone. Gone. Gone. Gone. Gone.

The abstract notion of lightening the load was more cathartic than the excruciating book-by-book process. I had to keep reminding myself that each item sold translated into that much more time I wouldn't have to spend in a gray cubicle. A neighbor squabbled when I refused his pitiful offer for *Italy: The Beautiful Cookbook*. He didn't understand that this was no ordinary garage sale, that we weren't getting rid of these things because we didn't like them. They were our only assets and we were exchanging them for a new life.

It's not that our old life was without its pleasures, but we were bone-tired. Dave was the managing director of a Shakespeare festival and I was the assistant to a vice president of marketing at a software company (back in the glory days of corporate-sponsored staff-bonding ski trips and free Snapple lemonade for all high-tech workers). I was too lowly a peon to get stock options, but my boss was a nice guy who thanked me daily for my competence. Having spent my twenties toiling in employee-morale disaster zones at supposedly progressive political and arts organizations, the software company's esprit de corps and catered lunches had been a revelation.

Quitting was Dave's idea. He was thirty-nine and barreling his way to an ulcer from the stress of managing the theater's never-ending backstage dramas, while juggling the demands of fatherhood, husbandhood, and gigs with his experimental jazz ensemble. He was seeing both a therapist and a career counselor, trying to figure out a way to make money that might also make him happy, or at least happier. Architect? Therapist? Jazz history professor? Vice president of something? Bookstore owner? Record-shop clerk? Hander-outer of putters at a mini-golf course?

None of these ideas stuck; more than a new profession, he needed a break—time to catch his breath, find his bearings, rekindle his spirit. He needed a lot more than a two-week vacation. While stuck in Bay Bridge traffic one Thursday night, the solution came to him. With desperate clarity, he bounded in the door and swooped Annalena up into his arms.

"Honey, I've figured it out. We don't have to buy a house. We can quit our jobs, sell everything, and become expatriates instead."

We had habitually entertained fantasies of life abroad while on vacation, but this time Dave was serious. My first impulse was to dig in my heels: "But I finally like my job."

"I thought you wanted to be a writer. Think about it. We're not tied down to a mortgage. I haven't embarked on a new career. We only have one child and she's not in school yet. This is our window of opportunity."

He made it sound so reasonable. I was thirty-one and had been coasting on my "creative potential" since college. This move felt like put-up-or-shut-up time, like my artistic bluff had been called. My work at the software company was pleasant, but it was meaningless. I needed to sit still long enough to find out if I had anything to say as a writer. I also yearned to see our little girl during daylight hours.

We contemplated relocating to Holland, Spain, Italy, or France, but settled on Mexico, where we'd vacationed three times, because we loved the mariachi bands and the brilliant colors, because families were revered there, and because rents were cheap. And we were, indeed, a family with limited resources—$23,732.45 after the sale, to be exact. We thought it would be enough money to carry us for a year, maybe two.

When the last of our furniture was carted away, Dave and I sat on the hardwood floor and surveyed the empty space. There was no remaining evidence of our personalities. We no longer had proof that we were intelligent people of distinguished, if modest, accomplishment and quirky good taste.

The closer we came to our departure date, the less coherent I was when people asked, "Why Morelia?" Nobody'd heard of this inland city. I tried to sound rational, explaining that we thought coastal resorts were well and good for vacations, but that at heart we weren't beach people and we didn't want to live surrounded by tourists. The guidebooks intriguingly described the state of Michoacán as the "Switzerland of Mexico," the "Hills of China of Mexico" and the "Land That Time Forgot." We specifically chose the capital city of Morelia because we were suckers for colonial architecture and cobblestones, and, with its universities, music conservatory, and nearby crafts villages, it just seemed like the place for us.

Of course, we'd never been there, we didn't know anybody there, and we didn't speak Spanish.

We ended up spending the first of what would turn into four years in Mexico in Pátzcuaro, a Purépecha Indian town on a mountain lake about an hour's drive south of Morelia. The capital itself had felt too sprawling and cosmopolitan, too similar to California. There was a gourmet grocery where we could buy imported coffee and Häagen-Dazs, and that felt like cheating. We wanted to live in the Land That Time Forgot, and in Pátzcuaro there wasn't even coffee to go.

We lived on a nameless cobblestone road in a little adobe house that had no telephone, no washing machine, no microwave, and no television. The kitchen counter was a glorious crazy quilt of Talavera tiles decorated with bananas and jalapeño peppers, and the bathroom walls were painted *azul añil*, a deep ultramarine blue believed to ward off evil spirits. Two stone angels, carved in the nearby village of Tzintzuntzan, held up the mantel above the fireplace in the living room. We bought wood from an eighty-three-year-old *campesino* named Don Ambrosio, who delivered it by burro. Stoking the fire, I felt like a pioneer bride.

Dave planted a stand of calla lilies and hung a hammock in the backyard. We learned how to finesse the water and gas tanks and (after our first miserable round of amoebas) to soak vegetables vigilantly in a disinfectant solution. Just walking to the post office was an adventure because we invariably stumbled on one fiesta or another—boys blasting fireworks at dawn in honor of the Virgin of Guadalupe, a mariachi band serenading a bride and groom on the church steps, children bashing a piñata strung up in the middle of the street, a drunken brass band careening through town in celebration of a win by their favorite soccer team.

Wandering through Pátzcuaro's outdoor market was a visual feast. Block after block was filled with the reddest tomatoes I'd ever seen, alongside pyramids of huge, ripe avocados, juicy cactus paddles, mangoes carved into flower shapes, baskets overflowing with dried chilies and pumpkin seeds, platters of chicken heads, candied sweet potatoes swarming with bees, and more cow parts than I'd ever imagined. Enormous bouquets of tuberoses could be had for a song. I'd dare myself to go back by the butcher stalls to look at the ghostly tripe, pig snouts on hooks, and glistening entrails. My legs would nearly buckle, the sensual overload was so confounding. When Dave wasn't around, I enjoyed a flirty dance with Juan, my favorite fruit seller. "A su servicio, mi reina (At your service, my queen)," he'd grin as he dug for the sweetest strawberries.

For people who had so recently shed our material trappings and piously sworn to "never accumulate that much stuff again," we had a hell of a lot of fun accumulating new stuff. There was such palpable pleasure in being surrounded by things that were hecho a mano (made by hand). We drank fresh-squeezed tangerine juice out of hand-blown glass goblets, wore hand-knitted wool sweaters and slept under a hand-loomed magenta bedspread. We brushed our teeth with purified water decanted from an earthenware pitcher. Annalena played with miniature toy frogs made of straw and she chased not only lizards, but dragonflies, ladybugs, grasshoppers, butterflies, pigeons, and all manner of mangy street dogs, as well.

We made friends with Lupita, who sold roast chickens in the market. She always gave Annalena a little cajeta (goat's milk caramel) cookie and advised Dave and me to make more babies. Mexicans rarely asked what we did for a living. They were more curious about the size of our family and, though ours was small, the fact that we were a family seemed to normalize us. Annalena, with her blueberry eyes and impeccable Spanish accent, became our goodwill ambassador. No matter how dusty-poor or remote the village, people made a fuss over her. *¡Qué linda!* (How pretty!), they'd exclaim. She was *preciosa* (precious), *una princesa* (a princess), *una muñeca*. "*No soy una muñeca. Soy un mono.*" (I'm not a doll. I'm a monkey.) She also took to telling anyone who asked that she had forty-nine brothers and sisters.

The view from my writing desk was one-third twisting cobblestone roads and red-tiled rooftops and two-thirds sky. When I sat down to work on my novel, it seemed ludicrous to try to invent a plot when the surrealism of everyday life in Mexico felt so compelling. I found myself trying to describe the sky outside my window—surging and cleaving clouds, thunder and lightning, cotton-candy sunsets and a profusion of shooting stars. The constant drama of that sky seemed a testament to celestial will, grace, and fury, an explanation of why there are so many believers in this part of the world. Instead of poetry, I wrote letters home.

Sent via email, these monthly dispatches to friends and family took on a life of their own. My loved ones forwarded the letters to their loved ones, who in turn often asked to be added to my mailing list. What began as a list of thirty grew to nearly three hundred recipients. A fledgling writer couldn't ask for a greater gift. Knowing that there was an audience eager to read my words helped me develop confidence and discipline.

Through the letters, I began to discover my voice and core literary themes (death, lies, and room service). Eventually I found work as a guidebook correspondent and published two books about Mexico—one about Day of the Dead and the other about the architecture and interior decor of Mexican inns. Dave also thrived creatively. He practiced playing his horns several hours a day and found work with an art-rock band from Mexico City, as well as jazz gigs at various resorts.

We loved living in Mexico, but ultimately tired of being

outsiders. The downside of a culture rooted in family clans is that friends aren't as integral a part of life. Annalena's classmates rarely invited her home to play, because at home they played with their cousins. We had genuinely warm but stubbornly superficial relationships with our neighbors. While it was possible for us to feel gloriously swept away by the splendor of saint's-day celebrations, these holidays would never belong to us. And because most of the expatriates we met were either cantina-hopping college students or cocktail party–hopping retirees, we didn't fit in with the foreigners, either.

After four years away, it was time to engage again with our own tribe; to let Annalena get to know her own cousins; to taste Black Diamond cheddar, sushi, and real maple syrup; and to hear the *thunk* of the Sunday *New York Times* on our doorstep. We returned to a Victorian house in Oakland and made dates to meet old friends for lattes at our favorite cafés. Annalena learned about the wonders of drinking fountains and central heating. Dave got another arts-administration job and my old boss at the software company hired me part-time to write brochure copy. Our community welcomed us back with open arms.

But we've been home five months now, and I'm not sure we belong in California anymore, either. We're struggling to reconcile the Mexican sky that now fills our hearts with the daily grind of a more or less upwardly mobile life. I find myself willfully spacing out, trying to slow down the pace, trying to hold on to the sense that time is simply time, not money. Perhaps we've become permanent expatriates—neither fish nor fowl, forever lost, no matter our location. But this fluidity also means that we're now like mermaids and centaurs—magic creatures who always know there's another way.

# Making a Difference

## Gunter David

On an overcast September morning I met with my first patient. He appeared to be in his early thirties, and had a tanned face and muscular arms protruding from his short-sleeved shirt. A man who spent a lot of time outdoors. A construction worker, perhaps. He shifted in his chair, folding and unfolding his hands.

"What brings you to the clinic?" I asked.

He looked down.

In his silence I heard the rain. I had learned to wait for an answer, not to press, as the former journalist in me wanted to do. After a while I started to worry. Suppose he didn't say anything? How long should I wait before prodding for an answer? What if he walked out? I glanced at the clock on my desk. Five minutes passed, then ten. I felt I had to do something. I rose and opened the window. Air as moist as tears invaded the room.

"It's my brother," the man said in a hoarse voice.

"Yes?" In a moment I was back in my chair, facing him.

"He . . . killed himself. Last month."

A suicide. His brother committed suicide. What could I say? What would the supervisor say? I didn't know. But I knew how I felt. "That's awful. I'm so sorry. So very sorry."

He looked up at me, and his dark eyes, large and sad, met mine.

"He . . . cut his wrists . . . I found him."

I shook my head. Don't say anything, just let him talk, my inner voice said.

"I wish I could cry," he said.

Silence.

Waiting.

"But I can't."

"Why?"

"I keep hearing my father's voice from when I was a kid . . . I keep hearing him say, 'Joey, don't be a crybaby.'"

I moved my chair closer to his. "Joe," I said. "It's okay for men to cry. Men have feelings, too. I cry sometimes."

"You do?" he whispered.

I nodded yes. "Go ahead, Joe. Go ahead and cry."

He did, then.

❖ ❖ ❖ ❖ ❖

I came to the clinic to change my life.

Just a few months earlier I had been a senior reporter on the *Evening Bulletin* in Philadelphia. For twenty-five years my life had been wrapped around the newsroom. I was a newsman. A Pulitzer Prize nominee.

At City Hall, at the White House, interviewing Ben-Gurion, reporting from the Middle East about the Yom Kippur War, exposing corruption, or rushing out to the scene of a fire, I felt I was making a difference.

One day the *Evening Bulletin* died. There were no vacancies for me on other area newspapers. I was fifty-two.

When you're doing what you've always yearned to do, when every day is a gift—and then one day you get up in the morning and have no place to go, it's more than the loss of a job, it's the loss of an identity. I had always been Gunter David of . . .

the *Bulletin, Newark News, The Baltimore Sun, Philadelphia Daily News*. Now who was I?

When I found myself struggling to get out of bed and not wanting to face the day, I sought help from a psychologist. Bit by bit, over months, my depression lifted. Then I wanted to help others as I had been helped. I found that I wanted to make a difference again.

I got my second chance when Hahnemann University in Philadelphia admitted me to the master's program in Family Therapy. My wife, Dalia, and I agreed to invest my *Bulletin* severance pay in this new career. On the first day of the semester, I attended an orientation for new students. I had exchanged my journalist's garb of shirt, tie, and suit for a sweatshirt, blue jeans, and sneakers.

I sat in the front row of the auditorium, flanked by youthful, hopeful faces. I had just turned fifty-three. Yet I was one of them.

Long, narrow, gray halls in need of a fresh coat of white paint. Voices from one therapy room bursting into the next through thin walls. Men with vacant faces from an adjacent day program wandering into the clinic.

This place, where the poor and desperate sought help for free or on a sliding scale, was to provide me with practical experience. For the first few weeks I only "sat in," observing Steve, my supervisor, at work. Abused women. Violent men. A man and his stepdaughter, who accused him of rape. Suicide attempts. Major depression. Schizophrenia. Manic depression.

Day after day I silently watched the suffering. Would I ever know enough to provide help? Would I ever be able to make a difference?

Then Joe became my patient. I saw him for several months.

One afternoon he told me, "I can do it on my own." He shook my hand. "Thanks," he said.

In my heart I thanked him.

Millie, a former patient of Steve's, followed Joe.

She appeared to be about fifty, but the intake sheet showed

her age to be thirty-nine. According to her chart she had tried to commit suicide three times.

"You're new here," she said, settling into the chair opposite me.

"I'm not just new here. I'm new in the field." The words sprang from my lips before I could stop them. My age made me look like a veteran. Steve and I had agreed that I would not discuss my background unless a patient asked. My novice status might unnerve some of them.

Millie's light blue eyes lit up. "What did you used to do?"

"I was a reporter. I'm making a change." Well, she had asked.

"That's quite a change," Millie said. "That's wonderful."

I liked her right away.

"I can tell you lots of stories," she said, sighing. "Might as well bring you up to date."

I sat back in my chair, pad and pencil in hand.

"My father is an alcoholic," she said. "Write that down. He beats my mother when he gets mad. When I was a teenager, I used to run away. Once I stole a car. I've also tried to commit suicide."

My pad and pencil seemed glued to my fingers.

"I don't see you writing this down," Millie said. Then she smiled.

I smiled back, relieved. She was pulling my leg, teasing me, taking advantage of the new guy.

"It's all true, though. I'm here because I took too many sleeping pills, and . . . "

I began taking notes.

There was much more. She had a son in the U.S. Army. She had a boyfriend, Carl, an unemployed auto mechanic. The boyfriend drank heavily. They were to be married in a month.

"But I'm afraid," she said. She started to cry. "He's a good man. But when he drinks, I don't like him. He's nasty. So I run away."

Tears rushed down her face. I wanted to hold her, but I knew it was against the rules.

"If I marry him, I can't run away," she said.

Didn't she see what she was doing? That she was repeating a pattern? The daughter of a violent, alcoholic father was involved with an alcoholic boyfriend who became mean when he drank.

There was a knock on the door and Steve came in. He sat beside me.

"I don't know why I'm living," Millie said.

I felt my heart beating rapidly. I moved my chair closer to her. "You're a human being. You live and you breathe. You have worth."

Steve put his hand on my shoulder but said nothing.

"Do you have any skills?" I asked.

She shook her head and dried her face with a tissue. "I dropped out in ninth grade. I'm stupid."

Not stupid. Just stuck. And lost. Suddenly it hit me. "You could try and go back to school. At night. And then you could get a job and support yourself," I said. "You can get a GED. You take a test and you get a diploma that's the same as if you graduated from high school."

Millie sighed. "I used to be a waitress," she said. "I guess I could go back to that. Big deal."

"It takes skill to be a good waitress," I said. "I was a waiter once, and I got fired after three weeks. I couldn't remember where the people sat and who ordered what."

Millie and Steve laughed.

"Thanks," Millie said. "I haven't laughed in a long time."

She made an appointment for the following week.

"Maybe she can be helped," I said to Steve after Millie had left. "And maybe I will have played a positive role in her life. That's what this is all about, isn't it?"

There was a little smile on Steve's lips. "Don't get your hopes up," he said as he rose.

On the appointed day, I waited for Millie. The phone never rang. She neither canceled nor rescheduled. As the minutes passed, I tried to figure out why she wasn't coming. Maybe I shouldn't have told her I was new. Maybe I'd pushed too hard.

"My Millie was a no-show," I told Steve plaintively when the hour had silently passed.

"She was my Millie long before she was your Millie," he said with a laugh. "And if you hang your ego on whether patients show up, you're going to be in for a lot of trouble."

✦ ✦ ✦ ✦ ✦

Sandra was in her late twenties. She had long, greasy brown hair. Her gray sweatshirt needed washing. She looked away from me. Steve came in at the beginning of the session.

"What brings you to the clinic?" I asked.

She shrugged her shoulders. "I don't know. My family doctor sent me."

"What happened that he sent you to us?"

She shrugged again. "I don't know."

"There had to be some reason," Steve said.

She shrugged and yawned.

The shrugging! It was so annoying, and it was also so familiar. The gesture belonged to Ronni, my fifteen-year-old daughter, from whom a shrug was a frequent response.

"Sandra!" I burst out. "Don't you care about your life? Don't you care about what's going to happen to you?"

She started to cry. Her right leg shook violently.

"Why are you crying?" Steve said gently.

"There are too many people in the room," she said.

Steve turned to me.

I rose and left, softly closing the door.

Driving home, I berated myself. Clearly Sandra didn't care about her life—her hair, her clothes, the shrugging. She was depressed. Too depressed to speak, to lay herself bare before two men.

And Millie, I thought. Again she had been a no-show. I was not allowed to call her. A form letter would be sent out by the front office, noting her absence and asking her to call for another appointment.

I was two months into the program, and instead of helping people, I was scaring them away. Maybe I had rushed into this big change. Maybe I had not thought it through enough.

That night I dreamed I was back in the *Bulletin* newsroom. Sitting at my computer, facing a blank screen, I suddenly remembered that I was supposed to be in class, at Hahnemann. "But I'm a newsman," I cried out.

Dalia shook me and woke me up.

✦ ✦ ✦ ✦ ✦

Millie returned the following day, without an appointment. Her face was puffy, her eyes filled with tears. I ushered her into my office.

"It's Carl," she said, wiping her eyes with her hands. "He's drinking and drinking . . . and he screams at me all the time. I can't stand it."

I felt hopeful. Maybe she was ready to get away from him.

"Millie," I said. "Who does he remind you of?"

"My dad," she said without hesitation.

"So, you see the pattern. You know you're repeating the pattern."

She nodded.

"Then, Millie, what's the answer?"

"Leave Carl."

"Right!" She understood! "Do you have a place to stay?"

"I can stay with my sister and brother-in-law."

At the end of the session, as she headed for the door, Millie turned around, her hand on the doorknob. "I know what I got to do. But to know something and to do it are two different things."

"I know you can do it," I said. "I know you have the inner strength to do what needs to be done."

She looked at me with a brief, sad smile. "What if I can't?"

Then she was gone.

✦ ✦ ✦ ✦ ✦

Back at the clinic, Sandra returned after two no-shows. I watched her and Steve going into his office. She walked past me, looking away. Was there anything I could do to make it up to her? Perhaps I could apologize.

After a few minutes I knocked on Steve's door. He came out. When he saw me, he waved me away. I could feel the blood rushing to my face. An editor's criticism of a story had never made me feel rejected. Well—of course, I thought. In my previous life I was a self-assured veteran. Now I was a student whose teacher was twenty years younger.

An hour later, Steve came into my office. "First, you never interrupt someone else's session," he said. "Except in an emergency."

I nodded wordlessly.

"Second, each patient has his or her own pace. You must match the pace to the agenda. If you tell a depressed person that they really shouldn't be depressed, as you told Sandra, and as you told Millie, you are saying to them that you are not in tune with their feelings. It makes them feel worse."

I recalled the time when I had been depressed about the end of the *Bulletin*, and Dalia had pointed out to me all the good things still left in my life. I had replied that she wasn't helping. Now I understood why I had felt that way.

"How can I make it up to Sandra?" I said.

His stern face relaxed. "Learn from the experience. Then use what you've learned with someone else."

Millie canceled her two sessions for the week following our last conversation. She left a message saying she was going hunting with Carl.

I closed my eyes. I wished I could shake Millie and say, "Don't you see what you're doing? That you're ruining your life?"

I was prepared for the worst when Millie arrived two weeks later. Instead, I saw a smiling woman, her usual sweats replaced by a light blue dress matching her eyes.

"I'm done with Carl," she said. "I'm dating a new guy."

Steve, I thought, I did help! Page One story!

"And I'm taking a course."

"That's wonderful, Millie."

"In bartending."

Good grief! "Oh . . . "

She laughed. "I know. It's not the GE something."

"Okay," I said. "But why bartending?"

"Check it out," she said. "There's lots of jobs. And I used to be a waitress, so . . ."

"Bartending? With the alcoholics already in your life?"

"Look, you wanted me to do a couple of things," Millie said. "And I did some of them. I left Carl, and I'm taking a course."

"Yes, but . . . "

"Remember when I said I know what I have to do, but what if I can't do it?"

"Yes."

She clapped her hands. "But I did! I did! I left Carl. Right? So, I didn't take the GE whatever. I just took another course."

"Yes. Of course. Congratulations." I reached out and shook her hand.

"You see," she said. "You and me, we talk good."

✦ ✦ ✦ ✦ ✦

The phone rang, and it was the metropolitan editor of *The Philadelphia Inquirer*. "Congratulations," he said. "It took you twelve years, but you've made it. You're on staff."

"You son of a bitch," I said. "Twelve years?!"

Then I woke up.

Other nights I lay awake. What if I failed? What if I couldn't find a job? Or build a private practice?

At a meeting to evaluate my progress, a faculty member said, "Your main problem is that you want to heal the patients too fast. You want their pain to go away so that your pain will go away."

It was true. When Joe cried about the suicide of his brother, tears filled my eyes. Millie's suffering haunted me long after the session's end. At times I would dream about the newsroom after a painful day at the clinic. That was the link, I realized, between the patients' pain and my most deeply felt one.

Sometimes my two identities became blurred. One such instance took place in an auditorium at the university, during a live presentation of a troubled marriage. About a hundred students faced a psychiatrist and a couple seated on stage. The session was followed by questions from the audience.

My hand flew up, as it had done during countless press conferences. I addressed my question to the husband.

"Did I hear you correctly earlier when you said you hoped to join the Philadelphia Police Department?" I asked.

"Yes," the man said clearly, nodding. "That's my dream."

"But didn't I also hear you say that you had a police record?"

I heard the scraping of chairs on the wooden floor.

"I did," the man said. "As a kid. Petty crimes."

"Were you ever detained?"

The man paused. Then he looked at me intently. "In Juvenile Hall," he said.

"So you were in jail as a juvenile delinquent."

The man pounded his fist into his left hand. "What's your point, mister?"

"My point is that you're deluding yourself," I said. Inexplicably, I stood up. "In twenty-five years as a newspaperman I've never met a cop with a prior criminal record."

"Sit down, Gunter!"

The order came from the program director. "This man is a patient. You are a clinician-in-training. This is not a newspaper. And you are no longer a reporter."

Slowly I sat. Laughter and guffaws. I put my head in my hands.

✦ ✦ ✦ ✦ ✦

Millie came in, hesitant as she walked across the threshold.

"Carl smashed up his car," she said, looking down to the floor. "And . . . when he comes out of the hospital, I'm taking care of him. Tomorrow."

"Millie, please look at me," I said. "I'm not your father. You don't have to be afraid of me. I'm your friend."

She raised her head and there were tears in her eyes. "I didn't know how to tell you . . . that I'm going back with Carl. You have so much faith in me, more than I have in myself."

"I still do. But Carl is no longer your responsibility. You broke up. Remember?"

She shook her head. "He needs me. I can't desert him. I couldn't live with myself if I didn't take care of him."

That last sentence put me on alert, reminding me of her suicide attempts. "If you feel that strongly, then by all means, take care of him."

"I feel like I'm letting you down . . . " Her voice trailed off.

"I still have faith in you," I said, although deep in my heart I was not sure.

"I'm trying," she said, smiling faintly.

"That's all you can do. So long as you try."

A week later she was admitted to the psychiatric unit of the local hospital. She had come to see me and broken into sobs. "Carl keeps drinking and screaming when he's supposed to be resting. This morning . . . I ran away, back to my sister's. A couple hours later I went back to Carl. I can't leave and I can't stay. I just want to die . . . "

I had seen it all coming, and I could not prevent it. I felt totally powerless, as powerless as when I saw the *Evening Bulletin* heading toward its final edition. My feelings must have been reflected in my face.

Millie leaned forward. "It's not your fault," she said. "You did your best."

"So did you," I said.

I arranged for Millie to be evaluated by the clinic's psychiatrist. Soon afterward, he reserved a bed for her at the hospital. "Thank you," she said to me, crying. "I know I'd have killed myself if I didn't get into the hospital today."

Some time later I visited Millie at the hospital. She smiled broadly when she saw me. We settled down in the patients' lounge. Millie prepared coffee for us. "You'll be very proud of me," she said. "I asked the doctor to make sure that they don't put through any calls from Carl. Also, that they don't let him in if he comes to visit me."

"I am very proud of you," I said. "You need time out."

"Yes. I do."

The resident psychiatrist, with whom I had met before meeting Millie, told me she was on antidepressants and tranquilizers and received individual and group therapy. She was responding well.

"I'm self-destructive," Millie said matter-of-factly. "I got to learn how to change."

Learn how to change. Yes. That was the key to her survival. It had been my hope all along. But she had been unable to change. Would this, her fourth major depressive episode, make the difference? I did not know.

She put her coffee cup on the table before her. Then she looked at me. "The last time I was in this place, it was because I tried to kill myself," she said. "This time I'm here because I knew better. I came to see you. So you see, I'm better than I was."

❖ ❖ ❖ ❖ ❖

The following evening, on the first anniversary of the *Evening*

*Bulletin*'s death, I went to the newsroom reunion party. It also was the end of my first semester. When I'd first heard of the plans for the reunion, I didn't think I was ready. But I had gotten my first report card—two As and one B—and a glowing review from Steve. And then there was Millie. Millie's progress.

The party was at the Pen and Pencil Club, the traditional hangout for newspaper folks, just up the street from Hahnemann. I had not gone very far away after all.

Amid the raucous reminiscences, clinking glasses, and tales of new employment, I felt a hand on my shoulder. It was a former colleague, now with *The Inquirer*. "How's the new therapist?" he asked.

For a moment I felt a twinge of envy. But soon my report card flashed into view in my mind, then Millie's face. "It ain't easy," I said. "But I'm getting there."

✦ ✦ ✦ ✦ ✦

After several weeks at the hospital, Millie was discharged into my care at the clinic. She moved back in with her sister and brother-in-law. Her relationship with Carl was over. I saw her twice a week for several months.

"Millie, you remember that when we first met, I told you I was in a major change in my life," I said one afternoon. "That I was at the clinic as a student."

A deep furrow marred her forehead. "Yes."

"Well," I said. "My year here is ending. Soon it'll be time for me to move on. To a hospital, for my second year."

She hung her head. Then she looked up. "I'll miss . . . talking with you," she whispered.

"I'll . . . it's been a great . . . experience working with you," I said.

"Maybe . . . maybe I can stop coming here. After you leave, I mean."

"Maybe."

"Because," she said, "I want to move on, too. I've started

looking for a job. And not as a bartender, either."

"Congratulations!" I held out my hand.

She grabbed it, squeezed it. "Congratulations to both of us."

For our final session she wore her blue dress and carried a small knitted white dog atop a crocheted blue pillow. "I made it myself," she said, handing me her gift. Her eyes glowed. "You saved my life. I wouldn't be here if it wasn't for you."

I cleared my throat. "We learned together, and from each other."

At the end of the session I opened the door and she walked out without looking back.

From a window in the hallway I watched Millie get into her car. She backed it up, then drove to the exit and into busy Main Street.

I stood there, by the window, until she disappeared.

That night I dreamed about the clinic. Not about a newspaper, not about the phone ringing with the news of a job offer from *The Inquirer*. I dreamed about my office in a building with long, narrow, gray halls in need of white paint, and in the morning I could not wait to get to work.

# Epiphany in F

## Juliet Eastland

Have you ever had a religious experience? A time when you entered a house of God—distracted perhaps, searching for something you couldn't name, maybe a bit skeptical—only to be blasted by the heat from the pulpit, which made your body boil and melt under the fervor of True Faith? You come out of the experience transformed. Your soul has been re-hammered into an alloy, shot through with brilliant, steel-strong strands of belief; you have found a purpose.

Or maybe a purpose has found you. This was my experience. The house of worship was a secular one, thick with cigarette smoke. Beer and whiskey replaced the holy wine; the acolytes wore jeans; and the high priest played a saxophone. I suppose it makes sense that, being a musician, I had my epiphany at a jazz club. It was a low, narrow building, its striped awning drooping like the remnant of a small-town circus. RYLES JAZZ CLUB curled over the door in neon script from the bell of a neon saxophone like smoke curling from a genie's lamp. I was just out of college, living in Somerville, Massachusetts. Every day on my way to work as a research assistant at MIT, I would head toward Inman Square—a triangular slice of park formed by the intersection of three streets—and pass Ryles.

It never occurred to me go in. Despite the fact that I grew up playing classical piano, or perhaps because of it, I didn't really know what jazz was. Besides, I was a researcher, a writer, a thinker. What did I want with a jazz club? I pictured characters from the revival-house B movies of my youth: dissolute sad sacks, fedoras pulled low, tossing back shots of bourbon; shellacked molls, lolling at the bar in evening gowns. Their scarlet lips would kiss and betray; possibly they carried a gun in their garter belts. They certainly wouldn't wear glasses, or worry about getting a date, or work at MIT compiling sociological data on racism in Brazil.

And yet . . . and yet, I was restless and lonely, and trapped inside my priggishness. I was ripe for conversion, and the universe obliged on one chilly December evening. I had finished up a late night at work and was heading home toward my roommates and my flannel pajamas and a frozen pizza-for-one. As I rounded the corner into Inman Square, there was Ryles. Alive! Candles flickered behind the steamy windows and I heard the beat of drums. Without stopping to think, I strode to the door and paid the five-dollar cover charge.

The den of sin turned out to be a long, narrow room with a tiny stage tucked at the far end—a wooden platform barely large enough for the four-piece band. Windows lined the wall along the street to the left, and a mirrored bar ran the length of the room on the right. About fifteen pockmarked wooden tables, surrounded by mismatched chairs, faced the stage, but it was a weeknight and only a few tables were filled. A few unattached men appraised me as I came in, and, finding me wanting, turned their predatory gazes back to the silent football game unfolding on the television above the bar. The bartender, a bearded man in a lumberjack shirt and Red Sox baseball cap, sat under the television reading a book. Two waitresses leaned against the counter, bored. The band had just finished a tune.

My feet squelched on the gummy rug as I made my way to the bar and ordered a club soda and lime. "Teetotaler's special," the bartender announced with a smile, putting down his book—Baudelaire's poetry. I blushed. As I perched on a bar stool with my drink, the saxophonist nodded to the pianist, and a somber chord resonated from the stage—and another and another, the quarter notes unfolding with hymn-like gravity. I recognized the tune, dimly, but couldn't place it. I recognized, too, the chords—major thirds, minor thirds, dominant sevenths—but there was something unfamiliar about it, a dissonance that made the hair on my arms stand on end. (I found out later that these added scale tones are aptly called "tensions.") Above this disquieting murmur, another sound emerged: a growl from the horn, rumbling and roiling into a wave of sound until I thought the foundation of the building would buckle under the force. Out of the chaos, a melody began to unfurl, pure and relentless.

The men at the bar turned from the television to study the band, and the bartender looked up from his book, his finger poised over the page. Conversation died. I sat without moving, holding my breath, but I felt my body surging and subsiding with each note, my insides shifting like particles in a kaleidoscope. I was splitting open, overflowing, and sitting at the bar, clutching my ticket stub, still wearing my coat, I began to cry. I wept with an inchoate yearning, aching for someone I might never meet, someone whose deliberate and tender touch would penetrate me and unclench the fist inside me.

And then the beat shifted into a higher gear, and the horn player took off into the stratosphere on a crest of eighth notes that swung so ferociously that every cell in my body started to dance, and I twitched as if possessed by St. Vitus, my fingers drumming on the bar counter and my feet stamping on the floor. Just when I felt I would be swept off the stool and carried up to the sky with excitement, the wave subsided, and the sound began to seep out of the room until the only noise left was the spit rattling through the metal body of the horn like the breath of someone dying. As the last bit of air rasped through the room,

I realized I had been holding my breath, and I exhaled. The piano sounded with the finality of a grave's lid closing.

Then silence.

The horn player stood with his instrument to his face, his eyes closed as if in prayer. No one moved. Then one person started clapping, then another, then all of us, our energy flowing back to the musicians just as their music had surged over us. I clapped until the palms of my hands hurt. The lights went up, the waitresses dispersed among the tables, and the world began to turn again.

Leaving my drink at the bar, I made my way to the horn player and waited for him to replace his horn on its stand.

"Excuse me," I quavered. "What was the name of that song?" He turned to me, wiping his shiny dark face with a towel.

"'My Funny Valentine,'" he said, smiling.

Of course! I knew where I'd heard the tune: at my parents' house, Ella Fitzgerald giving voice to the music. But that version felt like an artifact from the past, the music diminished and filtered through the record player and made safe by the familiar surroundings of home and by the presence of my parents, my guardians. What I'd heard tonight was created and communicated on the spot, a ferocious "valentine" addressed without mediation or mitigation to the audience. To me.

I don't remember the walk home. My roommates were asleep, so I let myself in, tiptoed up to my room, and changed into my pajamas. I wrote the words on a pad of paper and stared at them: "My Funny Valentine." They were just words, and the sounds I'd heard tonight were just sine waves. So how to explain what had just happened?

The rest of the week passed in a haze. My roommates teased me—"you must be in love!" they said. I was, although not in the way they thought. I bought five tapes with different instrumental versions of "My Funny Valentine," and as I absorbed the music each night, alone in my room, I had a revelation: I didn't just want to listen to this music, I wanted to create it. The more I took it in, the more certain I became that no other activity in the world was as worthwhile, as powerful, as relevant as playing jazz. As I contemplated this, my heart leapt. I was a fairly accomplished classical pianist—a bit rusty, but I had good technical facility and an excellent ear. Why not?

I contacted Berklee College of Music, across the Charles River, and arranged for an audition. Despite my stiff performance, I made it in, and two weeks before the spring semester began, I gave notice at my job and enrolled as a full-time piano student in the jazz department.

It was a painful and humbling semester, but with every chord I learned and every eighth note I swung, I rejoiced. Not once did I doubt that this was what I should be doing. Whenever I stumbled, which was often, I pictured the absorption, the complete, all-body intensity, of the horn player at Ryles. Someday, when I had mastered the mechanics of the craft, I, too, would be able to lose myself in the music so utterly. I, too, would be able to make my audience melt without saying a word.

I had embraced intellectual passions before. I'd preached to classmates about colonialism after reading *Lord Jim* in college, and my research at MIT had excited me with its political implications. But this was different. This was not just about what was out there to learn; this was about what was inside, about what I had to say. And if I said it well, if I played with as much power and honesty as the horn player had, I might touch somebody more profoundly than he or she had ever been touched before. I longed to bestow upon someone else the experience the horn player had bestowed upon me.

But could I achieve these goals within the familiar confines of my home city? I didn't think so. Armed with the rudiments of my new, powerful language, and feeling braver than I ever had, I did something out of character: I moved. To California, of course, land of opportunity and self-reinvention. My plan was, simply, to form the world's greatest jazz band and take the West Coast by storm.

+ + + + +

I did form my own trio, with bass and drums, but I ran into trouble with part B. After a year of slogging through loud, low-paying, smoky gigs in San Francisco clubs, my commitment began to waver. I loved jazz, but did I have the stamina and the discipline to keep plugging away, night after night, year after year? I wasn't so sure. Many nights I wouldn't get home until two or three in the morning, and I would sleep through the sunny California days, emerging, vampire-like, in time to watch the sun set. I was lonely, and I yearned for a "normal" schedule, one where I could work during the day and see my friends at night. My verbal abilities began to atrophy; my band members, so eloquent on their instruments, were painfully shy men who spoke only when spoken to, and then only in monosyllables.

At each gig, a few audience members would sit and listen, clapping respectfully at the end of a tune, but more often, we were background music for people's more immediate dramas and conversations. I still felt the desire to reach out and grab listeners, just as I had been grabbed; the problem was, I couldn't catch anyone's attention.

I finally dissolved the band, and while I still play jazz for myself, I no longer play professionally. My epiphany at Ryles changed the course of my life, but in the end it taught me the most basic lesson of all: Keeping the faith is hard work, and not everyone is a priest. Some of us are just appreciative members of the congregation.

# Taking My Lumps

## Sachin V. Waikar

The poison dripping into me is platinum, like the dull band around my finger. Unlike my ring, the metal is liquid. And clear. The bag that holds the poison—Platinol, to be exact—hangs above me, a chemo-zeppelin. I lean back on the bed, blinking at the white-light tubes in the ceiling. This afternoon, the first of five, my home will be the Infusion Therapy Room at the University of Chicago Hospital. It's 2001. My cancer odyssey.

A little over one centimeter. That was the lump's diameter. Last week, they plucked it out of me, along with its host, my right testicle. Beyond its diagnostic value, the surgery—minor, though it didn't seem so at the time—offered at least two benefits: (1) It was one of many medical events that would excuse me from work for months; (2) I could no longer say, "I would give my right nut to . . . (insert much-desired activity here)." Actually, the second one wasn't much of a perk—I've always hated that expression.

Now, if someone had said, "Sachin, here's the deal: You get to skip work for a while! Special introductory rock-bottom price: an embryonal carcinoma with vascular invasion! Act now, and we'll throw in an orchiectomy and two rounds of chemotherapy!" I would have passed. Given that I had no choice, however, I was happy to take a long, unplanned vacation.

✦ ✦ ✦ ✦ ✦

I hated my job; the feeling was mutual. "Fit issues," my second-year review read; they weren't talking about my waistline, though that, too, was having issues. The management-consulting company that had made the mistake of hiring me, a lapsed clinical psychologist, proffered euphemisms to describe flailing employees: "Great team player" meant, "This guy can't do the work by himself; you don't want him on your team"; "strong social skills" indicated that those were the only talents evident; "solid," which peppered my reviews, stood for "shitty."

Maybe it was my mood—"solid" in the consulting vernacular—but I noticed a unifying theme to the work. "At the *end* of the day, what matters is this move's effect on the *bottom* line," we told each other, as one of us erased our fifth full whiteboard of the morning. (Note that our "end of the day" was often celebrated around eleven P.M. with soggy nachos in a dim hotel room.) "These guys are *screwed*," we whispered in the gray basement offices and windowless conference rooms of our clients. Of course there was the occasional talk of "going forward," usually reserved for client meetings, but my perception of the job cohered around ends, bottoms, screwings. In this context, testicular cancer kind of made sense.

✦ ✦ ✦ ✦ ✦

In the Infusion Therapy Room, the infusee beside me, a smiling, middle-aged, jeans-wearing woman I'll call Ann, is not here because of cancer. Ann's in line for a heart transplant and doesn't think she'll get one in time, but if she does, the IV drugs might convince her body to accept the new organ. The same general treatment—and by now I understand that "chemo" refers to myriad agents, a wet bar of colorless anodynes—that is flushing cancer cells from my body is pleading with hers to welcome a cardiac Trojan horse. "It's okay if I don't get a heart," says Ann. "I've seen a lot of life." I nod, cringing inside—both for this big-hearted woman and for myself.

My son is not yet one year old. Kayan has black-brown eyes, scattered teeth like pale little pills, a mad-scientist laugh like his father's. No, I haven't seen enough of life. Not yet.

I don't think I'm going to die. The probability I'll beat this cancer: 97 to 100 percent. I'm not a gambler, but I've always thought about rates and odds. Maybe it's because my dad's a statistician. I beat the odds to get into my college—less than a 15 percent chance. And again for graduate school—about 5 percent. Getting the strategy-consulting position, depending on how you calculated it, was an even lower-odds outcome. Now the numbers are on my side. Ninety-seven to 100 percent, I tell myself. Better than 30 to 1. My numerical mantras.

But I'm afraid. When the chemo's over, about a month from now, and the allotted disability period—another month—is up, I'll have to go back to work. What if I leaned over to Ann, or to one of the others here under the white lights, most of whom would give anything for my 97 to 100 percent, and said, "Hey, I know you've got it tough, but soon I have to return to a basement in Columbus and fake my way through twelve-hour days." Yeah, not a whole lot of sympathy would flow my way.

To the side of my narrow bed, on the floor, is a backpack, a funky green, ergonomically strapped Tumi I picked up for all the traveling I would be doing for work. Inside the pack is my laptop, and on its hard drive, along with dense financial spreadsheets and BS-laden PowerPoint slides, is a folder called "Story." A document—less than ten thousand words long—in the Story folder is the only file I would mourn if my laptop crashed. The document, which contains the tale of an arrogant management consultant's sudden demise (for now, the irony of this choice is lost on me), is my first attempt at fiction in more than fifteen years.

✦ ✦ ✦ ✦ ✦

I have a knack for English. In seventh grade, I advanced to the regional spelling bee, only to be felled—in the first round—by "ecru." That still burns me, and I sometimes boycott beige-colored items. In high school, I won the Four-Year English Award, and I believe my application essays sealed admissions to several top colleges.

But writing as a career? "Never," I whispered to myself as I biked to psychology classes at Stanford. Okay, maybe I just thought that, but the whispering sounds more dramatic; the biking part, at least, is true. "There's no money in writing," I argued, in what I now term the Voice of the Conventional, as I applied to clinical-psychology graduate programs. I looked past the fact that Los Angeles, the city where I landed to pursue a doctorate, probably employs more highly paid writers—in Hollywood— than any other.

But the act of writing, of creating with words, persisted. I've always enjoyed penning skits. In fifth grade, I helped write a Western parody, casting myself as a southern belle. (Don't ask.) In graduate school, I drafted a spoof, "(Unresolved) Fantasy Island," that brought down the proverbial house at our annual talent show. And the only time in my tenure as a consultant I didn't sit like a silent lump—it was more than a year before my tumor spoke up—at the end of the table was on the last day of a long training program, when we broke into teams to make mini-movies. The films were supposed to be humorous. When two of my teammates, a physicist and an economist, suggested we put non sequitur nicknames (made-up example: Bill "The Crazy Man" Smith) in the credits, I said no. "But why?" they said, tears in the corners of their bespectacled eyes (sorry, going for drama again— but one of them did look a bit tearful; maybe an ocular condition?). "Because it's not funny," I replied. For the first time in two weeks, they were silent.

✦ ✦ ✦ ✦ ✦

In the chemo room, I power my laptop and scroll through the story. I started writing it between consulting projects, at night, after my son went to bed. I understand now why I pursued clinical psychology: I had mistaken an interest in observing—and generating—life stories for a desire to help people alter their own. Writing my first fiction in years, I've lost track of time, I'm falling through the notebook's pages, diving into the computer screen. "Why didn't you tell me it could be like this?" I want to ask my few friends who enjoy their jobs. The metaphorical phone is ringing, my future on the other end. Or, more likely, a metaphorical telemarketer.

"Just because you think it's your calling, " speaks the Voice of the Conventional, my only companion in the hospital, "doesn't mean you have to answer." I shut the laptop, listening. "You have a six-figure income that barely covers your bills." Almost hissing now. "Your wife doesn't have to work anymore; she's already supported your first career switch and you're going to ask her to . . . " I glimpse a yellow shape at the room's end; it's moving closer. "And what about him?"

My son, dressed in a yellow fleece pullover, is being wheeled toward the bed by Kalpana, my wife. From his stroller, Kayan smiles. "And you two want another," continues the Voice, more confidently. "Think stories are going to put food in their mouths?" It rises in pitch. "No, stories are the realm of teen trust-funders, twentysomething bartenders, and bored housewives." I squelch the Voice, reaching for Kayan.

But I think the Voice is right.

✦ ✦ ✦ ✦ ✦

Between chemo treatments, my white-cell count drops more than expected, prompting the doctors to delay the next round. If I contract an infection, I'll be taken to a "special room"—

another euphemism, I fear—in the hospital. I'm to wash my hands frequently and avoid raw fruits and vegetables. But I can't avoid thinking about work.

Kalpana and I know that my company will not tolerate "solid" on-the-job performance much longer, even from a cancer guy, especially in the declining economy. We understand and accept this. But what are my options? On the couch in our condo, we've discussed organizational-behavior consulting—"it's kind of psychology-related"—and executive recruiting—"you like talking to people." But we know these jobs, which are not even easy to get, would be Band-Aids at best. The sweat I ooze at night has little to do with my illness.

✦ ✦ ✦ ✦ ✦

The epiphany—like this story's end—comes with little warning. It's the evening before my second round of chemo. We're on the couch, staring through the TV.

"How's the story going?" asks Kalpana. She has read most of the pages I've written.

"Okay. Don't know if I'll work on it much this week, though." I feel weak. I'm not looking forward to the morning's needles and white light. Outside the window behind us, Chicago is dark.

"You're not going to give up on it, I hope."

"Don't think so."

"I was thinking . . . " she says, looking at me. "Maybe you should take some time away from work to, you know, write."

I laugh. Maybe she's bought a lottery ticket, I think. That would be a first for either of us; remember, I have an interest in odds. "That would be nice," I say, shaking my head. We have no savings. Kalpana left her sales job when Kayan was born. Not once has she mentioned missing work. The Voice clears its throat.

Then, at the same time, I say, "I could stay home with

Kayan, but you'd have to go back to work," and Kalpana says, "You could stay home with Kayan, but you'd have to be okay not working."

Silence, as our world rotates 180 degrees. We blink at one another.

"Yeah, good plan," sneers the Voice of the Conventional. "How are you going to . . ." I press a couch pillow into its flapping lips.

And I smile at Kalpana—and our future.

## *Epilogue*

It's been almost three years. My follow-up CAT scans—twice a year—have revealed no signs of cancer. These hospital visits are the only times I think about the disease much.

We live in Chicago's suburbs. Three of our four bedrooms hold beds; Sarika, our daughter, joined us nine months ago. The fourth bedroom is my office. "What does your dad do, Kayan?" my son's day care teacher asked him last year. "My daddy goes to the gym," he said. After a moment, he added, "He writes books and movies."

Kayan left out the part about my having no income. That, for now, is Kalpana's job; she works in sales again, while pursuing an MBA. I've written two screenplays I view as practice. And a novel that will hit the desks of several publishers—via my agent—next month.

When I left the consulting job two years ago, I gave back the company's laptop. The only folder I saved: "Story." I haven't opened that folder again, leaving my arrogant fictional consultant in limbo. But in a sense, that story's over.

And a new one has begun. As this tale opens, the handsome—if somewhat hairy—protagonist emerges from a fluorescent-lit cavern, where he has peered into a dark pit with no end. Though shaken, he is more aware than he thought possible, more alive. Like a reveler who escaped the Masque of the Red Death—like

Fortunato freed from his brick tomb—like someone who's been reading too much Poe.

The road before the hero is wide, his path clear. At his feet, a painted gold line. He crouches behind the line, one knee on the road. But wait—a low voice from the copse of black trees to his side. "Going somewhere?" it hisses. The hero rises; he glances at the trees, frowning. Then he shakes his head, his eyes back on the road. The voice continues, but he can't hear it, its sound reduced to an ant's tread. Smiling, the hero waits.

And when the silent starting gun goes off, I fly.

# In Her Hands

## Paola Gianturco

"One of the most well-known advantages reach stackers have over lift trucks is their capability to access a container from the second or third row of a stack without removing containers in the front rows."

Magazines full of news like this cover my desk every morning, delivering information that is crucial to understanding my corporate communications clients' businesses. I stuff them into my briefcase. How many evenings it takes to read forty trade publications about container shipping, railroads, and lumber! After spending twelve hours in the office, I commute home to be a single mom, then work in my silent house long after my son goes to sleep. I finish a client's budget, then pick up another magazine: *The National Hardwood Lumber Association is offering one of its most popular short courses at its headquarters in Memphis: grading lumber.*

I dream of living a completely different life.

1995: I sit in the boardroom at a client's headquarters surrounded by men in handsome business suits, expensive contemporary furniture, and paintings created by famous artists. Before the meeting, someone has set out a silver tray of coffee and cookies. Air-conditioning cools the building but outside, the sun shines on the corporate campus's perfect green lawn, pond full of ducks, splashing fountains.

1997: I sit on the floor of a mud hut in the desert of India interviewing twenty-five tribal women who make mirror embroidery. It is hot. The only furniture is a cot standing against the wall. Flies buzz around. There are no windows but I know there is dusty desert for miles in all directions. The women wear bright silk dresses that glitter with sequins. When the sun goes down, someone hands me a grimy flashlight so we can see each other and continue our conversation.

For more than thirty-five years I worked in advertising, marketing, public relations, and corporate communications. When my son was in the first grade, I was the only mother in the class who had a job. By the time he graduated from college, lots of women were working, but they were not yet holding many leadership positions in corporations. I was senior by then, and often for six months at a time, I was the only woman in meetings.

It was a lonely life. I longed for a break from the stress. I was tired of always being on deadline. I longed to pursue my own interests rather than my clients'. I dreamed of doing something that might make the world a better place.

For a while, I wondered, "What's wrong with me? I am good at what I do, well-paid and, people say, successful." Nevertheless, I began to entertain a heretical idea. What if I aligned "who I am" with "what I do"? If the two matched, surely my life would proceed more smoothly, like a sleek train on a track.

The first hurdle was that I didn't know "who I am." For years, I had focused only on my son and my work, without time or inclination for introspection. I entered therapy with a wise woman who listened to me—no matter what came out, from drifty thoughts and half-baked ideas to memories, questions, fears, tears, dreams. Her example taught me to listen to myself.

One day at a therapy session I saw, in my mind's eye, a sunflower—and recognized myself as tall, strong, and energetic, radiating creativity and intelligence. The insight stopped me cold. How effectively I had hidden those attributes from myself! I had seen myself secretly as a child: short, not tall. Creative? In advertising, a "creative" person is a copywriter or an art director, not a businessperson like me. Intelligent? My father and brother have always been the intelligent ones in our family.

In 1995, my ninety-year-old father died. I went back to our family house in Illinois, where every room spoke of his imagination and ingenuity in the form of his countless inventions. They were delightful, useful things: a snuffer to prevent candles from smoking as they go out, a clip to hold the straw steady in a drinking glass, nails poking through shelves to keep figurines from falling. My father cooked up these household gadgets in his spare time. It was his medical devices, which saved many lives, that were his real contribution to the world. As his oldest child, I sensed that it was now my turn, my obligation, to begin doing more important work. Given my genes, I might have thirty or forty more years in which to do it.

I asked myself, what can I do? On weekends I hiked alone on shady trails under the redwood trees, following paths through sunny fields, over streams, toward the ocean. And I questioned myself. Could I really begin again in a different field, jettisoning all my professional experience, being older than the other beginners, earning a starting salary again? I couldn't imagine how to apply my knowledge and skills to a new field. I couldn't envision anything that might interest me more than communications, which first captured my fancy when I was fifteen. What else could I offer that anyone would pay for?

I began dreaming about taking a one-year sabbatical to test-drive a life that included only the things I love most, know best, and wanted to learn. I made a mental list: *I love: travel, collecting folk art, and taking pictures. I know: communications, business, and women's role in it. I want to learn: about women who run micro-businesses in third-world countries (how are they the same as, or different from, the women I work with in large companies?).*

Across the Pacific Ocean, the United Nations Fourth World Conference on Women was beginning in Beijing. I read about it in *The Economist* magazine, which reported that women all over the southern hemisphere who live on a dollar a day spend the money they earn to send their children to school. Men, the article said, spend their income on other things. I was stunned. These women, I thought, are invisible heroines! If they succeed over time in educating the next generation, they will change the future—not just for their families, but for their communities, their countries, and for the world. I wanted to meet them, to talk with them, to document their lives.

Suddenly I knew what I would do on my sabbatical: create a photographic book about women artisans in other countries who are using the money they earn to send their children to school. It was pure alchemy, combining all the things I'd been considering doing.

But I was also worried. Could one person complete such an ambitious project? Was it possible for a woman to travel alone in the countries where I planned to go?

I invited my friend Toby Tuttle to share the project with me. We had been friends for years, and had worked together and photographed together. Serendipitously, the day I called her, she had just finished reading a magazine article advising women to do something new every ten years if they want to stay young. She deliberated for about six seconds before saying yes.

For the next year, I taught in addition to consulting, earning two years' income in twelve months. I read endlessly to find out which crafts are considered "women's work" in many cultures. I enrolled in photography workshops. Toby and I purchased new camera equipment and did test shoots. I joined a writers' group for coaching and encouragement. Shamelessly, Toby and I asked virtually everyone we knew for help. Friends who work at universities, art galleries, nongovernmental organizations, and retail stores connected us to craftswomen in other countries.

We applied for grants—without luck—and decided to proceed anyway. We sent proposals to fifteen agents, but when we finally found one willing to work with unpublished authors, he couldn't find a publisher willing to give us an advance. Again, we decided to proceed anyway. I was so passionate about the project that—with absolutely no evidence—I was confident that everything would turn out all right.

Flying over the Atlantic Ocean en route to Poland and Turkey, where we were going to shoot the first two chapters, I did get butterflies. I thought to myself, Toby and I are not like the craftswomen we have arranged to meet. Many of them are illiterate; we are well educated. They are heartbreakingly poor; we are affluent enough to collect their work. Many of them cook on open fires, even crush chilies between rocks; we have microwave ovens and blenders. What hubris to have assumed that these women would talk openly to us about their lives!

I need not have worried. Everywhere we went, our interpreters knew the women personally and introduced us as friends. We began our conversations by sharing pictures of our own children, so that immediately we had something in common with the craftswomen. They welcomed us generously, even when their cupboards were bare. In Indonesia, a woman borrowed coffee from a neighbor and brewed it with river water. In India, we were served *chai* in the best china in the house—a saucer.

Patiently, the women responded to my 119 questions (not for nothing did I supervise marketing research). The interviews, during which every question and answer had to be translated, sometimes consumed six hours. (Later, I sent chapter drafts to all our interpreters. They read the stories to the women so that they could correct the facts or confirm that they had been represented accurately.) At the end of each interview, we invited the craftswomen to ask *us* questions. Usually, they inquired about where we lived and how we'd gotten to their villages. They often told us they were flattered that we were interested enough in them to travel so far. Always, they won our hearts and became our friends and teachers, showing us how women can create an economic, social, and artistic legacy. Every encounter made us feel that the world is smaller, and women's spirits larger, than we had ever imagined.

Toby and I traveled by dugout canoe to islands off the coast of Panama to interview the women who cut and sew the colorful appliqué pictures called *molas*. We moved boulders off the road after a landslide en route to weaving villages in Guatemala. We ventured so far into the countryside of South Africa that the banks had never seen traveler's checks. We photographed Shipibo potters working together in a women's pavilion high above the Amazon basin. We visited an AIDS craft project in Thailand and documented meetings of craft cooperatives in the Ring of Poverty, the river of slums around Lima.

In India, we hid on the floor of a Jeep to get through military checkpoints, because local officials did not want two American women anywhere near the Pakistani border. The distant desert villages were hardly tourist destinations. In one of them, Muslim women covered their faces when I approached; they had never seen a woman with short hair wearing pants, so they assumed I was a man. Children rubbed our arms to discover whether, under our pale color, we actually had dark skin like theirs.

Almost a year into the project, after a day of photographing and interviewing knitters in Bolivia, I was riding back to town on the flatbed of a blue Toyota truck bumping through the wheat fields south of Cochabamba. Leaning against the cab as the stars began to shine, I felt the warm evening breeze and was suffused with happiness. At fifty-four years old, I knew I was blessed to be right there, at that moment, in that fertile countryside, doing that challenging work.

During six trips, we interviewed and photographed ninety women artisans in twenty-eight villages in twelve countries on four continents. The result was *In Her Hands: Craftswomen Changing the World*, published in 2000. Apparently it struck a chord, because the book sold out and was reissued in paperback in 2004. Toby and I worked tirelessly to promote it. We appeared on *The Oprah Winfrey Show* and gave slide lectures at the

American Craft Museum, the Peabody Museum, and the Museum of Women in the Arts, as well as at dozens of smaller venues. We were proud and delighted when the Textile Museum in Washington, D.C., asked us to repeat our talk because twice as many people as they could accommodate had bought tickets. Our pictures were exhibited at the Field Museum in Chicago, the United States Senate, and the United Nations.

We began our book tour at the opening of the Progress of the World's Women exhibit at the UN. We used the last of our frequent-flyer miles to bring two Ndebele tribal women from South Africa to the United States to demonstrate their bead-work. They had never traveled outside their country, much less flown on an airplane. "Heaven must be like airplanes. You look *down* on the clouds!" Dinah Mahlangu marveled as she and Marley Mahlangu disembarked.

Eight *In Her Hands* pictures were hanging on the wall above Dinah and Marley as they sat on the floor of the UN General Assembly Building lobby, their bodies wrapped in Ndebele ceremonial blankets and their legs covered with tradi-tional beaded bracelets. The only indigenous artisans present, they were the most colorful of all the women artists who had come from seventy countries to participate.

As soon as Kofi Annan finished his speech to open the exhibit, he came across the lobby to meet Dinah, Marley, Toby, and me. The craftswomen, hobbled by their leg bracelets, couldn't get up quickly from the floor, so the secretary-general of the United Nations promptly and gracefully sat with them on the shiny marble. Dinah reached out to his lapel and pinned on a beaded AIDS-awareness pin she had made. "How do you say 'thank you' in your language?" he asked Dinah, who taught him on the spot. Flashes popped, television cameras rolled. It was a heady beginning for our book tour.

✦ ✦ ✦ ✦ ✦

For all the success and excitement that accompanied *In Her Hands*, the most gratifying results of the project came because readers were inspired to take action. A woman whom Toby and I had never heard of wired $10,000 to the mirror embroiderers in India when their houses were destroyed by an earthquake. Another donated $50,000 to Aid to Artisans. All in all, the book generated $120,000 for indigent women all over the world.

Nor was it just a matter of money. I received an email from the Girl Child Network in Zimbabwe, which runs a program for 20,000 girls ages four to sixteen, perhaps half of whom have been sexually abused. GCN programs aim to give the girls the self-esteem they need to respect and protect themselves. One of their tools is *In Her Hands*, wrote the founder, "because the book shows the girls that they can grow up to *be* somebody."

I, too, had become someone else. What began as a one-year sabbatical from a career in corporate communications became a right-angle turn in my working life. I had morphed into a photo-journalist, and I began working on another book, this one about festivals in fifteen countries that celebrate women's attributes, accomplishments, roles, rites of passage, and spiritual lives. *Celebrating Women* was released in October 2004, when the International Museum of Women in San Francisco opened an exhibit based on the book.

Today I look around my office—much as I did years ago, when I peered down at that heap of magazines about container shipping, railroads, and lumber—and see textiles, puppets, dolls, masks, costumes, pottery, beadwork, and baskets made by women in Turkey, Thailand, Bolivia, Guatemala, India. One whole wall is covered with purses the craftswomen made to hold the money they earn. The bags are bright with flowers, fringe, and pom-poms; some are shaped like animals, others like children. Many women's creative spirits inhabit my office. One of them is mine.

# Flat Follies

## Phyllis Johnston

*I*'d often wondered if spending my junior year abroad would have altered my life. Now, suddenly, I had the opportunity to find out—without the boorish demands of course-work or the constraints of the parental purse. True, I was thirty years older than the average exchange student and married to the man who had been asked to head up the London office of an American consulting firm, but these would surely be attributes, I thought. I'd be free to learn London at a leisurely pace, develop lasting friendships in the bustling international city, see plays in the West End every week, dash off to the Continent for long weekends, eat scones with fresh clotted cream. I would be living *Masterpiece Theatre.*

These enticements, coupled with the promise of injecting spontaneity and adventure into my life as I started my fifth decade, propelled me over the course of the six weeks I was given to put my consulting career on hold, sell our house, and put all our belongings in storage before boarding the flight to Heathrow in January 2001. What actually transpired during those 357 cloudy and eight sunny days in London would make better fodder for a Dennis Miller rant than for any teleplay introduced by Diana Rigg. Suffice it to say that I will never again call Dorothy a whiner for wanting to go home.

Within days of landing on British soil, I realized that I was going to have to stiffen my upper lip and squelch what one taxi driver termed—"no offense intended, madam"—my American naiveté when confronting the daily onslaught of astonishments, snubs, and conundrums that befall American expats in London. I must silently accept that being ignored in shops is true British service. I must keep from bristling when the first response to any question I asked was a disdainful "you're an American." And I must keep a copy of the British-American dictionary next to the telephone. My greatest survival technique was retreating to my computer and seeking solace by sharing observations, quandaries, and discoveries with friends back home.

In short order, I was proving the Heisenberg uncertainty principle. By merely observing things, you do change them. I found myself moving from maddening frustration, gasping disbelief, cultural alienation, and profound loneliness to varying degrees of catharsis, clarification, comedy, and comfort. My change in perspective might have been incremental, but my English vocabulary was enlarged immensely. Had this knowledge been accompanied by the acquisition of a British accent, my foray into flat follies might have been less jarring.

I knew it would take time to become familiar with the newness of living Britishly, but I did not think that getting the flat in working order would pose any difficulty. Over the years, I have lived in about a dozen apartments, and four houses, in four states. I have had years of experience setting up short-term campaign offices in many U.S. cities.

Yet no past experience had prepared me for my journey into this twilight zone. It was just as Rod Serling had described it. I had landed on "the shadowy tip of reality . . . on a through route to the land of the different, the bizarre, the unexplainable."

With only one week to find a flat in a city I had only seen on televised travelogues, I leafed through the phone directory and made bookings with five different real estate agents. This was not overkill. The concept and attendant convenience of multiple listings is not a British thing.

After seeing countless flats short on space and long on price, we made the decision to let a 1,400-square-foot, three-bedroom flat, furnished à la JCPenney, on Queensway in the Bayswater section of Central London for the king's ransom of £700 a week.

On moving-in day, we were forced to sit in the lobby for more than an hour waiting for the inventory specialist to arrive. His charge is to prepare an excruciatingly detailed list of the flat contents before any tenant sets a suitcase on the floor. Watching this wry Brit dash about the flat dictating into a handheld tape recorder proved that Monty Python was indeed alive and well. His innumerable references to the wall color "cream as in cow" were interspersed with what would have been charming euphemisms for "battered," "worn," and "filthy"—"well in use," "age discolored," and "not clean"—were he not referring to the place I was about to call home.

The next step was to arrange for telephone service. Using a prepaid mobile phone—an absolute must for new arrivals—I rang up British Telecom. A representative quickly arranged to activate the phone within twenty-four hours, and then put me on hold for twenty minutes in anticipation of speaking with another BT representative to arrange for Home Highway, the 128 KB Internet connection service, to be installed in two to three weeks.

A mere week later, the BT phone installer arrived, and the phone did work—but not right away. Once the lines were connected, the installer said the phone would be operative "in a bit." Apologizing for sounding the skeptic, I asked whom to call if it didn't work. He said not to worry. Jaded me pressed on until the installer promised he would call me himself in an hour. Well, an hour and a half later, no dial tone.

Unlike the stereotypical American, I did not call and complain. I opted to adapt. After all, the installer promised service "in a bit." And, as I had already learned, "in a bit" and "fort-night" are often synonymous. Luckily, that particular bit lasted only six hours.

There was plenty to do in the flat that did not require out-side intervention. I sat down with two operating manuals in preparation for doing the laundry. After an hour of reading, I put in the first small load and—just ninety minutes later—the wash was done. After another brief ninety minutes and two drainings of the water reservoir, all five bath towels and two tea towels were dry.

Buoyed by my success, I decided to plug in my Danish-made, American-wired stereo system. That proved to be an undertaking requiring previous training. Electrical service in the United Kingdom is not simply different from the American sys-tem—it is physically demanding, not to mention dangerous.

To plug in an English-made device, you need a three-prong adapter plug that you force into the socket before inserting the device plug and flicking the outlet's on/off switch—which, of course, is not marked (apparently you just intuit the distinction). For an American device, the sequence is: (1) insert the adapter plug in the wall socket; (2) insert a transformer into the adapter; (3) determine the wattage of the device you wish to run before sliding the transformer button to either 50W or 1600W; (4) insert the device plug into the transformer; (5) switch on the wall socket; (6) say a quick prayer; and (7) turn on the device. Beyond the obvious time and expense entailed, the weight of the now properly connected device is increased by nearly fourteen pounds—aptly termed a "stone" in local parlance.

When the day finally arrived for the Home Highway installa-tion, I was unabashedly excited. Being Internet-incommunicado in a foreign land is like being the title character in *Robinson Crusoe*. However, in the two hours preceding the scheduled appointment, the phone lines went dead, the power in the flat zapped out, and I sliced a three-inch gash in my finger. These circumstances called for British resolve and American tenacity.

First aid first, then a call from my mobile (this is exactly why both land-based and cellular phones are mandatory) to BT for repair and a plea that the line be activated prior to the arrival of the long-awaited high-speed-access installer. Next, a call to the building porter, who arrived on crutches, without a flashlight. Peering into the darkness at the fuse box, he said he had not seen one of them before and, of course, the building management was not responsible for repair.

"Perhaps you would like to ring up an electrician?" said the young porter.

"Perhaps not," I said. "Why not ask one of the workmen refurbishing the flat on the ground level if he would just take a quick look in the hope that power could be restored before the Home Highway man rides in?"

Minutes later, a wee bit of a man with a large brogue appeared at the door and said, "I am not an electrician, miss."

I replied warmly, as I do to any human who still calls me miss, "Neither am I. Shall we have a look."

My mobile rang. It was the Home Highway installer outside the building. I went to let him in, and as we were riding up in the lift, I casually mentioned my tendency for poor luck, citing this morning's events as examples. In true Brit form he politely inquired, "Should I expect to leave the flat alive, madam?"

By the time I ushered Melvin, the BT installer, into the flat, the workman had discovered that the new toaster was the culprit. By simply disconnecting the appliance, the power returned. Ah, but didn't that make me proud of my heritage!

The Internet connection was not resolved so easily. The process took three hours, largely due to the fact that one of the two phone lines in the flat was linked to Whiteley Mall, a nearby shopping centre anchored by the ubiquitous generic-brand food and clothing store Marks & Spencer. When I asked Melvin how this could have happened, particularly since his colleague had recently activated the lines, he resorted to what I suspect is a genetically British tactic for conflict avoidance—a bit of wry humor.

"I'm surprised that you haven't been deluged with phone orders for Estée Lauder."

However, all was still not right. Though I'd engaged AOL as my Internet service provider a week earlier, the company had failed to mention that it doesn't support ISDN lines. This would have been patently impossible had I not been in London seeking service from AOL UK, which is based in Dublin, which is not part of the U.K. So after receiving two conflicting yet mutually unhelpful responses from two AOL tech support people, Melvin and I decided to call his company, good old BT, and engage it as the ISP.

Just three short phone calls later, I was signed up, but the CD-ROM needed to load the software wouldn't arrive by mail for five days. Of course, if I wanted to pick it up at a BT store, I needed only to call yet another number to get the location. Of course, the number I was given was incorrect. Enough. I listened to the Greek chorus invoking the London mantra for expats: Know when to quit.

When the computer disk finally arrived, I did a series of Pilates breathing exercises to calm myself and began loading the software. During the hour-long process, I received a call from a research firm conducting a BT customer satisfaction survey. As I responded "extremely dissatisfied" to all of the questions except the courtesy of the seven phone representatives and two engineers I had had far too many lengthy conversations with over the past weeks, the computer screen popped up a warning message saying "loading canceled." Indeed.

After being forced to listen to this string of boorish complaints from one of *those Americans*, one would have thought that BT would have flagged my account with a "bitchy expat—do not disturb" warning. But no. The occasional provider of phone and Internet services remained undaunted, and dug in as a true contender for the *Catch-22* award with a confounding series of phone bills.

BT issues quarterly invoices for phone service. And, as is the practice of many London service providers, each bill is for past and future use. However, after receiving my third invoice within thirty days of having my phone connected, I noticed that I have been double-billed for one item. Just one call and three transfers later, I had an answer.

Yes, I was overbilled for £33. No, BT could not send a revised bill. Yes, I could deduct the amount from my payment, but my phone service would be disconnected. Yes, my next quarterly bill would include a credit. No, it was not illegal for BT to keep my £33 interest-free for three months. Round one to BT.

When I received the next quarterly bill, shockingly, there was no credit. Again, the call and multiple transfer process. After relaying the details, I heard an audible gasp from the customer service representative. Weakness in the opposition! I smelled victory. BT could not issue a revised invoice, but could post a counterfoil (the first page of the invoice with the total amount due on it). Seems I had been misinformed back in March. An amended counterfoil arrived within two days. Round two, a TKO for the visiting team.

The practices of the justifiably maligned British Telecom tend to be more the rule than the exception when residents attempt to deal with utility companies, government agencies, and real estate entities. Customer service is an oxymoron, billing procedures are virtually incomprehensible, and "dispute resolution" is a term that apparently cannot be translated from American into British.

Flush with victory from my encounter with BT, I rang up the City of Westminster about an overbilling on Council tax, a levy somewhat akin to property tax that the renter—not the property owner—must pay. This government group sends a bill for a twelve-month period to be paid on a monthly installment basis. However, my bill ran from April 2001 through March 2002, a full two months after I was to leave the rock forever. When I called in April, I was told to put these facts in writing and assured that my account would include a notation that the bill is in dispute and payment is not due until a corrected bill is provided. Seven weeks later, I received a demand-for-payment notice. So, I called and waited for only ten minutes before engaging in an impromptu theatre-of-the-absurd dialogue with a staff member.

Yes, the copy of the lease I sent does prove the tenancy period. No, the Council cannot issue a corrected bill and payment schedule. Yes, the Council did respond to my letter by phoning, but there was a hang-up. Yes, dialing a phone number but getting no answer and leaving no message on voice mail is considered a response. No, she has no idea whether or not I am telepathic. No, she cannot tell me exactly what my total bill should be, as it is determined on a per diem basis. Yes, I could calculate it myself. Yes, I should pay at the overbilled rate and four weeks prior to leaving the country I could notify the Council, whereupon a refund would be issued. No, she does not know if I believe in God.

As a courtesy, I informed this woman of my resolution. Yes, I would pay according to the inaccurate payment schedule through December. In January, I would send a check for £5 to cover the remaining balance. There would be no need for a refund. Thank you. Cheers.

# The Beginning

## Rita Golden Gelman

### 1985.

J am living someone else's life. It's a good life, filled with elegant restaurants, interesting people, and events like the Academy Awards and the Grammys. My husband of twenty-four years and I dine with celebrities, we see the latest movies before the rest of the world, and we're invited to all the book parties in Los Angeles.

Because of his job as an editorial consultant to some top magazines, we've been able to create a life that is privileged and glamorous. But now that I'm there, I realize that I don't like feeling privileged and I'm uncomfortable with glamour. I am living in a designer world that has been designed for someone I no longer am.

I prefer Goodwill to Neiman Marcus, Hondas to Mercedes, and soup kitchens to charity banquets. My house is too big; my garden, too trim; my friends, too white and American.

I first realized something was missing about five years ago when a woman wearing a floor-length muumuu and sandals sat next to me on an airplane. She told me she was in the business of booking sailing tours for captains around the world and was returning from the Mediterranean, the Adriatic, and the Gulf of Mexico. As she was telling me about her trip, tears began streaming down my cheeks.

"I'm sorry," I said, embarrassed. "I don't know where that came from." I wiped my eyes.

But I did know. I was crying for my lost spirit. As the woman spoke, I remembered that once I'd dreamed of sailing around the world, of paddling down the Amazon, of sitting around a fire with tribal people and sharing their food and their lives. I had loved the person who had those dreams. She was daring and idealistic . . . and gone. My husband had no interest in boats or tribal cultures.

"If I were to take a sailing trip," I said to the woman, "there are three things that I would want: a salty old captain who has tales to tell and philosophy to spout, a crew that likes to sing, and a place that is rich in experiences. I hate lying around on beaches."

She didn't even have to think. "Go sail on the *Tigris* in the Galápagos Islands."

Three months later, I boarded the *Tigris* without my husband, toured the spectacular volcanic islands, interacted with sea lions and blue-footed boobies, snorkeled the tropical waters, and touched the magic of otherness. I was never the same again.

When I returned from the Galápagos, that long-dormant fire of adventure had been rekindled and the glamour of my life turned gray. The gourmet dinners, the exclusive press screenings, the concerts, the parties, and the evenings at the theater suddenly felt like empty substitutes for discovery, for learning, for penetrating the unknown.

I knew that I couldn't run around the world adventuring, not if I wanted to stay married, which I did. But after the Galápagos trip, I needed something more in my life. I came up with a compromise. I would go to graduate school in anthropology and get my adventure from books.

The timing was right. My two kids no longer needed a full-time mom. Mitch was in his freshman year at Berkeley, and Jan was about to graduate from high school.

I had a fairly successful career as a writer of children's books. I enjoyed the wild and imaginative leaps into fantasy and the visits to schools and the modest recognition, mostly among first- and second-grade teachers; but I happily put my work on hold and plunged into academics.

I spent the next four years at UCLA, reading ethnographies, studying with anthropologists who had lived in exotic cultures, watching films, listening to lectures. By 1985, I am finished with most of the course work for the Ph.D., and I'm ready to choose a place and a topic for my dissertation research. Although my husband puts up with the hours I have to study, I doubt he would join me or endorse the idea of my doing fieldwork for a year in some far corner of the developing world. So I plan to do my thesis among the urban tribes of Los Angeles.

Meanwhile, our marriage is foundering. Over the years, our divergent interests and our personality differences have pushed us deeper into opposite corners. I'm basically laid-back and sometimes careless. I tend to excuse my own mistakes as well as other people's; and from time to time I find it necessary to adjust my ethics to the situation at hand. He is a perfectionist, reliable, honest, and prompt. He sets high standards for himself and has high expectations of others. More and more we find ourselves in minor skirmishes. The bell keeps ringing and we come out bickering.

Finally, after yet another squabble that escalates, I suggest that we take a break from each other for a couple of weeks. I need time alone, I tell him, to figure out what's wrong with the marriage and how we can fix it. When I come back, I say, I'd like us to try some marriage counseling. He agrees to a break and counseling but adds that two weeks is not enough. He suggests two months in which we are both free to see other people.

His response surprises and frightens me. Eight weeks of independence is very different from a two-week break to clear our heads. And I hadn't even thought about dating. I'm not sure I can be with another man after twenty-four years of marriage; I don't really want to. But I accept his suggestion. When he leaves the room, tears roll down my cheeks. As in many of our conversations these days, we are talking different languages, and I realize that once I introduced the idea of a break, I could not control his reaction.

If the break had been for two weeks, I probably would have checked into a hotel near Los Angeles. But two months is too long for a hotel. I decide to go to Mexico. It's a place I've always wanted to go and my husband hasn't.

By the time I leave, we both fear that this is more than a "break."

✦ ✦ ✦ ✦ ✦

I walk weak-kneed down the steps of the plane into hot Mexico City. My eyes are red, my nose is stuffed, and I feel as though my head is filled with lead weights. I am more frightened than I have ever been. I've initiated something that has already taken off in a direction I never intended.

I slip my arms into my backpack and follow the signs out of the terminal. In spite of my heavy load, I warm to the musical sound of Spanish all around me. I've loved the language from the first day I entered Mrs. James's Spanish 1, as a sophomore in Bassick High School in Bridgeport, Connecticut.

When I step outside, I am greeted by five young men waving brochures. The hotel I decide on looks decent, the price is right, and I don't have to pay for a cab. I'll only be there for two nights anyway. In two days I begin a Spanish-language course in Cuernavaca; the school has arranged for me to stay with a family. It's the only plan I've made for the two months.

It is seven-thirty at night when I check into the hotel, which gives me plenty of time to clean up and find a restaurant for dinner. As I salivate for Mexican food, I realize that I have never, in my forty-seven years, had dinner alone in a restaurant. When I was young, I had plenty of friends to share meals with. I married at twenty-three, and then I had a husband. I have never eaten out by myself . . . and I don't feel like beginning tonight.

I use the phone in my room to call for room service.

"*Discúlpeme, Señora. No hay comida en el hotel.*" My high school Spanish registers the words. There's no food in the hotel.

When I think about going out, an advance video runs through my head: I am sitting at a table trying to look content. The restaurant is filled with smiling, chatting people. I am the only one alone. They are staring, pitying me, wondering where I'm from and why I have no companion.

I sit on the bed and think about having to choose a place, get there, eat the meal while pretending to be happy, and then return to the hotel. How do I pick a place? Do I take a cab or walk? Is the neighborhood safe?

I can't do it. I'd rather not eat.

So I shower, put on my nightshirt, and curl up with the guidebook. Tomorrow I will go to the market. I plot the route to the central market on buses, and then I turn out the light, hungry and disoriented, as though I am not connected to the body lying in the bed. Who is this person in this strange hotel, alone for the first time in her life? Why am I here? What have I done? I feel as though I'm in a play, following a script that was written by a stranger. Part of me is scared, but there is another part, deep inside, that is excited at the idea that I am about to enter the unknown.

As a child, I loved the unknown. Every summer my parents, my brother, Pepper the dog, and I went on a one-week vacation in the car. My father would drive and my mother would sit next to him, a map on her lap. Every once in a while, when my mother said, "Turn right," my father would get a funny look on his face and turn left. Within minutes we would be lost. Then we'd have to knock on a farmhouse door (when it happened, we were always in farm country) to ask directions. Sometimes we'd be invited to see the newborn calves. Or watch the cows being milked. Often we'd get to throw a handful of grain to the chickens. Lost meant adventure, and I loved it. It's been years since I've been lost, and I can't remember the last time I stepped into the unknown.

I am out on the streets at six-thirty in the morning. The day is sunny, the Spanish language sings its musical sounds all around me, and cars whiz through the city ahead of the morning rush hour. Early mornings have a special energy that I like. I decide to walk the couple of miles to the market and get something to eat on the way.

Entering the market through a side entrance, I am immediately surrounded by piñatas: Mickey Mouse, Goofy, Donald Duck, and an assortment of animals and aliens dressed in their colorful papier-mâché skins. They are standing on the floor and hanging over my head, hundreds of donkeys and dinosaurs, cats and dragons, boys and girls, hogs and bugs. All the colors of the rainbow are swirling in front of me, swinging to the salsa music that is blasting out of unseen speakers. I am swinging, too. The brassy, percussive rhythm of the Caribbean is contagious.

Then I am out of piñatas and into avocados, shades of green and brown in massive piles on flowered oilcloth. Then mounds of sweet-smelling mangos fight for my attention with the pineapples. There are booths of papayas, red, yellow, and green; bananas, big and small, thin and fat; dozens of varieties of peppers and chilies fresh and dried and mounded in cubicles; tomatillos, jicamas, carrots, tomatoes, and bunches of green leaves. For a while, cilantro dominates the air, until I pass a table full of oregano. Seconds later, I stop next to a table covered with yellow squash blossoms and wonder what they taste like.

There are children in the booths, babies swinging in tiny hammocks, nine-year-olds wooing customers: "*Señora*, buy my watermelon. Good taste. Sweet."

The music streaming through the fruits and vegetables is a whiney, unrequited love song that I know from the Mexican radio stations in Los Angeles. It's called ranchero music. Though the music is sad, my body is light. My fears of the night before have turned into excitement.

I pass through mountains of green- and red- and brown- and rust-colored pastes, three feet high, the essence of mole sauces, redolent of cloves and garlic, oregano and cinnamon. Nothing is wrapped in plastic or sealed in containers. It is all out there to be smelled and seen and tasted and bought. I am surrounded by the colors, the smells, the sounds of a culture that lives life full out.

In meats, fifty little butcher shops compete for the shoppers' business. There are brains and stomachs and kidneys and tongues, feet and tails and intestines. Butchers are slapping and smashing meat on huge wooden blocks, beating red blobs into tenderness. They are scissoring and chopping up yellow chickens that have been fed marigolds so their skin and flesh are gold. Heads here, feet there. Innards sorted.

The butchers are mincing beef and hacking pork, sharpening knives and chopping slabs. Cleaving, slapping, scissoring, beating. It's a spectacular percussion band, with its own peculiar instruments.

The shoppers, thick in the aisles, are carrying string and plastic and cloth bags full of newspaper-wrapped packages of their purchases. I walk among them, enjoying the touch of our bodies.

I wriggle through the crowd to peer into waist-high vats of thick white cream and barrels of white ground-corn dough called *masa*. I cannot stop smiling at the explosion of joy I have felt since I passed under the canopy of piñatas. It's exciting to be exploring a world I know nothing about, discovering new smells, and moving through a scene where I am a barely noticed minority of one, swallowed up by the crowd.

I follow my nose to the eating area of the market. Sausages are frying, soups are bubbling, chilies are toasting. I sit at a picnic table and eat and smile, surrounded by Spanish-speaking women. I bite into my quesadilla stuffed with stretchy Oaxaca cheese and strips of sweet, green chilies.

"*Muy sabrosa.*" Delicious, I say to the woman sitting on my right. She asks me where I am from. I answer some simple questions and ask her name. When our conversation runs out of words, I move to another table and try a *sopa de flor de calabaza*, squash blossom soup with garlic and onion, zucchini, corn kernels, green leaves, and bright yellow squash blossoms . . . with strips of sweet chilies on top. The blend of flavors, the texture of the different vegetables, the thickness of the broth are like the Mexican people, filled with spice and spirit.

Then, at about noon, after nearly five hours in the market, I head off to the anthropology museum. I have never been big on museums or churches or most tourist attractions. As I wander through, I am thinking that I want to move into the enclosed tableaux, to live with these people, to celebrate with them, to cook and eat with the families. I want to experience their lives, not look at them through glass.

Many of the exhibits represent cultures that no longer exist, but there are plenty of living, breathing indigenous people in Mexico today. How I wish I could live among them.

Then it hits me for the first time . . . during these two months, I do not need anyone's permission to do what I want to do. I am free to make my own decisions, follow my whims, and take whatever risks I choose. For me, these two months are not about dating or being with other men; they are about doing the things that I can't do with my husband. I decide, while looking at a Zapotec family behind glass, that for some part of this Mexican journey, I will live in a Zapotec village.

By five o'clock I am thinking about dinner, and yesterday's fear is back. It is not a fear of people; I loved being in the market, surrounded by people. Nor am I afraid that someone will hurt me or rob me; I'm not a worrier. What I am feeling is a deep psychological fear with its roots in adolescence: a fear of being seen alone. Alone means unpopular. Alone means you have no friends. Alone means that you are an outsider. In the context of Mexico City, it makes no sense. But it is there, this vestigial fear, left over from my teenage years. Sitting alone at a table, where everyone can see me, is like shouting my inadequacy to the world.

I understand what I'm feeling and how foolish it is. But I still don't want to eat alone. I need to find a dinner companion, anyone, male, female, old, young, a family, a loner, a three-year-old. I've never been shy about talking to strangers. It doesn't matter whom I find; what I need is a human across the table.

I decide that it would be easiest, and safest, to look for a dinner mate in one of the better hotels. I study the guidebook and find my way to the most expensive hotel in the city, where I sit in a lounge chair by the pool and try to look as though I belong.

A family is sitting at the umbrella table next to my chair. "Where are you from?" I open. We talk: about Mexico City, about kids, about New York (where they are from and I used to be). An hour later, they gather up the kids and leave. They are a unit unto themselves; they don't need me.

A few lounges over, there is a man sitting alone. I am thinking that he will probably be joined by a wife full of shopping bags. What the hell. I can try. I smile at him, nod an opening, and we begin to talk. He's an engineer from Indianapolis, on business. Alone.

"I'm traveling by myself for two months," I say in answer to his question.

"Are you finding it difficult? I mean, what do you do about dinner?"

Yes. Yes. "Is that an invitation?" It wasn't, of course. "If it is I accept." I try not to sound as though I'm propositioning him.

He laughs and tells me that he is waiting to hear from a friend who usually calls in the morning. He suspects that their signals may have gotten mixed up. He'd be happy to have dinner with me, unless he hears from the friend. We make plans to meet.

I go back to my hotel, pleased with my ingenuity. I shower and get dressed. Then the phone rings. The friend has called; our dinner appointment is off. Back to zero. Okay. I'll start again at a different hotel. It is 8:15 P.M.

I choose a hotel with three stars and take a taxi there. The lobby is small. No one is sitting in the stuffed chairs, so I stand near the wall opposite the reception counter and observe the activity. Nobody is hanging around this lobby. I stand with a silly smile on my face and watch people on their way out for dinner. The pace is brisk. There's no chance to make eye contact, which is a necessary part of picking people up. And no one lingers, so there's no opportunity to hook someone with a spontaneous comment. It is nearly nine o'clock.

I find myself watching the young woman who is checking in guests. She has a warm smile and expressive eyes. And her English is excellent. I wait until there is no one in line.

"I'm sorry to bother you. I know you're busy, but I'm here and I wonder if you could recommend a restaurant where I wouldn't feel uncomfortable eating by myself."

"Hmmmm. Let me think about that for a few minutes. I'll get back to you."

I feel less alone already.

She continues checking in the guests and I retreat to my post near the wall. A line grows in front of her. It keeps getting longer. A half hour goes by. I am feeling more and more uncomfortable standing there. Just as I decide that she has forgotten about me, she calls me over.

"Excuse me," she says to the man at the front of the line. "I'll be just a minute. This woman asked me to recommend a restaurant where she could eat alone, and I promised I'd get back to her."

He smiles and looks at me. "An Englishman never lets a lady eat alone. I'm John and this is Lionel. We'd be delighted if you would join us for dinner."

I look at the woman and then at the men. "Thank you," I smile to all of them.

John directs the taxi driver to a small restaurant in Zona Rosa, the elegant part of the city. The tequila comes in a shot glass along with a small spicy tomato juice, and we begin our meal, all of us, with ceviche cocktails, raw fish "cooked" in a marinade of lime juice with diced peppers, tomatoes, chilies, green onions, and cilantro. Even before the main courses arrive, they buy me a wilting rose from the old lady who is selling them from table to table.

My chicken mole is fabulous. The three of us drink bottles of wine and laugh and talk a lot. Lionel is John's boss, recently arrived from London. He's about seventy years old, fit and funny. John, who is a few years younger than me, is tall and slim. He has a little twist in his nose and brown hair that flops over his forehead. They are both wearing suits and ties. John has been in Mexico for six months, traveling in backcountry, negotiating and doing deals and being propositioned by all the eligible young women in the villages he visits. He mentions only the propositions, not what he did about them.

The men are vague about their mission in Mexico. As the mariachi band plays my requests, I have visions of drugs and Mafia and spies. Then Lionel lets something slip about guns. I ask and the answer is evasive. I leave it alone.

I tell them my story, including my apprehension and fear that my marriage may be over. I can feel the tears in my eyes as I talk. They say nothing except, "Have another glass of wine."

We walk back to their hotel, singing songs from the fifties, holding hands like old friends, me in the middle. The streets are empty and our voices are loud. It is half past two; most of Mexico City is sleeping. John and I deliver Lionel to his room. Then we walk down the corridor and around the corner. Suddenly he stops and puts his hands on my shoulders.

"Rita," he says, "I think you want to cry."

He opens the door to his room and locks it behind us. Then he puts his arms around me and I cry.

The next morning, I am confused as I walk back to my hotel. Who was that woman who just spent the night with a stranger? Two days ago I could never have done it. In twenty-four years, it has never happened. Is it possible that leaving the country has turned me into someone else?

I try to look at myself from another dimension, detached and nonjudgmental. This person is not wife, mother, daughter, writer, anthropology student, L.A. sophisticate. She is, of course, all of these things; but alone, without the attachments, she is a woman in limbo, whose identity has been buried in her roles. Away from those roles and alone, she is someone she doesn't know.

Clearly, my job over the next two months is not only to think about the state of my marriage and to discover new worlds, but also to uncover the person inside my skin.

I collect my things and check out of the hotel. They are expecting me today at the Spanish school in Cuernavaca.

The city bus is crowded. People are pushing. I have switched my backpack onto my stomach so I can see it, and I am clutching my shoulder bag around the bottom. I've been warned about the dangers of city buses, but I like getting the feel of a city by riding the buses.

Five minutes into the bus ride, approximately thirty-six hours into my adventure, the bus lurches and a couple of teenagers standing next to me are thrown against my side. I fall to the floor. One of the teenagers helps me up. I don't even know that my wallet has been taken until I'm at the terminal looking for money to pay for the bus ticket to Cuernavaca.

Luckily, I'm wearing a thigh belt where I put most of my money, my traveler's checks, and my passport. I've lost about twenty-five dollars cash, $150 in traveler's checks, and a Visa card. I rush to a phone and try to call the American Express office in Mexico City to report the stolen traveler's checks. The line is busy. I try about ten times over the next week, and the line is always busy. (Months later, when I return to the States, I call them and they honor my loss.)

The money is negligible. The worst part is having to call my husband to cancel the credit card, which is in his name. The call is awkward and I feel like the stereotype of a helpless wife.

❖ ❖ ❖ ❖ ❖

The school has made arrangements for me to stay with a young couple and their baby; I'm their first foreign guest. Pili is twenty-one, slim with long black hair, sparkling eyes, and a bouncy personality. Raul, her husband, is strikingly handsome. His eyes are deep and dark, his shoulders are broad, and his smile is real. But there is something weighing him down. I can see it when I look into his eyes. Perhaps it's the responsibility of a wife and a one-year-old baby at the age of twenty-two.

Neither Pili nor Raul speaks English, so I'm forced to communicate in Spanish, which is the reason the school houses its students in homes. I am amazed at how much I remember.

The classes are one on one and I'm flying through the lessons. It feels great. I've never studied a language in context; it makes so much more sense than sitting in the United States with a book. Here, everything and everyone around you is a classroom.

Then, one week into my visit, I wake up with a rash on my chest. I decide it's nothing. I'm in a new environment, new foods, new water, new everything. I ignore it. The next day the rash is all over my body. And two days later, it turns into something that feels and looks like a stage-three sunburn. Every inch of my body is bright red. Wherever I touch, it hurts. I also hurt when I wash, sit, and put on clothes.

I leave the house that morning clutching the little pamphlet that the school has given me; instead of going to school, I go to the recommended doctor a few blocks from my house. I say nothing to Pili and Raul. I'm hoping it's nothing, so it doesn't make sense to worry them.

"It's varicella," the doctor says. "The whole family must come in immediately to get gamma globulin injections."

I have no idea what varicella is, but I am humiliated. I have just arrived and I have brought disease. When I tell Pili, in my halting Spanish, that they all have to get gamma globulin shots, she is skeptical. "That is not varicella," she tells me and then brings over her dictionary.

Varicella, it turns out, is chicken pox. She's right. I know what chicken pox looks like and this isn't it. She calls another doctor, who agrees to come to the house the next day. I go to bed early and wake up in pain—my back hurts and so does my scalp. My ears and my eyelids and the bottoms of my feet are the color of tomatoes. My entire body feels as though it has been dipped in boiling water. And I have a fever.

It is frightening to be so sick in a place where I don't know anyone. And my Spanish is not good enough to ask all the questions I have. I keep asking myself if it is safe to be treated by doctors trained in Mexico; I have no idea about the quality of the medical schools here.

Before the doctor arrives, I sit with a dictionary and prepare a list of possible causes. I am terrified that those village women who propositioned John have given him, and me, a disease. I'm embarrassed to mention it to the doctor, so I bury it in the middle of my list.

*varicella*
*food reaction*
*water reaction*
*cat allergy*
*venereal disease*
*reaction to Aralen, the malaria pills I've taken twice*
*hives*
*some tropical virus*
*a skin disease*

The doctor examines me in my room. I hand him the piece of paper. "It is not chicken pox," he tells me. He looks at the rest of the list without commenting. "I don't know what it is. I will have to consult my colleagues."

When he leaves, Pili says, "My father is a doctor. He gets back from vacation tomorrow. I'll call him."

Pili's father doesn't venture a diagnosis either. He sends me off the next day to the top dermatologist in Cuernavaca. By the time I get to his office, my skin has changed again. It is not hurting anymore. Now it is peeling, and when I take off my shirt in the office, thousands of tiny flakes of dead skin fall off onto his floor. I am snowing.

"It is a reaction to something," he says. "But I have no way of knowing what. It is not chicken pox or a virus or venereal disease. It is probably a response to the malaria medicine. Stop taking it." He prescribes prednisone, a steroid. I ask if my illness is contagious. He says no.

As I ride home in a taxi, I am trying to decide what to do. "Probably" is not very reassuring. I cannot, will not, go back to Los Angeles to my family doctor. I'm not even going to call my husband. This is my trip, my freedom, my problem.

I feel very alone. Not only have I never had such a strange illness, I've never gone through anything on my own. I decide that if I don't get a confirmation of the diagnosis, I will go to Miami, where I have a friend who is a doctor.

I walk in the door and Pili greets me. Doctor number two has called. He and his colleagues are calling my condition Stevens Johnson syndrome, a reaction to medication, probably the malaria prophylaxis, Aralen, although none of the literature discusses this side effect. He too prescribes prednisone. Okay. There's consensus. I decide to stay.

My condition gets worse. The fever brings on hallucinations and my vision becomes blurred. My legs blister so badly that when I stand still, the pressure and pain are intolerable. I have to sit on the shower floor while I bathe and brush my teeth because when I stand still for more than a few seconds the blisters feel as if they are going to explode.

Midway through the ordeal, I begin to see the illness as some kind of Herculean challenge that I must endure in order to become a new woman. I have also convinced myself that I am not in serious danger. (Months later, when I see my doctor in L.A., he tells me that Stevens Johnson syndrome is, in fact, extremely rare and dangerous. He has seen it twice, and both times he hospitalized his patient. The danger is infection; people die from it. He also tells me that the illness can do permanent damage to the patient's eyesight.)

After two weeks, I still cannot stand still. I have to sit

with my legs up to reduce the pain. Occasionally I go for walks, pushing the baby in the stroller. One day I go to the bank and discover that there is a line. I jog in place like a runner at a traffic light.

Every inch of my body is peeling. The more delicate parts of me flake onto the floor. Even my nipples and my earlobes are peeling. The skin on my fingers peels off, like the skin of a snake, intact. And my legs are still blistered. I have turned into one of those hideous pictures in a medical book.

Then, as I lie in bed one night, burning up and in pain, I get the first spiritual message of my life: In shedding my skin, I am being reborn. I am symbolically peeling away the person I have become and releasing the woman who has been trapped inside all these years. Soon this new me will be going out into the world on a journey of self-discovery.

The next night Pili and the baby go to bed at nine o'clock and I sit with Raul, my feet up on the coffee table, until two in the morning. Until now we have never had a conversation in depth. We have talked about food, about school, about his baby, and my illness; but language has always prevented our conversation from going beyond the superficial.

Tonight is different. We talk with dictionaries on our laps, and we share an extraordinary conversational intimacy. We are not an old American and a young Mexican. Nor are we man and woman in any sexual sense. There is certainly a mother-son component to our discussion; but it is more than that. We are friends, sharing feelings.

We begin when I tell him my revelation about rebirth. Like most Mexicans, he is Catholic, but he has never thought much about what he believes. We talk about souls, inner selves, the basic nature of human beings. He asks me about my marriage and I tell him, with tears in my eyes, that I don't know if my husband will want to stay married when I return, and that I am both afraid and challenged by the thought of being alone in the world. Raul confides in me his fears for his own marriage. Ever since his son was born, Raul has been noticing other women, wanting them, fearing his fantasies. We talk on and on, much of the time with tears in our eyes. Somewhere in the middle of our talk, I realize that I am comfortable speaking Spanish.

Slowly, I heal. My fever disappears; my blisters dry up; my skin is renewed. From beginning to end takes less than three weeks. When I am well enough to go back to school, I have no patience for the classroom. I no longer want to study. I am ready to move out into the unknown, to experience life with a new sensibility, to embark on my journey of inner and outer discovery.

On the Sunday morning before I leave, Raul, Pili, the baby, and I pile into the car and drive off for a farewell tour of Cuernavaca. The first stop on our tour is to buy *chicharrón*, fried pigskin that's been boiled for hours in a vat of lard, left to dry, and then boiled again. You can buy thin, non-fatty pieces, or the fattier middle part, or you can look around for pieces that have a little meat attached. Raul buys a bagful and I reach in for a hunk.

I've been a health-food nut for years. I can't remember when I last had bacon in my house, even though I love that crispy smoky meat surrounded by mushy fat. I banished it years ago when I became concerned about what went into my kids' bodies. But now, it is my body, and my host can't wait for me to taste this Mexican treat. Neither can I.

I crunch through the tasty, crisp cells that have puffed up into a light and airy snack; it's wonderful. I reach into the bag for another piece, feeling exhilarated when I bite through sections of fat.

I feel no guilt as I demolish some long-cherished no-fat rules along with the *chicharrón*. I'm not sure why I am guilt-free. Perhaps it is the setting; rules tend to reduce their grip when you cross borders. Perhaps it is the *chicharrón*, crunchy, light, and bacony; it's easy to put aside guilt in this enthusiasm and taste of the moment. But more likely, the joy I feel at this guilt-free moment is a sign that I really have peeled away the old and begun the process of self-discovery.

As I reach into the bag for my third piece, Raul informs me that "*el domingo sin chicharrón no es domingo.*" Sunday without *chicharrón* is not Sunday. With *chicharrón*, he affirms his place in a stable world.

My experience of *chicharrón* is a different kind of affirmation. It suggests that I have let go of the old and given myself permission to move on.

# Voices

## Penelope S. Duffy

I hear voices. Irish voices. When I least expect it—driving
to the grocery store, or sitting at my desk struggling to
make a character come alive, or dreaming and drifting as I look
out the window.

*"Fancies herself a writer now."*

*"The cheek of it. How is she then?"*

*"At spinning out tales? Fair to middling, I suspect."*

*"Aye. But what's the point of it all? Has she nothing better to
do than fritter her time away with stories and dreams?"*

The brogue is ironic. After all, aren't the Irish known for
their storytelling, for the value they place on lyrical language?
Ironic or not, there the voices are, casting a running commentary of doubt over the value of my work and my new life as, dare
I say it, a creative writer. It's not my talent they question—that
I can do in my own voice, thank you.

The job of the voices in my head seems to be to highlight
the self-indulgence, self-involvement, and self-promotion associated with the craft of writing, with the process *and* the product.

I expected fear, loneliness, some regrets, and lots of self-doubt when I shifted my identity two years ago and went from
a twenty-five-year career in clinical research to creative writing.
I expected new challenges, new learning, and new growth. But I

didn't expect the suffocating "all me all the time" feeling that can be part of the process.

Let's start with self-indulgence. Wake up, stir a cup of tea, write for a bit, take a long walk, observe life about you, do some library research, drift into the imaginal space, work out, take care of the household, and write some more.

*"Isn't that a fine life, now?"*

It gets better. I'm comforted and buffeted against fear and doubt as best as can be by a husband who supports me emotionally and financially, who encouraged me to take up writing full-time, who generously reads and edits whatever I write, and, what's more, is really good at it.

I have an agent in New York, which sounds so ridiculously inflated that to keep things in perspective I call her "Agent B," as if she works for the CIA or the FBI, and isn't really connected to me. I have a new manuscript on Agent B's desk. I have a book on a shelf at Barnes & Noble, plus a story, essays, and a poem published. I've been on a book tour. I'm working on a novel (though, really, isn't everyone?).

I have my old wool sweater, my tea, and my dog for the long contemplative walks. I know the high-flying, spirit-reeling feeling of words racing across the page when creative mystery strikes and the universe sings. I've known the immense pleasure of living in the lives of the characters and settings I've created or re-created, the favorable reviews, the stranger who tells you they were moved by what you wrote.

All of it is balanced, of course, by times when the words stutter and start, sputter and peter out into clunky, half-formed approximations of inner imaginings. I've known the crippling fear of laying myself bare on the page, the inevitable rejections, the exposure of failure. But I've lived long enough, experienced life fully enough, known enough of success and failure in my previous career, to know that struggle only makes success all the sweeter. Most of the time, anyway.

I have no schedule and am responsible to no one but myself

for the work I produce until it is out to Agent B. Could there be a more self-indulgent life?

It's not that I view pleasure with Calvinist suspicion, nor that I didn't love my former profession. As a speech-language pathologist, I was involved in clinical research with the goal of improving the communication abilities of adults for whom the threads of normal communication had become tangled, people who had lived full lives, raised families, worked hard, and talked just fine—until one day they didn't. Following a catastrophic event like head injury, stroke, or the onset of degenerative neurologic disease, they might suddenly call a pencil a "filbert," or struggle to insert emotional tone into their voice, or, holding a pencil in their hand, be unable to grasp its function or meaning. Aphasia, apraxia, aprosodia, agnosia—these strange-sounding terms are disorders that, when severe, can wreak havoc and shatter lives.

That was my profession, one not well understood by the public until they are faced with someone whose ability to speak is damaged. Certainly, it is a profession with laudable goals. Of course, there's the usual striving to make a mark through grants and publications, to be recognized, to have one's contributions stand out. Ego quite happily crosses all professional borders, I've found. And it's a good thing, too. It helps fuel the drive to achieve.

The difference is that in my previous life, it was a little easier to look at personal success in terms of fostering the greater good. Mine was a profession in which advancement and achievement were married to human need and suffering. I had worked as a clinician and knew only too well the needs of the patients served by the research. They were never far from sight, never forgotten.

Like many of my colleagues, I won grants and had publications and was invited to lecture around the country. Unlike them, I hated math. I still do. What kind of a scientist hates math? I asked myself that for twenty-five years. I hate time, too, and am almost as bad with time as I am at math. I get things done on deadline, but that's dates. It's the numbers on the clock, the minute hand ticking, the hours passing, that I can't seem to keep track of. I have to work very, very hard to estimate time, to be *on time*. Truth be told, I have a fear of being early—but that's another story.

So, no, I don't miss the eternal struggle to deal with statistics and design experiments. I managed to do it, but with about three times as much effort as everyone else. Even when I did it well, it felt like I was wearing a costume, as if I had on a fake lab coat. My reputation rested on a body of work about the nature and mechanism of certain patient deficits, some of which had not been described, let alone understood, and on a facility for synthesizing information from widely disparate sources. Internally, it also rested on a passion for helping people for whom the normal routes of self-expression were no longer functioning.

Like my friends in the field, I had articles, chapters, and even a book to my name. Mind you, these were articles with titles like "The effect of visual and inferential variables on scene descriptions by right-hemisphere-damaged and non-brain-damaged adults," published in journals with equally esoteric-sounding names, like *Aphasiology*.

My writer friends in my new life assume that if you are a writer, and you once published scientific papers, you must have been a "science writer," that is, a journalist or reporter, rather than a researcher or clinician sharing your findings in a data-based article in a peer-reviewed journal. Peer review by other scientists focuses not so much on the clarity of the writing as on the soundness of the science. Like science itself, the process is meant to be unbiased, objective, removed from self—both the one doing the science and the one doing the judging.

Blind, objective, distant, removed from self. Could these ideals stand in any sharper contrast to those of the creative arts? As much as you try to remove the self from science, you strive to insert it into creative writing. It's the whole point, really. Your voice, your imagination, your story, your vision. If you don't make an intimate connection with the reader, you fail to bridge the gap between their experience and the one you've created. Literature is nothing if not subjective. Both the reader and the writer bring their own sensibilities to bear. I like that. I like the subjectivity, the intimacy, the sense that words are not ends in themselves but require interpretation. There's plenty of interpretation in science, too. But let's face it, two plus two equals four unless, God forbid, you are into imaginary numbers. A piece of data is significant or it is not. I appreciate the clean coolness of it, but I like the messy gray areas better.

Not long before she died, I spoke to my mother on the phone. She asked me what I was going to do. I started to outline the next study I was working on, the next conference I was speaking at.

"No," she said. "What are you going to *do?*"

The question took on new meaning. Someone near the end of her life was asking me what I was going to do with mine.

I sat down slowly on a kitchen chair, phone pressed to my ear, head bowed with the import of the question. "I'm going to write, Ma," I said.

"I thought so," she said. "Stories. You should write your stories."

How had she known what I hadn't known myself?

She died about two months later. After suffering with her through the difficult hospitalization, I found my work did not inspire the same passion it once had. I felt too close to the suffering around me to maintain my distance. I could hardly bear seeing patients, which was a problem because I worked with patients. I could hardly bear being in a hospital, which was a problem because I worked in one. I've made my contributions, I thought.

Having worked hard to give other people their voices, I considered my own in a new light. Had it changed? It had. An inner voice, long silent, led me out of the hospital and into my new life. I even changed my name. Before, I was Penelope

Myers, known too well in my field to change it to Duffy when I got married. Now, as Penelope Duffy, my personal life and professional life are married to each other.

It didn't happen immediately, this identity switch. It took time and adjustment, and it wasn't until I was well into it, truly committed, that the Irish chorus welled up. Writing away, I first heard them speak on what turned out to be a favorite topic of theirs: self-involvement. When I'm on a roll, can't stop, don't want to, forget to eat, forget time, when all I think about is writing, even when I'm not writing, when I lose track of where I am, appear distracted and distant instead of my normally connected, gregarious self, the Irish take note. I am immersed, absorbed, and by what? By *my* words, *my* story, *my* imagination.

*"Can she never get beyond herself?"*

There are words in my head, I say to the voices. There are settings and moods, plots and characters. They have voices of their own and want to be heard.

*"Well, if that isn't grand."*

No, listen, I say. Stories serve an elemental human need, to feel connected, to share in the larger human experience. Good ones transcend the particular, resonate with universals, and enrich our time on earth.

Sometimes I have to shout at the Irish to be heard at all.

And if there is success? Oh, then they come on full bore, adding quite a bit of head wagging to their disapproval of the arrogance and self-promotion. *Art for art's sake,* they caution. Yes, I whisper, I know. But how does a book get noticed, let alone read, without promotion? And I want it to be read, to be noticed. I admit it.

You have to promote your book. The publisher expects it. Bookstores expect it. There are entire books written on self-promotion, and even one on Amazon on how to improve your Amazon ranking. I haven't read them, of course, but they're out there. Oh, yes, it's a different world I'm in now.

It reminds me of a conference on right-hemisphere brain

damage in Chicago some years ago at which I was the invited speaker. On the second day of the meeting I found myself alone during the lunch break. I walked down one of those wide, windy avenues near the hotel conference site and ended up in a noisy Italian restaurant. At the table next to me a group of four men were shoving pizza into their mouths and talking over each other about a weekly publication they were starting up on medical science. The politics of it, the money behind it, the insider's look at fast-tracking grants, the hot new studies. Their conversation went something like this:

"No, look. I'm telling you," said the one leading the discussion. He planted beefy forearms on the checkered tablecloth, and leaned over his plate toward the other three. "There are people out there—scientists, doctors, whatever—that publish all the time in these journals and get paid nothing. *Nada.* Write stuff up, don't get paid dick. Don't even ask to get paid!" He leaned back, eyebrows raised, nodding. "I'm telling you . . ."

The other three froze, pizza suspended en route to open mouths.

"Like where? Like what publications?" said the skinny man next to him, slowly lowering a slice of pepperoni.

"Like the *Journal of New England Medicine*," Beefy Man retorted.

"You mean the *New England Journal of Medicine?*" Skinny asked.

"Yeah, whatever. The point is they do all this work and then publish for *nothing*. Do it all the time. *This* is a source we definitely need to tap. What great stringers they'd make! They'd give us articles for peanuts. I'm telling you. Unless they're too dumb to *want* to get paid!"

Laughter all around. I laughed, too. Irony all around.

I thought back to the morning's session, where my book was being promoted during the break by the conference organizers. There's no book tour for academic books. Rarely are you even asked to sign a book. Your book is sold and promoted, but not by you. You sip your coffee at some remove, wrapped in your cloak of scholarly disinterest. You chat with conference participants, answer questions about their patients, review your notes. You don't so much as cast a glance at the table where your books are stacked up. Bad form. Well, maybe a glance. You aren't entirely uninterested in whether your book does well. You're hoping above all that the book is respected. That's the true coinage of the scientific realm. Above all, the book is not *you*, it's the *work*, objective, removed, something you hope adds significantly to the body of knowledge. At least, that's the goal.

Consider, on the other hand, the goal of the standard author event at the local Borders, Barnes & Noble, lecture hall, or talk show. It is almost as much about promoting the author as it is about promoting the work. How many times has an author of fiction been asked how much of what he or she has written is autobiographical? I've attended these events myself, and like everyone else, hoped to make a connection between the writer and the words on the page. You want to experience something of the person who evoked your tears and laughter, called up feelings of joy, sorrow, excitement, irony, who lifted your spirit, commandeered your attention, and took you on a journey to another world.

Most author events are not celebrity affairs, but rather quiet signings by unknown authors nervously hoping to attract some notice. Two years ago, on just such a book tour, I found myself in New England, a thousand miles from home, sitting at a table in a bookstore, whose name I now forget, that was located in a busy upscale mall between a Pottery Barn and a Victoria's Secret. I had my pens and my stack of books, and was surrounded by a crush of holiday shoppers doing their level best to ignore me. Smile, I told myself. Look inviting. Well, not inviting, but interesting. Or open. Friendly. Something. Because behind you are books upon books upon books, packed into the shelves, teetering on tables. How in the world does any one book stand out? This is your chance, I told myself. Remember what Agent B said, what your publisher said. You have to promote. It's no more uncomfortable for you than for any other author. Promotion, promotion, promotion. Think you're above it? Don't be an idiot.

An Asian man stopped and stood before the table. I tried to look interesting, interested, friendly. He just stood there staring at the books. He was tall and bony, dressed in a long black raincoat. He was bare-headed, and flecks of snow were melting on his shoulders, shimmering wet on his round glasses. He removed the glasses and wiped them on his shirt for some time. He had a boy with him, maybe ten or eleven years old, in a blue parka with a Boston Red Sox cap on his head. They spoke in Chinese to each other. Then the man picked up one of my books and asked if I'd read it. Yes, I said. Somehow I didn't want to tell him I'd also written it. The boy ran his finger across the brilliant blue cover of one of the books. I handed it to him to hold. He turned it over and over in his hands.

"My English is not so good. But the boy could read it," the man said. "What is this book about?"

I told him that, oddly enough, most of it takes place in China, that it was a true story that had occurred during the Communist Revolution in the late 1940s. He arched back and smiled. He told me he was from mainland China and that his parents had lived through Mao's revolution. My family, too, I explained. My father was an American, teaching at Huachung University, I said.

Who wrote this book? he wanted to know.

I admitted that I had. He frowned. "You wrote it?" he said. "You wrote a book?" Yes, I said. "You have also read many books?" I said yes, I had. "She wrote it," he said to the boy, smiling now. The boy glanced up with a quick, shy smile of his own, and then down again at the book.

"I cannot read very well. I cannot read English," the man continued. He put his arm around the boy's shoulders. "But he can. He could read this book to me. It will be very beautiful."

He took out money, and I explained that he had to pay the

cashier at the counter. I signed the book and thanked him. "When I hear the words, I will think of this moment, of the person who wrote them," he said.

A month or so ago, I attended a book club meeting in a town not far from my home. They were reading my book, and, upon learning that I lived nearby, the members had invited me to the discussion. At the end of our time in the church basement, a woman asked if I'd mind if she read a few of her favorite passages out loud. Mind? I sat back against my jacket on my metal folding chair and listened. I heard my words in someone else's voice, and they became not my words, but something independent of me, larger than me. It was magic. As I listened, I thought of the Chinese man, of the boy reading the words out loud, of the moment shared between them, between us. Magic.

✦ ✦ ✦ ✦ ✦

Why do I write? Why do I fritter away my time with stories and dreaming? To the voices in my head, I say this. I write because I can't help it. And, I add, is it not helping to enhance the greater good? Is it not about something more than me?

"Aye," they say back. "Aye, *it is. Try to do it well.*"

I will, I say. I promise.

# Confessions of a Drug Dealer

## Li Miao Lovett

I sorted the limp bodies into two piles. Red eyes. Purple eyes. Red eyes. Purple eyes. And then another little red-eyed monster, with two gleaming rubies set into a coal black head. The legs dangled lifelessly.

In the biology lab, I was surrounded by college students taking the lives of fruit flies for the sake of science and knowledge. We were yellow, brown, black, and white, a diverse group thrown into the petri dish of a world-class university. For those of us who were Asian, going into medicine was par for the course, like playing the piano or getting better than just "good" grades.

But that science experiment was the final straw. The day I had to commit that terrible act—gassing hundreds of flies and then sorting the lifeless bodies by their genes—was the last day I pursued medicine. I would disappoint my mother, who could no longer say that her only child was going to be a doctor. I would disappoint myself, having once vowed in an essay contest that I would prevail through life's challenges and never give up my pursuit of medicine.

Like other immigrant Chinese parents, my mother saw my career choice as a reflection on the family's honor. A degree from a prestigious university was a coat of arms my parents could hold up for relatives and friends to see. A white coat embroidered with the letters M.D. would be a symbol that our family had found success in America.

"Well, if you don't want to be a doctor, you can be a lawyer," Mom said when they came to visit me on campus that year. Was there no other choice? She forgot to mention being an engineer, which my roommate from Taiwan gamely pursued among a sea of men in her program. But I wanted to be none of those things that brought prestige to self and family, yet seldom seemed to guarantee personal fulfillment.

I had no desire to torture more fruit flies and God knows what else before swearing the Hippocratic oath that I would do no harm to my patients. No, I didn't want to be a doctor, but in the last quarter of my senior year, I came up with the next best thing. I still wanted to be in the health-care field, and I was the ambitious sort. I could be a pharmaceutical sales rep, rubbing elbows with all the doctors in town as I promoted a company's prescription medicines.

I was hired right out of college by a respected pharmaceutical firm. The first order of business was going through sales training. Then I had to stock my car and home office with samples of our medications, like so many Cup-a-Soup packages—dry little nuggets in a big fluffy box. I gave away the pin-striped suit I'd worn to job interviews and bought a few fashionable outfits. I thought of putting a wink in my outgoing phone message: "If you wanna buy some drugs, please leave a message for Li," then thought better of it. Yes, I had become a legal drug dealer. But those relatives and friends of the Miao and Teng families, who had once approved of this diligent daughter . . . oh, they might get the wrong idea.

Surprisingly, my parents didn't seem that disappointed in my career choice. After all, I had a company car, nice clothes, and a steady paycheck with healthy bonuses for hitting my sales targets. But what they didn't know about was the daily humiliation endured by medical salespeople, who occupy the lowest position on the health-care totem pole. Doctors were GOD spelled in big illegible scrawls on prescription pads. Patients were noble creatures, despite their runny noses and endless coughing. They paid the bills. But salespeople were flying insects who snuck in the door every day without warning. They swarmed around the White Coats and buzzed incessantly. They were no more important to the practice of medicine than those poor flies I'd gassed.

"Doctor, if I could show you a more convenient, less costly way to lower blood pressure, would you consider our drug for your next patient?" Translation: "Doctor, will you help my company capture a fat little piece of the profit pie, when you see your next stressed-out patient suffering from the disease of Western affluence?"

My favorite line from sales training boot camp was, "Doctor, if you could prevent one more heart attack with our drug, would you prescribe it to your patients with high cholesterol and low HDLs?"

To which the doctor probably wanted to respond, "If I could swat one more fly buzzing in my ear, would I?"

"We're paid to *bother* people," said a colleague of mine in her sultry voice. She was destined for Latino TV stardom in a not-so-distant future. We both knew we weren't doing this job for the rest of our lives, but I still hoped to be more than just a pest.

I spent weekends at the Stanford University medical library, searching for a wider array of studies so that I could provide honest information to my physicians. I was going to put my college degree to use. I would make myself an asset to the harried physician.

"So when you see the next patient with high low-density . . . no . . . low HDLs but high total cholesterol . . . " I repeated to myself that evening, determined not to flub my lines when I approached the White Coat.

Early one Monday, I decided to visit one of my most challenging physicians in San Francisco, whose disdain for drug reps was well known in the sales community. I showed up with a little package of sweet treats for the office staff. Stuck on the front was a bright company decal declaring, "Up Your HDLs." I always thought that line was like giving someone the New York finger, but the caffeine-starved staff didn't seem to mind. Chocolate was the way to an office assistant's heart. As I made small talk with the girl at the front desk, I kept searching for the apparition of the White Coat out of the corner of my eye.

Finally, after the doctor had finished with his patient, he appeared behind the receptionist's small window. Here was my moment. Big smile. Shoulders back. Copy of medical study cradled in my arms. "Doctor—recent studies show that patients with heart disease benefit significantly from increasing their HDLs—our drug raises the good HDLs while lowering total cholesterol—would you consider . . . "

"I don't talk to drug reps," the doctor said, looking me squarely in the eye. "Just let me sign for samples."

My voice faltered, shrinking to the size of the point of the ballpoint pen I held out for him. My shoulder-padded suit slunk down toward my briefcase, and I took out that familiar colored pad of forms. Since the doctor's signature was legally required for the transfer of prescription product samples, this was often the only way we could catch a second of a busy physician's time.

For the next two and a half years, I learned how to open doors. I bribed office staff with sweets and clever presents: fortune cookies in pretty red wrapping, delicate fans I found at Japantown—three for a dollar. I took pride in being the only sales rep that some of my physicians would see. I learned to sit attentively in waiting rooms, watching patients come in with the hope that this doctor, this remedy, would cure their ills and ease their suffering. I got away from the "Doctor-when-you-see-a-patient" scripts, and spoke frankly about what I saw as the limits of the medication I was selling. All day, these physicians saw people ill with heart disease, cancer, arthritis, chronic pain, and the common cold. And the reality was that their medical bag of tricks stopped short of a cure for many of these conditions.

Doctors were expected to be gods, and I was expected by

the management to be a walking commercial for my company. But, from the beginning, my job took a toll on my health.

San Francisco is a city filled with one-way streets, jaywalkers, honking horns, homeless beggars sharing the road with harried men and women in stiff gray suits. Doctor's offices seldom feel like the promised land of healing. Their phones ring incessantly; each call is a cry for help, but there is too little time to give patients the attention they really need.

"Medicine isn't what it used to be," a physician in his sixties once told me. He had to run it like a business, he said, but the paperwork seemed to run his practice. To make any money seeing HMO clients, he could spend only about fifteen minutes with each patient. Fifteen minutes, I thought. I could barely park my car and schlep my samples to his office in that time. I was glad that I had changed my mind about pursuing medicine.

But as I chalked up more and more pairs of torn pantyhose, I realized that this, too, was not the life I wanted. I came home every day with frayed nerves, limp bangs across my face, and the swallowed pride of a drug dealer in a suit. My integrity was put on the line with each sales call. Did I believe I was really doing any good for that patient with high blood pressure, two jobs, and too many mouths to feed?

Which is not to say that I had no golden moments on the job. There was the portly receptionist, known as Attila the Hun, who finally opened the gates to let me see the doctor one day. Why? Because I'd given her a thirty-three-cent fan that came in handy during an attack of hot flashes. Thank you, menopause.

And then there was the time I took my friend Helen, an eighty-one-year-old artist, to meet Dr. Dong, one of my physicians in Chinatown. Helen had been struck by arthritis in her fifties. "I could no longer use my thumb," she said. "But there's no Western cure, so the doctor told me, 'You don't need your thumb.'" But she did need it—she'd been a painter all her life. Helen discovered a book of dietary remedies by Dr. Dong, and followed the plan religiously. The pain and swelling went away and never returned.

Now Dr. Dong was in his nineties and still blending Eastern and Western principles in his practice. And thirty years after Helen had regained her health, she had the chance to meet Dr. Dong. His office felt warm and inviting, filled with mahogany furniture and testimonials on the walls from grateful patients. My octogenarian friend marshaled all the wrinkles on her face into a big smile.

"Thank you, Dr. Dong," Helen said. "You saved my life."

My own life seemed to be falling apart. I turned to yoga and meditation to counter the physical stress. Besides the pressures of the job, I felt increasingly conflicted about the path I'd chosen. All we did was bother these doctors, enticing them with drug samples and free dinners at company-sponsored talks. No matter how much integrity I tried to maintain in my job, I could not accept the fact that profits seemed to overshadow patient care in the business.

A few months after visiting Dr. Dong, I had a particularly taxing day making the rounds. Nobody in the offices wanted samples, and everybody driving on the road seemed to own it. By late afternoon, all my reserves of patience, energy, and positive attitude were spent. I drove to Helen's house to meet her for supper. She saw the desperate look on my face.

"Come here," Helen said in her calm, resonant voice. I sat next to my friend, and my face fell into her lap, sobbing. She held me as one would hold a small child, and my pent-up frustrations poured out in long, heaving waves. Her bony hands glided over my hair and shoulders with the loving strokes of the painter who knew her brush so well. When I finally sat up, I cleared the filmy glaze from my eyes and looked around. There was a portrait from her Van Gogh phase, in vibrant, warm tones. Another work was a city scene that blended collage cutouts and delicate Asian brushstrokes. My friend had been an artist all her life, a prolific painter for seventy years. For Helen, there had been no struggle, no question about following her heart's desire. Her life seemed like a Bach concerto, its harmonious rhythms as deep as the grooves in her old vinyl records. I often looked at a small portrait of Helen in her forties that sat on an armoire in her living room. She seemed self-assured in that portrait, staring into the distance toward a promising future, looking a bit like Queen Elizabeth at the same age. Where would I be at forty, I wondered. And another forty years after that, would I look back on my life with joy or regret?

A few months later, I quit my job. I had not achieved my goal of winning the company's sales contest, but I was ready to give up those old, stale ambitions. I decided to enroll in a graduate school program in marriage and family counseling. In high school, psychology had been my first love, but as though it were an unsuitable boy, it was a field I did not pursue. Now it was time to reclaim those dormant passions.

The day after I announced my resignation, my manager showed up at the house. The company files were packed into a plastic crate. The company car, which I'd filled to the brim with the remaining samples, was parked outside. The end was unceremonious. My boss asked a few standard questions, packed the crate into my car, then drove it away. Gone were the perks, the job pressures, the half-baked dreams of youth. I was ready for a new life.

The next morning, I put on a flowing skirt and dangling earrings, and dashed off to my interview for the graduate school program. The car was gone, and I had to depend on the good graces of city transit. But there was a skip in my step as I headed down the hill. Suddenly, the season's first rain came down in pellets—hard, cold, and cleansing. The bus appeared in the distance. I knew there would be obstacles in my new life, but as I lifted my heels off the ground, I was ready to meet them.

# Choosing Africa

## B. Susan Bauer

Why would a fifty-year-old American woman choose to abandon her comfortable home and lucrative job to live in Africa for six years? That is a question I often asked myself as I sat in my tiny apartment in Windhoek, the capital of Namibia, and later in Accra, the capital of Ghana, five time zones away from almost everything that was familiar to me.

Was it a longing for adventure? A desire to peek inside the lives of people living in an exotic country? A quest for meaning and purpose outside the comforts of home in the United States? It was all of those things, and it all began with my decision to attend a church convention in the spring of 1992.

I had never attended such a meeting, even though I'd been married to a clergyman for twenty-five years. I wasn't exactly a typical pastor's wife. I was shy and didn't much care for mingling with strangers. But when I heard there would be a Sunday morning breakfast for clergy spouses, I thought perhaps it was time to meet some of my counterparts.

At the end of the breakfast, a vibrant, gray-haired lady stood up and said, "I will be leading a study tour to West Africa in October. If anyone is interested, I have brochures."

My husband, Lou, and I had been living in Chapel Hill, North Carolina, for six years. Our son, Jason, was twenty-two years old. Our daughter, Megan, was sixteen. I was the director of the Office for Human Research Studies at the University of North Carolina's School of Medicine. Although my work in the area of research ethics was satisfying, my life seemed devoid of challenges. I felt restless, and I asked myself if the job was what I still wanted to be doing ten or twenty years down the road.

The idea of traveling to Africa had never really occurred to me before, but I found the invitation compelling. By the time my husband and I arrived back home, we'd made up our minds. We were going.

During the next six months, we renewed our passports, updated our vaccinations, and read travel books. I learned that West Africans consider it disrespectful for women to wear slacks, so I bought cotton skirts and dresses. I listened to French-con-versation cassette tapes while driving to work to reacquaint myself with the language. Our friends and family considered us brave and adventurous for choosing such an exotic vacation.

For three weeks, we traveled the rough roads of West Africa, visiting mud-hut villages and women's-empowerment projects. Everywhere we went, the villagers greeted us with danc-ing and singing and gentle hospitality. The children giggled, pointed, and sang songs to us. We slept in tiny hotels and freshly swept huts. We learned to eat *foufou* (millet porridge) and chewy pieces of goat.

In Burkina Faso we met a retired government official who said, "We watch your TV shows, like *Dallas*, and we see that you Americans have so much. Why can't you share with the poor who have so little?"

Although we tried to assure him that most of America was not like what he saw on *Dallas*, his question lingered in our minds.

West Africa not only saturated my senses; it assaulted my conscience. Against the romantic images of teeming markets and Fulani dancers, I could not stop seeing the ragged village farmers, the polio victims, and the children. Especially the children.

On our final day in West Africa, Lou and I were sitting at a small table in an outdoor café with John, our tour guide. John had been living in West Africa for seven years. We sipped our Cokes and watched the market women peddling bananas and fried pastries. When Lou asked John, "What, exactly, is it like to be an American who lives here?" I knew that he had already begun to wonder, "Is there any way we could do this?"

At the time, the idea was too big for me. I had too many "Yes, but . . ." thoughts.

Yes, but our children needed us.

Yes, but what about our secure, lucrative jobs?

Yes, but what would we actually *do* in Africa? We aren't exactly trained for life there.

The more we shared our experience with people back home, the more compelling I found the thought of living and working in Africa. But we were no longer twentysomethings. A lot was at stake. We had to test our desire and our physical stamina. We contacted John, and he told us if we wanted to visit West Africa on our own, he could make available a vehicle for us. He said his assistant, Yacouba, would be honored to be our guide and driver.

When we returned to West Africa the following year, we visited places even more remote than before, villages where Westerners were rarely seen. In Mali, we were within a half-day's drive of Timbuktu, but Yacouba strongly discouraged us from going there. "I've been there many times," he said. "Trust me—there's nothing to see, and we'd probably have several flat tires along the way."

The trip was physically demanding. Although our zeal to live and work in Africa had not diminished, we had discovered our limitations. I, for one, could not live in a mud hut, pee in bushes, and wash my clothes in the river.

As 1994 drew to a close, Lou was eligible for a three-month sabbatical leave from his congregation. We asked ourselves, Why not try a sabbatical in Africa? We approached our national church's Division for Global Mission. Was a three-month opportunity available?

Six months would be preferable, they said, but a seminary in Namibia needed lecturers, and they would be happy to use us for three months. We would not be paid, but Lou's salary would continue. We would be able to come back to our home and our jobs. The university allowed me to take a three-month leave of absence.

We had been told that Otjimbingwe, the village where we would be living, had electricity for only twelve hours a day. We bought our first laptop computer. Roger, our computer guru, created a power source for us that could be hooked up to a car battery—a metal box with wires and plugs attached to it. It looked like a bomb! I still wonder how we got it through customs.

We spent a week in a Windhoek guesthouse, walking into town and enjoying the city that travel writers consider one of the continent's cleanest and prettiest, with its palm trees, jacarandas, and bougainvillea. Roads are wide and well paved, and traffic lights, which the locals call "robots," function most of the time. If it weren't for all the African faces and the street vendors selling carvings, drums, and batiks, it would have been easy to forget that we were in Africa.

In Otjimbingwe, I taught English. Lou's specialty was pastoral counseling. I am embarrassed now when I think of my terrible teaching during those three months. Fortunately, my Namibian students were forgiving and eager learners who also taught me what living in a community is all about. On my forty-eighth birthday, they all gathered outside my bedroom window at five A.M. and awakened me with songs. "It's how we honor our lecturers," they said.

The sabbatical in Otjimbingwe ended, and we returned to life in Chapel Hill, but Africa had captured our hearts. The following year we again contacted the Division for Global Mission, and told them of our desire to return as contract missionaries. We would have to be paid this time. The process was lengthy.

New positions had to be created and funding had to be approved. Eventually, we were approved for faculty lecturer positions in Namibia. We signed contracts for two years, with the option to renew them. We learned that the seminary had relocated from Otjimbingwe to Windhoek, so our living conditions would be less primitive than before.

When I announced my resignation to the doctor who was my supervisor at the university, he grinned and told me he wasn't surprised. He said he thought I had made the right choice. In fact, nearly everyone in our Chapel Hill circle of friends said the same thing.

We rarely had second thoughts, if only because there was no time—we had too much to do. The paperwork for our visas and work permits seemed endless. We sold our house and put our furniture in storage. We bought a new laptop computer and packed up ten cartons of books, clothes, and housewares to be shipped to Namibia.

Before our deployment, Lou and I were required to attend a monthlong orientation in Chicago, where we learned what it meant to be overseas missionaries. The Evangelical Lutheran Church in America (ELCA) had adopted what it calls an "accompaniment" model. According to this model, American missionaries are called to be co-workers with their colleagues in foreign lands. We learned that Lutheran missionaries today, unlike those of the previous century, are rarely expected to convert non-Christians. Rather, the American missionary will usually find herself working with members of established churches. Since the ELCA places a high priority on leadership training, many missionaries today are placed in teaching positions, especially those involving the training of church leaders.

I remember having a "What have we done?" moment as our plane crossed the equator, but those thoughts disappeared as we entered the arrivals terminal at the Hosea Kutako Airport in Namibia. There, on the other side of the plate-glass window, were more than twenty students and faculty from the seminary who had come to meet us. We were ready to take up our new roles as African missionaries.

Seventy-five percent of Namibia's people are Lutheran, a testament to the persistence of German and Finnish missionaries of the nineteenth century. For many decades the leadership of Namibian Lutheran churches was firmly in the hands of their European mother churches. Over time, this leadership shifted to Namibian pastors, and the need arose for local training. In 1963, Namibian Lutherans of various tribal backgrounds came together and, with the assistance of the Lutheran World Federation, formed a seminary for the training of their pastors. By the 1980s, the seminary was also accepting women, a relatively rare phenomenon among African Christians. The seminary became accredited by the Joint Board for Theological Education in Southern Africa, and grew to become a respected institution of higher education in Namibia, offering a four-year course of study.

We lived in a small apartment on the campus. I had assumed the continent was always hot, but here, in the southernmost part of Africa in the midwinter month of July, the temperature dipped to freezing at night. Our flat lacked central heating, so we wrapped ourselves in blankets and turned up our little space heaters to the highest setting. There was plumbing and hot water, but no shower, only a European-style spray attachment on the bathtub faucet. Lou decided that he absolutely could not manage without a shower, so one of our first trips into town was to a bathroom-supply shop. Lou installed a showerhead with a drill borrowed from our German colleague.

Our tiny second bedroom became an office. We filled it with two desks, a small photocopier, and a bookcase. When we were both working in our office together, we had to learn not to bump into each other with our desk chairs. This was togetherness taken to a new level.

Despite the upscale restaurants and ATM machines in Windhoek, we discovered that the veneer of sophistication and technology was actually quite thin. Phone service, water, or electric power might suddenly cease—for no apparent reason. Visits to banks and post offices became tests of endurance and patience. And we had not yet seen the sprawling squatter areas, euphemistically called "informal settlements" by the government, discreetly hidden behind the mountains, out of the tourist's view.

Six weeks after we arrived, the campus was paralyzed by a student strike. Most of Namibia's tribal groups were represented on our campus, and we were distressed to see, among the students and faculty, some of the most blatant forms of racism we had ever experienced. Prior to gaining independence in 1990, Namibia had been under South African rule for decades, and the Namibian society had been cruelly fractured by the imposition of apartheid. Tribal groups that had been living peacefully with each other were divided and forced into a caste system. Although independence had officially broken down these structures, intertribal suspicion and animosity remained. Some students, tired of being victimized by what they perceived to be racism within the faculty, initiated a boycott of classes. A few of us attempted to hold classes anyway, but this soon proved to be fruitless.

We would sit on our balcony in the mornings and watch small groups of agitated students gather to plan their next move. The students were demanding the removal of two faculty members, and they threatened to take their case to the media if the seminary's governing board did not respond to their satisfaction.

We were dismayed. Any romantic illusions we may have held about Africa were shattered. Had we made the greatest mistake of our lives? How could we endure the remainder of our two-year contract in such a situation?

The chairman of the seminary's governing board patched together an uneasy truce, and classes resumed for the remaining two months of the academic year. In February, the board had to choose new seminary leaders. Fearing a repeat of the tribal hostilities, they chose a neutral faculty member to be dean of students—my husband.

One of our students, Namusha, told us the story of a woman

who had attended a wedding. She arrived at the celebration with her baby bound tightly to her back in a swatch of brightly colored cloth. During the festivities, she discreetly stepped behind a bush to relieve herself. When she returned and resumed dancing vigorously, she was unaware of the crowd that had gathered around her, laughing and pointing. She did not know that she had inadvertently tucked the hem of her dress into the cloth that bound the child to her back, exposing her backside to the crowd each time she bent over. The moral of the story, Namusha told us, is to always be aware of what other people are saying about you, because you might learn something valuable.

What we learned was to be cautious. The two troublesome African faculty members were also suspicious of the white Americans, especially the one who was now the dean of students on their campus.

In time, the contempt abated, and we became involved in the normal routine of campus life. I learned the true meaning of hospitality from our Namibian friends. In all my years of being a pastor's wife, I had never hosted so many dinners as I did in Namibia. The sitting room of our flat was tiny, but we would collect all the chairs we could find, and host buffet dinners for as many as ten people. We learned from our Namibian friends the value of lingering, as well.

Once I got over the initial stage fright, I was surprised to discover how much I enjoyed teaching. In Africa, elders are respected, and my few strands of gray hair gave me status. Students would often stop by our flat in the afternoons and evenings. They might have questions about an assignment or need an aspirin for a headache, but just as often they would simply come to visit. We learned, from our own experience, the African concept of *ubuntu*, in which "a person is only a person through other people." It felt comfortable to be living in that community.

Over time, I acquired other responsibilities—I was faculty secretary, accommodations manager, and development officer. Back home, I had been cautious about taking on new tasks, but now I welcomed these opportunities, which helped me to feel useful and accepted. And for the first time in my life, I found myself looking forward to meeting strangers.

It was the students, though, who captured our hearts. One after another, they would come to our flat and tell us their stories. Hainane told us he was sent to tend cattle as a young boy.

"My father was an uneducated man who did not believe in sending his children to school."

When Hainane was eighteen years old, he was hospitalized for a serious medical condition.

"A kind nurse began to teach me to read and write. I was very determined." He remained hospitalized for about a year, and when he was finally discharged, he chose not to return home, but to live with some friends who helped him get into school.

He said, "I was embarrassed to be a twenty-one-year-old student in the fifth grade."

After he finally graduated from high school, he held a series of jobs, and as a seminary student he worked for construction companies during the term holidays.

Listening to our students' stories humbled us. We were able to help a few of them with medical expenses and transportation to the clinic. When their family members began dying from AIDS, which happened all too often, we'd give them a few dollars so they could travel home for the funerals.

Our contracts came up for renewal, and we agreed to remain for another three years.

I was grading papers one hot summer afternoon when I received a phone call from the doctor I'd seen recently.

"Mrs. Bauer," he said, "I'm afraid I have some bad news. I've just received the pathology report on the lesion I removed from your leg. I am so sorry to have to tell you this. It's melanoma."

I immediately sent an email to a friend in the States who is an oncologist. He told me that surgery was the usual treatment. I considered my options. I could have the surgical procedure in Namibia, return to the United States, or go to Cape Town, South Africa, a two-hour flight from where we were living. I tried the Namibia option first, but became frightened when the surgeon I visited told me to have a seat while he searched his bookshelf for a reference book about skin cancer. I chose to go to Cape Town instead.

I recuperated from my surgical procedure in a Cape Town guesthouse. When a missionary colleague stopped by, I told him about the treatment options I had been given. He reminded me that *choice* is one of the fundamental differences between the lives of people who live in the Western world and those who live in Africa. Several days later I prepared to return home to Namibia.

On our way to the airport in Cape Town, I looked out the car window and saw an urban ghetto extending toward the horizon as far as the eye could see. It was the infamous Cape Flats. I peered intently at children playing in the dirt, a woman hanging her washing on the clothesline, a man repairing the corrugated tin roof of his tiny shack, and I thought again about choices. The medical choices available to me—and the gut-wrenching poverty that obliterated any choice for many.

Lou and I lived and worked in Namibia for more than five years. When our contracts ended, I felt ambivalent about returning to the United States. Part of me yearned to be closer to my adult children, and to put down roots in my home country. But another part couldn't let go of the African experience.

People often ask me what it feels like to return to America after living in Africa for so long. I wonder what they are expecting me to say. That the culture shock is overwhelming? That it feels so good to be back home?

Before we went to Namibia, a wise man—an older Jesuit missionary who had lived in Africa for a long time—said to us, "Once you become a missionary, you will never be fully at home in either culture." He was right. No culture is stationary. My return to America felt like a crash course in relearning my own country. During the first few weeks, I savored the pleasure of being able to walk into a shop and find what I wanted, having Internet access in my home and, of course, seeing my children and friends. But over time I became aware that changes had occurred while I was gone, and it wasn't simply the new gadgets, like DVD players, that I had to learn about.

I had become accustomed to life lived at a slower pace. I had grown used to having fewer choices. I still spend too much time in grocery store aisles bewildered by all the new products. I see TV commercials for medicines to treat conditions I wasn't aware were so serious. At first, I couldn't seem to get enough of news programs on television—until I realized that there wasn't any news of Africa.

At odd moments, I find myself remembering images of skinny African children playing in the dust. I see sleepy-eyed donkeys plodding along a dusty road, their backs bowed by heavy water jugs. I remember brilliant purple jacaranda trees announcing springtime in Windhoek. I hear the crow of early-morning roosters awakening a village.

Six years in Africa taught me that I must, somehow, continue to live my life with passion, and I am still passionate about doing what I can to help Africans. This takes the shape of what Lou once jokingly called our Robin Hood Ministry. We don't have great financial resources, but we are connected to people who do. No longer shy, I am not above shamelessly approaching such people and pleading with them to support those we know in Africa who have such great need. I remember things the old Jesuit missionary said. "Managing transitions is tough," he told us. Perhaps, as he said to us, I will never again feel entirely at home in either place. But Lou and I have also learned that we can't live without a dream. As we enter retirement this year, we are careful to keep intact our African connections. We have purchased a low-maintenance townhouse. One day soon, we will give away our houseplants, tell the post office to hold our mail, and set off on a short-term mission assignment.

Feeling at home on two continents, however incompletely, is not a bad way to live.

# A Different Kind of Recovery

## Jennifer Karuza Schile

"My name is Jen, and I am an alcoholic."
That's what I would say if I were at an AA meeting. But I'm not. I haven't been to a meeting in almost ten years. That's what I'd say if I believed it was true. But I don't.

✦ ✦ ✦ ✦ ✦

It is the springtime of 1996, and I am a twenty-one-year-old English major. Only, this morning, instead of being in class, I am propped up against several pillows on my bed. Vomit and a bath towel lie on the carpet beside me, but I don't remember being sick. I don't remember much from the night before except that someone hid my bottle of vodka. After a frantic search, I'd discovered it behind a bag of potato chips on top of the refrigerator. My stomach turns to ice as I remember one more thing—the way I blacked out repeatedly while driving on the freeway on my way to the party.

I clench the cordless phone in my trembling hand and spend a moment debating whether to even make the call.

"I don't know what to do," I announce in a shaky voice when my mom answers. "I'm scared to quit drinking and I'm scared not to quit drinking."

I no longer have any idea how to function without alcohol. I don't know who I am anymore and I need help. I need to learn how to live again.

✦ ✦ ✦ ✦ ✦

What didn't make sense was how I'd even arrived at that place. I hadn't even *tasted* alcohol until I was seventeen. There was no history of alcoholism in my family; my parents didn't drink, and there was never any liquor in our house. During high school, I'd secretly preferred staying home with my parents and sisters to partying with friends. In my youth, I'd been athletic and involved in school activities. Suddenly I was spending my afternoons and evenings gulping screwdrivers and waking up before the sun to write English papers and study for exams. My college friends had a nickname for me: Designated Drinker.

What I did know was precisely where it had all started: my first drink. Just a few experimental sips of cheap strawberry wine with friends one night had created a sensation unlike anything I'd ever experienced. It was magic. I felt giddy and relaxed all at once. I'd been miraculously transformed from a shy and insecure girl into one I didn't know existed, and one I liked far better: a smiling, laughing, confident young woman. I wanted to be her all the time. And I was, for a while. The problem was that five years later, she no longer existed. She wasn't smiling anymore and she certainly wasn't sparkling. She was a sick, pale, tired mess. She needed help, and help she would get—but almost a decade would pass before any of it made sense.

One week after I made the call to my mother, she took me—on Mother's Day—to the all-women rehabilitation facility to which I'd been admitted. Along the two-hour drive, I became increasingly less sure this was the step I needed to take. Surely, I had overreacted.

"I don't think I need to go after all," I told my mother. "I'm sure I can just quit drinking on my own. I think I was just scared."

My mom did not agree. She listened but continued driving until she stopped at the entrance to the facility. She climbed slowly out of the family car and stood, clutching her purse with small white hands. Her face was pale and her brown eyes were pained. I glanced quickly at her and then down at the ground, hating myself.

Two nights earlier, I'd been knocking back screwdrivers alone on my front porch and, later, dancing with friends at the Royal Room. Now, here I was, ninety miles from home, standing with my mother in the driveway of a rehabilitation center, clutching a pack of Newport menthol cigarettes and a pink flowered suitcase. I tried to hide behind my hair, which hung limply down to the middle of my back. My face, fuller than usual with alcohol-induced bloat, was twisted into an expression of grief. I folded my arms against my chest, set my mouth in a tight line, and looked with watery eyes at what would be my home for the next thirty days.

Because of the way I had used alcohol—basically, to deal with all aspects of my life—and the amounts I'd consumed, combined with my history of bulimia, the intake counselor declared me an emergency case and said that I probably wouldn't live to see my twenty-second birthday unless I got help.

I didn't care about living to see my next birthday.

I wanted to go home.

I wanted to get back in the car, go home to my family and friends, and pretend this had never happened.

"I'm not staying," I said. "Please take me home. I don't want to stay."

My mother looked at me with an expression in her eyes I would never forget, and surprised me with her response.

"I think you should stay," she said. "I want you to be safe. I want you to be taken care of for a month."

I glared at the counselor who stood next to us.

"This is the best Mother's Day present you will ever give your mom," she said calmly. I looked back to my mother, who nodded in agreement through the tears now running down her face.

With that, Mom got back into her car and drove away, leaving me with that stranger. I hauled my suitcase to my new room and flung it on my new bed.

I fell asleep that night to the sound of a ticking clock in the room I shared with thirteen women. The tick-tock-tick-tock from the clock on the wall mesmerized me, and its steady rhythm provided a calm reassurance that accompanied me to sleep that night, and every night I was there. I woke up each morning in sheets soaked from the toxins I was sweating out of my body.

During the first week, I sat and glumly took notes during classes on anger management, healthy eating, and assertiveness training. I was at least fifteen years younger than the women I'd joined in rehab. They ranged in age from thirty-five to seventy. There were corporate executives, mothers, artists, and professors. Others had no education beyond eighth grade and were on welfare. I had nothing in common with any of them. I isolated myself until the second week, when I unexpectedly began to experience my first and most critical steps toward healing.

That was when I discovered a form of therapy that wasn't taking place in classes. It was taking place outside on the patio. Drawn to laughter and the sound of women telling stories, I ventured outside to the smoking area where the women congregated in between sessions.

From then on I spent all of my free time with the smokers. We smoked first thing in the morning, before breakfast. We smoked in the evenings, sipping orange-juice nightcaps. We sat in white plastic deck chairs and smoked. We smoked two packs a day and had our families bring us cartons of cigarettes—Marlboros, Camels, Newports—on Sunday visits. We smoked and told stories; we smoked and somehow felt better. Some days I didn't talk at all. I just shuffled around in sweats, sat in a chair, and smoked.

I began to think that I might have things in common with these women after all, and I began to pay closer attention in our formal group sessions. We did have things in common: We were women who liked to laugh but had forgotten how. We had suffered similar abuses at the hands of others and of ourselves. We began to offer empathy and encouragement to each other. We had similar interests and hopes for the future. We had pasts we wanted to recover and then let go. At last, I opened myself up to the group, to the counselors, and to the idea of recovery.

My initial assignment was to write my "First Step," an autobiography that included both my personal history and my history with alcohol, and read it out loud to the group. It was easy to admit that I was a heavy drinker who had lost all control of my drinking habits; that I drank to forget who I was, to transform a person I hated into one I considered less vile. Other subjects were not as easy to write about, and I began to remember things I'd long forgotten—or had tried to drink away.

I wrote of a childhood spent reading *Little House on the Prairie* and *Anne of Green Gables*. I recalled the vacations I'd taken with my parents and two sisters, and of the ocean-side condominium we rented each year in Santa Barbara. I recounted the camps I'd attended in the summers and how I played "school" and "store" with my sisters in our front yard, and how we laced up our white leather roller skates with yellow wheels and raced up and down Vallette Street. I wrote about ballet and piano lessons, and of the long jump and sprinting competitions I won at track meets. I wrote at length about my ten years as a gymnast and the ribbons I'd won, about how it felt to be young, muscular, and powerful, to run and tumble and leap and swing and bend and twist and flip and stretch.

I recalled how I'd walked through the hallways of Shuksan Middle School with a group of ten giggling thirteen-year-old girlfriends, secretly memorizing lists of food I'd eaten the day before and repeating them backwards and forwards. Milk, cereal, sandwich, Cheetos, orange, ice cream, chicken, mashed potatoes, milk, popcorn. Popcorn, milk, mashed potatoes, chicken, ice cream, orange, Cheetos, sandwich, cereal, milk. If I messed up the order or forgot a food item, I'd start the list over. I'd repeat the list over and over again until I had it perfect. And then I'd do it again. I also memorized the outfit I wore on a given day. Pink shoes, white socks, miniskirt, pink sweater, pearl earrings, headband. Headband, pearl earrings, pink sweater, miniskirt, white socks, pink shoes.

I remembered how I'd burst into tears one day when Mrs. Wagner handed back my book report and I saw the B+. I sat glued to my chair after the final bell rang until the sting of not receiving an A had dulled. I wrote about how I couldn't fall asleep at night until all the clothes I had worn that day were folded neatly on the floor of the bedroom I shared with my sister. How I'd lie in bed each night convinced my headache was a fatal brain tumor.

I wrote about how I wept as I was pinned down on a blanket and raped in a wooded area of an unfamiliar neighborhood and how something that felt like a knife was rammed into me and how I felt like my insides were being sliced up and about how I bled for a week afterward.

I wrote about how it felt to eat popcorn and fudge and toast and cookies and then stand over a toilet and shove my finger down my throat and twirl it around until I gagged and choked and threw up everything inside of me. I wrote about how it felt when I was done and how tears ran down my face and I blew my nose and cried and checked to make sure my stomach was flat again and that I was empty.

I wrote about how it felt to be trapped inside my bedroom by my boyfriend, who kicked my shins and slapped my face and how my jaw was scratched and so sore I couldn't eat. I wrote about how it felt to be thrown against the futon in the living room and how my shoulder struck the frame on my way down and the bruise hurt so bad I couldn't sleep on it for a week and how the cut by my eye looked.

I filled a blue Mead spiral notebook with my writing. The same words turned up again and again as I wrote: ugly, worthless, pathetic, slut, disgrace, hideous.

It occurred to me that perhaps drinking was not my problem. Perhaps I was my problem.

My transition from girlhood to womanhood had not gone smoothly, and somewhere, I had gotten off track. My body had become a tool for abuse from others and from me. My young adult life had been defined by this abuse and I didn't know who I was outside of it.

Based on the contents of my First Step, my counselor assigned writing projects tailored specifically to my issues. I wrote an "Angry Letter" to the abusive boyfriend and a "Resignation as the Family Fuck-up." I wrote an "Angry Letter to God" and a "List of Losses" I had suffered since my drinking began.

And one day, a miracle happened: I laughed. I sat doubled over in one of the smoking chairs one afternoon and laughed and laughed until tears streamed down my face. I don't even remember why I laughed. I just remember that it was loud, wonderful, and genuine.

I remembered how much I loved writing, and I wrote. I wrote letters to my family and friends, and I continued to write in my Mead notebook. I remembered how much I loved reading, and I read. I sat on the floor by the bookshelf in the common room and read poetry out of a tall book called Spirit Walker. I remembered how much I loved singing, and I sang. I accepted a microphone from my thirty-year-old friend Paige and belted out karaoke songs in the cafeteria to an audience of ten clapping women. During our free time, Paige and I set up blankets and lawn chairs on the roof of the facility, put on our bikinis, and painted our fingernails red beneath the bright afternoon sun.

And finally, on another sunny afternoon, I stood with twenty-three of my newest friends and watched my mom and dad pull up the drive. I knew from a picture that was taken of me the day before that my face was lean, rosy, and tan, and my hair was shiny and healthy. I was delighted to be leaving. I felt refreshed, composed, and at peace. I was eager to put my new skills to use in the life that I had learned how to live all over again, and was confident I would follow the post-rehab program I'd so painstakingly planned out with the counselors.

✦ ✦ ✦ ✦ ✦

The plan was fairly simple. First, break up with my boyfriend. Abstain from alcohol by taking it one day at a time. Dutifully attend AA meetings and collect the coins marking pivotal days of sobriety. Find a sponsor. Go to AA picnics and dances. I was optimistic that life would go reasonably well for me if I did all of these things, and I assumed I'd never drink again.

But what actually happened was this: I never found a sponsor, and I attended about five AA meetings before I decided they weren't for me. Regardless, I didn't want to drink, and I didn't. I didn't drink at my sister's festive wedding that year, nor did I drink at her husband's funeral four months later. I didn't drink when, instead of breaking up with my abusive boyfriend, I married him. I didn't drink during the six months it took me to build up the courage to tell my family what I'd done, nor did I drink when he was convicted of a crime and sentenced to five years in federal prison. I didn't drink during our divorce three years later.

In spite of these events, I was getting my footing. Slowly but surely, I was learning to deal with trauma and tragedy with a grounded and clear mind, finding out exactly what I was capable of handling. I enjoyed being sober and alert as I discovered my boundaries. I understood that I had to actually feel grief and then deal with it, so I wasn't piling new pain on top of old. Although I never joined AA, I enjoyed being sober and alert as I began to create a life for myself, using strategies from rehab and some I developed myself, to strengthen my overall health and my ability to function.

Although I was not overweight, I joined Weight Watchers to learn how to properly manage food and to stop the binge-and-purge cycle that, now that I wasn't drinking, I feared I might turn to as a way to handle grief. And so every Friday morning at eight A.M., I sat in a folding chair among a roomful of women and listened as the group leader explained how to read and understand a nutrition label, and I scribbled down strategies for controlling food portions. I carried all of the pamphlets, charts, and books with me everywhere in a notebook and referenced it day and night for a year.

I turned my little apartment into a place I adored and enjoyed being in by myself. I'd been introduced to the calming and cleansing benefits of scented candles, bubble baths, and lotions—Riviera Sun, Patchouli, Strawberry Champagne—which I added to the nightly ritual to which I held fast. After making and eating a nutritious dinner, soaking in a bubble bath, and applying a sweet lotion, I'd spend the rest of my evening in a recliner, writing ten very honest and detailed, front-and-back pages about my day and what I was facing in my life. I ended my evenings by reading in bed until I happily drifted off into a peaceful sleep, grateful that I was not drunk.

I joined a gym and started each day with an invigorating workout. I attended Jazzercise conventions and participated in the fitness challenges the gym sponsored. I cycled, stepped, and danced until the sweat poured down my face and soaked through my shorts and T-shirt, and the endorphins pumping through my body produced the most natural and passionate high I'd ever experienced. I silently chanted "strong, strong, strong" and "healthy, healthy, healthy" to myself as I stood before the mirror with the free weights and watched my biceps grow and the muscles in my stomach tighten.

I made sure that I was constantly aware of what I was feeling, thinking, and doing. If I had a problem, I identified it immediately and addressed it. Instead of rushing to pour myself a drink, I asked myself a series of questions:

"What is going on in my life at this moment? Am I scared? Angry? Uneasy? Feeling threatened? Nervous? Am I simply having a down day? Am I hungry? Is it the rain? Am I lonely?"

I gave honest answers to the questions and then asked myself what I could do to improve the situation. Should I write? Call someone? Sit down and take a time out? Fix something to eat? What do I need *right now*?

And so, with gleaming new wings and a huge gulp of sunshine-filled fresh air, I burst out of my dark cocoon and flew confidently into the unknown. I had graduated from college years earlier, but wanted to continue my education. I took writing classes and became a correspondent for a national trade magazine. I traveled and met remarkable people on writing assignments, including a particularly kind, healthy, and gentle man whom I married. I entered writing contests and won a couple of awards, and published my work in other magazines.

Eventually, the struggle to decide whether I could or should drink no longer mattered, because I was no longer using alcohol as my coping mechanism. Have a glass of wine, or don't have a glass of wine. The choice was mine, and mine alone. I was now able to make that choice, because I was no longer the lost, scared, traumatized girl of a decade before who had been unable to handle any aspect of her life. Using the tools I'd learned at rehab, and others I picked up along my journey, I'd become the healthy and functioning woman I was meant to be.

One of the things I discovered was that I liked and trusted this new woman. I wanted to care for her.

I do not want to die. I do not want to be drunk. I do not want to stand over a toilet bowl and violently force myself to throw up. I am in no way tempted, after a glass of wine with my husband on a summer evening, to finish off the bottle. The ever-present memory of how things used to be, and the desire to never return to the person I was before, eliminates any and all temptation to abuse. I know that the life I now love—completing a story and sending it off to my editors, waking up early each morning without regret, leaving the gym after another soul-satisfying workout, taking my dogs to obedience class, my relationship with my husband—will not be possible if

I am drunk, or if my heart should finally give out or my esophagus erupt after one more purge. I know that my life of balance and health will cease to exist. And so it is easy to take my glass over to the sink, rinse it out, and set it inside the dishwasher. I'm eager to get on with my evening and already relishing the thought of the next morning, when I will get to wake up once again, savor a mug of coffee, and live one more blessed day.

# My Junior Year Abroad

## Edith Pearlman

Sometimes Nehama got annoyed at me. Fire flashed from her slate-colored eyes. My tenses were mangled, my spelling corrupt, and my penmanship!—a disgrace to civilization.

Most of the time, though, during our twice-a-week Hebrew tutorials, Nehama exercised a quiet vigilance: the very attribute you might expect from a woman who'd emigrated from Berlin to Palestine as a girl, lived under the British Mandate, endured World War II, hailed the Partition, and suffered through five further wars. At seventy-eight, retired from the classroom, she still worked privately in her apartment up the hill from the Jerusalem Theater.

And I? A *jeune fille* of sixty, I lived in an apartment *down* the hill from the Jerusalem Theater. I was taking a Junior Year Abroad. People were disconcerted by the airy claim. *You've left your husband at home?* (This question was accusatory if asked by a man, wistful if asked by a woman.) He's minding the shop, I'd answer. *You're writing a new book?* I'm writing letters only. *Then you're conducting an inner voyage—you're in Israel to get to know yourself!*

I let them think that. But they were wrong; or, to be as precise as Nehama would wish, they were right only in a general sense. We all—wherever we are—make daily voyages of self-discovery. I had come here to get to know not myself, but

Jerusalem. Why had I chosen that mysterious place? My pious grandfather had invoked its holy name; my Socialist uncle had scorned its political rigidity; my fashionable cousin wondered how, in a world that contained Paris, I could live in a city where nobody owned a necktie. It was time to form my own opinion.

◆ ◆ ◆ ◆ ◆

I was learning the city by tramping its streets. The map was my syllabus. My textbook was the local tradespeople, immigrants and their offspring who had been pouring into the country since its inception. I bought fruit from a Moroccan with a corrugated face and the manners of a correct Parisian. I bought pickles from an energetic Hungarian. A Romanian sold me bread. I got milk and newspapers from the nearby *macolet*, the store that sells everything. Its youthful proprietor had come from Russia a decade ago. This young man also supplied me with wine, a bottle every other day. To polish off a bottle of wine in forty-eight hours is not to have an uncontrollable habit; still, after a few months, I became defensive. "I want you to know," I said while paying for a Tuesday–Wednesday fix, "that I buy a lot of wine because I have a lot of company." He looked at me intently. "I'm so glad," he said, with Chekhovian economy.

I was dispatching the wine myself, of course, as both of us well knew. I never had a lot of company, and in the beginning I didn't have any at all. I was always out, widening my research. Wearing my customary pants and shirt, I wandered through the humble Katoman neighborhood. Respectfully donning a dress, I glided into the courtyards of God-fearing Mea Sharim. Back in drag, I lounged in hummus stalls on the crumbling Jaffa Road. I entered every shop and exchanged a sentence or two with every shopkeeper, from scholars who sold religious books to scrap ironware dealers and importers of Italian tiles.

When I wasn't poking my nose into other people's businesses or disturbing the dust of ancient alleys, I sat in gardens, eating figs out of a paper bag. I chose quasi-public gardens—the grounds of the Leper Hospital, for instance—and small private ones, their gates forgetfully ajar, like the fragrant forecourt of the Pontifical Institute.

I rode the buses. With determination learned from Israelis, I joined the bus queue even after threats, even after incidents. Scores of routes wind through the city. I'd board a bus on a whim and get off if I glimpsed an arbor, or a curve of pale stairs, or if a fellow passenger happened to mention some unpublicized place—archives open only every other Thursday, say. In this haphazard manner I managed to visit almost every section of Jerusalem. I went to Ramot Polin, where pentagon-walled apartments create a peculiar beehive effect. "We love it here," a kerchiefed woman assured me. Gilo is stiff with neo-Oriental arches. East Jerusalem is unroofed houses and backyard chickens. I took one bus to a convent selling wine and bread; I took another to a mall selling T-shirts and towels. In a café in a suburb I listened to Louis Armstrong on a jukebox. At the University on Mount Scopus I joined authentic Junior-Year-Abroads at the library. When I tried to withdraw materials I was asked who I thought I was. But I was grudgingly allowed to read the books on the premises.

Meeting people was a snap. Women alone—particularly women of a certain age—arouse interest and invite protection (women in pairs, by contrast, seem unapproachable). Some people became friends. Some I encountered only once, but unforgettably. In the Arab quarter of the Old City, a shop-keeper showed me slippers that I ended up not buying. He then invited me to have tea. I said no, thanks. He said: When you don't buy my slippers you are expressing a preference, but when you refuse my tea you are insulting me. I drank his tea, and took in also his lesson in civility. In the Armenian quarter, one languid afternoon, the cook of a tiny restaurant told me of the rich insular life of Armenians in Jerusalem. He revealed nothing about his own life, leaving me free to invent several unauthorized biographies.

And loneliness, too, became a friend: a slightly down-in-the-mouth visitor to be pampered with Brie, and a detective novel, and a refreshing shower of tears.

I telephoned someone whose name I'd been given. She asked me to a party. There I met the eager young organizer of a volunteer program in an Arab school just outside the city. "Join us!" he said. And so, most Wednesdays found me in the playground of that underequipped school, getting to know the children and several brisk female teachers and one harsh male, who indicated he'd rather be anywhere but here—did I have connections in New York?

A leftist introduced me to her ardent friends; I marched in demonstrations, learning political science on the hoof. One evening, waiting for a concert to begin, I fell into conversation with a retired diplomat who gave me an impromptu lecture on the importance of water to the Middle East. It was more important, he told me, his blue eyes looking through me as if *I* were water, than democracy, than autonomy, than human rights! Then, remembering his diplomatic manners, he invited me to a party, where I met . . . and so it went, until, every so often, in order to return hospitality, I had to buy *two* bottles of wine at the *macolet*.

✦ ✦ ✦ ✦ ✦

It is a Friday afternoon in late spring. I have joined the weekly procession of Franciscan monks along the Via Dolorosa, stopping at each Station of the Cross. We stop also at the intersection of the Via Dolorosa and El Wad Street; we must make way for the crowd of worshippers rushing pell-mell from prayers at the mosque. For a moment I am in the thick of battle, Christianity warring with the Infidel. Then the Muslims—who are only going home for dinner—pass through the square, and the Franciscans advance to the next station.

I break away, and leave the Old City through the Jaffa Gate. In modern West Jerusalem shops are closing; buses are

completing their last runs; people are carrying flowers; a gentleman in gabardine with a cell phone tucked under his earlock is
enjoying the final cigarette of the week. The city is closing upon
itself. Tomorrow there will be no buses and no entertainment.
The shutters of the stores will be down. I resent the Orthodox
stranglehold on city life, but at the same time I welcome the
sweet melancholy that descends every Sabbath.

Meanwhile it is still Friday. I take my usual detour to a leafy
cul-de-sac off the Street of the Prophets, where a plaque says that
the poet Rachel once made her home. I'd heard Rachel's name
before this year abroad, though I had not read her work; but I had
not even *heard* of Boris Schatz, Benjamin of Tudela, David Elroi.
Now I walk on streets that bear the names of these men. I can
recite their histories because I searched them out in the library
I'm allowed to read in. Boris Schatz founded the Bezalel
Academy of Art and Design. Benjamin of Tudela was a Spaniard
who visited Jerusalem in the twelfth century. David Elroi
rebelled against the caliph.

And Rachel? She came to Palestine in 1909, at nineteen,
the age of many college juniors, and she died at forty-one of
tuberculosis. In her poems she is "alone in a vast land." She too
has become a kind of friend.

❖ ❖ ❖ ❖ ❖

"Your grammar is slightly less muddled," praised Nehama at our
last meeting. Her eyes seemed more like velvet than slate.

"I'll miss you," I said: meaning Nehama; meaning Rachel;
meaning shopkeepers, monks, gardeners; neighbors, bus-riders,
children; Talmudists, secularists, fanatics. They made up a spirited,
enlightening faculty, and they didn't spring a single quiz.

# My Own True North

## Julie Seiler

Tonight is my last night along the White River in Vermont, and in the darkening spring woods the steady rain penetrates all the layers of my clothing, right down to my bones. As a whitewater guide, I can usually ignore dreary weather, cold water, and exhaustion. But tonight I am shivering and spent, as is everyone with me.

Misha, my co-leader, and I have been leading a group of six advanced paddlers aged ten to sixteen along this mountain river for a week. We've pulled our canoes out of the fast, green water up into the underbrush so as not to disturb the wildness of the river for any others who may pass this way tonight, though I doubt anyone would choose to paddle this evening. It is getting late, and hauling our soaked, heavy gear up to our campsite is only the beginning of our evening's chores. The tent and tarp must be pitched, the kitchen must be assembled, and I must search the dripping forest to find dry firewood, something that seems as unlikely as the journey that brought me here, to Vermont, in the first place.

There was a time when the only fires I experienced were those safely enclosed behind glass in the posh restaurants where I dined as a rising associate in a Baltimore law firm. I would often become mesmerized, losing myself in the dancing flames when I should have been paying attention to the "important" issues being discussed by the partners and other associates around the table. It was confusing to be so drawn to the fire, rather than to the job I had worked so hard to attain. I was proud of myself for having gotten so far, for finishing in the top 5 percent of my law-school class. I had pulled all-nighters, missed holidays, neglected my social life, and amassed tens of thousands of dollars in school loans. I knew I should stop gazing at the fire, join the discussion, and get back to work in my office high above the Baltimore harbor, with its wall of windows, a secretary I could buzz, and a high-backed leather chair that swiveled.

Instead, one afternoon, I went for a walk and ended up buying myself a pewter bookmark that quoted the writer George Eliot: "It is never too late to be what you might have been."

On the plateau above the river, Misha calls out that he has found a spot for our camp. He is the Russian-born director of the nonprofit wilderness education school I am working for: Kroka Expeditions, whose motto is "Where consciousness meets wilderness." Misha speaks quietly and deliberately, like the forest. I think of him as a large basswood tree, his mind as open as the branches, his words falling like leaves, importantly, into the world. Though he is only in his late thirties, he seems to me to be an old soul. He is handsome, with the lean yet muscular body of a gymnast and strong, weathered hands. His eyes, azure blue and wide, contain both an abundance of wisdom and a twinkle of mischief that matches his broad, almost goofy smile. He sports perpetual bed-head, because he believes "hair is self-cleaning," and most of his clothing is torn on both the left shoulder and the right knee from his pattern of kneeling to make fires and carrying boats. As he leads most of the group in carrying our gear, I take a few paddlers farther up the mountain to find dry wood.

At my first Associates Luncheon at the firm, I sat at a long conference table with my fellow associates and a few senior partners. We were debating the settlement value of a case in which we were defending a home for developmentally disabled adults that was being sued by one of the residents for the horrific burns he had suffered all over his legs and genitals from a scalding bath. His attorney sought a large settlement based on the victim's pain and suffering and "loss of consortium," a generally lucrative claim because it means that a person can't have sex anymore. We went around the room, each associate stating what he or she thought was a fair settlement amount and why. The figures were astoundingly low, and I found the rationale even more frightening: As one man put it, "The loss of consortium claim is worthless—the guy's a retard, he isn't going to have anyone to have sex with, anyway!"

Thank God for my fancy lawyer chair. If I heard a partner walking down the hall, I spun to the books and the briefs, looking busy and consumed with work. Partner gone. Spin to the sun and seagulls. What might I be? If only I could find the answer as fast as I could spin in my chair.

After a year and a half of having my nose pressed against the glass, I quit, moved to Washington, D.C., and became a bike messenger, of all things. Maybe it wasn't what I might have been, but it was the furthest thing from what I was.

✦ ✦ ✦ ✦ ✦

"Education," according to the poet William Butler Yeats, "is not the filling of a pail but the lighting of a fire." When I was a child, my family lived in Germany and we spent our vacations camping out of a beat-up white Volkswagen van, our trusted, rusted, busted bus, as a way of seeing Europe on the cheap. My parents slept in the back, my sister in the coveted pop-top loft, and me in a cot that spanned the front seat. Attached to the sliding side door of the van was a tent so large that my six-foot-four father could easily stand up in it. We stayed in comfortable campgrounds in France, Italy, and Switzerland—campgrounds with hot tubs and gourmet restaurants. We were hardly roughing it.

One spring, when I was about ten, my father and I went on a camping trip to the Black Forest. It was unusually cold, so we brought along our toboggan in hopes of finding enough snow for some sledding. What we didn't expect was a full-fledged snowstorm, a storm that dumped over a foot of snow on us overnight and made the roof of the tent sag down so low that I had to duck to get inside it. The next morning, right up the hill from our campsite, we found a narrow trail to sled on. My father lay down on the old orange toboggan and I climbed on top and wrapped my arms around his neck. I still remember the smell of the wet wool of his Army parka as we careened down the hill. At one point the sled hit a rock, stopping both my father and the sled, and I continued on, airborne. I ended up face-first in the snow, exhilarated and scared and so cold that I cried. On that trip, I experienced the outdoors in a new way, and I discovered the beauty of the forest and the pain of the cold. (I also relished the happiness of getting to sleep in the pop-top for once.)

I began collecting outdoor adventures the way some people collect old coins. Among my favorites: paddling over a sapphire waterfall at the headwaters of the Actopan River in the mountains of central Mexico; seeing a black bear and her cubs at close range while hiking in the Appalachians; scuba diving among Caribbean reef sharks in the Bahamas; surf kayaking the turbulent, wintry waters of the Atlantic shore; awakening at 3 A.M. on Mount Shuksan's glacier beneath the glory of the Northern Lights. Every so often I pull a memory out of my collection, dust it off, and hold it in my hand.

Even during my time as a bike messenger, an interlude that quickly depleted my savings and forced me back into law for four more years, I felt the ache in my legs and the wind against my face as I pedaled down the grimy city streets. Maybe I was just spinning my wheels, the way I had spun my fancy chair, but at least I was in motion.

While the rest of the group splits wood and sets up the tent, Chris and I carry the large cooking pots down the hill to gather our evening's water. We take a different route down to the river so we don't trample a path in the fragile vegetation; later in the season these banks will be covered by delicate fiddlehead ferns that we'll sprinkle with olive oil and salt for a wilderness salad. We dip carefully from the river, gently tilting the lips of the pots to avoid taking in river silt. I look out over the dusky White, one of the last free-flowing rivers in Vermont, the water slapping and hiccupping as it careens through the boulder garden just upstream from our campsite.

When I am in my kayak, hips snug in the cockpit, I am wearing the boat. I am the river. Paddling a difficult rapid reduces my world bit by bit, to a river, then a rapid, and finally to a moment, with room for nothing else. There is only me, trying to figure out how to best use the current to make my way. Even when all the water is rushing toward a deadly obstacle—a downed tree straining the river, or a dangerously undercut rock—it is only by using the current, not fighting it, that I can avoid the trap.

I notice the feel of my paddle slicing through the water, in at my toes and out at my hips, rotating my torso, my breathing matching the rhythm of my strokes. The early-morning fog whispers low across the river; it will later give way to the smell of sun-baked boulders. I try to remember to look at where I want to go, not at what I want to avoid. Where the eye goes, the boat will follow. Lifting my edge, I skid into an eddy. I am tossed upside-down in a hole, like a lone tennis shoe thumping around in the dryer. Rolling back up, I'm eager to see where on the river I am, not knowing which direction I'll be facing when I finally surface. I relax at the end of the rapid, as the lens backs out, zooms out, wide angle, and my world becomes the river, the mountains, the sky. It is as close as I ever come to having religion, to knowing God.

It was all these rivers rushing through my veins, the current pillowing up on me, that eventually dislodged me from my indoor job for good.

I first stumbled upon Kroka Expeditions through an Internet search for a summer whitewater kayaking job. Misha hired me for a two-week expedition to northern New Hampshire and Maine. We paddled by canoe and kayak, up the Androscoggin River and across choppy Lake Umbagog, to the mouth of the Rapid River. We camped on a tiny, wooded island and spent our days paddling the whitewater of the Rapid, swimming in the lake, and making primitive shelters in the forest.

The expedition was incredible, and completely different from anything I had experienced before. Misha does more than just impress his values about the earth and community living upon the kids; he encourages them to figure things out for themselves, and to be free to disagree. The students don't wear watches on our trips, and the "what time is it?" question is always answered with "a good time for kayaking"—or hiking, or cooking, or whatever activity is going on at that time. After a while, the kids start answering the question for each other, and eventually they stop asking.

What I found most striking about the trips is the space—both physical and emotional. There is space to have free time, to watch the stars, to burn the dinner, to cut yourself while carving, to get the entire group lost, to make mistakes. As a result, the students are responsible, capable, thinking beings, but still kids, which is wonderful. And, as an instructor, I gained far more than just a paycheck for playing outside with these students: I affected their lives and they affected mine. I am both a teacher and a student.

Years ago I thought that environmental law might be the answer to my career dilemma and that I would be happy using my legal skills to protect the wild places I love. What was missing from that picture was the experience of *being* outside, of living a life connected to nature. I didn't want to spend eighty hours a week in pantyhose, fighting an uphill battle to protect the environment. Stealing bits and pieces of wilderness time on weekends and holidays was not enough, and I hated watching the passing of the seasons from behind office glass.

When I moved to Vermont at the end of March, it was warming up in Washington but there was still four feet of snow on the ground in Vermont. My first task was to help finish the new office being built on the second floor of the barn. My desk, which I sanded myself, is made of a salvaged door with tree branches, the bark still on, as legs. I don't miss my leather lawyer-chair at all.

✦ ✦ ✦ ✦ ✦

The fire must be started, and Lauren, one of our two cooks for the day, carefully begins to prepare it. She works intently, patiently peeling the many layers of a piece of birch bark into papery-thin strips before rolling them into curls between the palms of her hands. She sets two bunches of kindling on end, leaning against each other, and sets the nest of birch bark in the space below. She strikes a match on a rock, lights the bark, and leans down low to the ground to blow life into the tiny flame. The fire catches the kindling and flares up for a moment before it begins to die out. Misha kneels down and tells her, "Don't stare at it, feed it. If you are not afraid of it, it will not burn you."

Before Kroka, I worked for two seasons at a camp in the Shenandoahs where D.C. private schools send students for "wilderness adventures." It was sterile, pre-packaged, canned adventure—we herded the kids through high ropes courses, man-made climbing walls, and trust falls. Even a simple pleasure like cooking s'mores over a campfire was over-instructed, with the assistant director giving a nightly s'mores speech: "Tonight we're having s'mores—if you can be mature and follow directions. So, everyone (Not right now! Sit down!) is going to go into the woods and find a stick—and not just any stick. Hold out your arm. The stick must be longer than your arm. Hold out your pinky; it must be thicker than your pinky. Hold out your thumb; it must be thinner than your thumb. When you find your stick, come sit on the benches around the fire pit and wait for your marshmallow to be handed out. Do not wave your stick around—keep it pointed toward the ground at all times." It was as if the speech had been drafted by a personal-injury lawyer.

Over the hot fire, a pot of water boils for our dinner. We are having *rababu*, a favorite Kroka dish of rice, lentils, tamari, and cheese. We'll eat it with the spoons we've carved out of cedar and hollowed out by burning the bowls of them with hot coals from the fire on the first night of our trip. I'm thankful now for my improvisational culinary skills, developed during my underemployed days as I discovered the joys of being penniless. I dig through our food buckets, pulling out onions, cabbage, several cloves of garlic, leftover kasha from breakfast, cream cheese—every leftover item from the past few days that could possibly be added to the stew. It is dark in the forest and we are cold and hungry.

Shortly after accepting Misha's offer of year-round employment, I went on a paddling trip to Pennsylvania's Youghiogheny River with my friend Jaime. Over beers at Uncle Tucker's Pub, I told him about my plans. Jaime, who owns a successful business, couldn't believe I was leaving behind the financial security of the legal profession for a guiding job. "I couldn't do it," he said. "Have you considered sticking it out as a lawyer for another ten years or so, saving your money so you can comfortably pursue an outdoor career later?"

My answer came surprisingly easily: I said, "Life is too short for that."

I eventually became more comfortable handling questions about my career change from status-conscious strangers, and even from my mother. "Isn't it about time," she wondered, "that you stopped playing in the water and got a real job?" When going out with friends, I found myself tuning out during discussions of the features on someone's luxury car or the expensive Spanish tile one of them had ordered for her home. I didn't feel judgmental toward these people, just disconnected and hungry for something more real.

✦ ✦ ✦ ✦ ✦

The steady rain has tapered off to a light drizzle as we finish washing our dishes. I toss a handful of fragrant hemlock needles into a pot of water for our nightly "tea" and we pass around some squares of chocolate for dessert. Though we're exhausted, we're not quite ready for bed yet. Something draws us closer to the fire, something beyond its warmth. No one wants to leave until the embers die out—it would be like leaving a show early. Standing around the fire, we begin to make music—without instruments. One person is clapping, another clucks his tongue, one girl swishes her hands along her rain pants in time with the beat. I feel blessed to be here, part of this unique tribe.

I am lucky to have two homes these days, one in the wilderness and one back in civilization, in Putney, a village of 2,000. The landscape of Vermont speaks to me, with the humpbacked Green Mountains growling softly and the West River jostling its way to its confluence with the Connecticut River. There is a slowness here that I love, with people moving in accordance with the flow of the seasons rather than abruptly bumping up against them. It sustains my need for a sense of place and community, a need created, perhaps, by a childhood spent moving from place to place every few years. Once, while hitchhiking after an afternoon of kayaking on the West River, I met a man who, like me, had moved here from Washington, D.C. "There's no slower place to raise children," he said.

My home, when I am not in the forest, is a yurt attached to Lynne and Misha's house. Modern yurts are based on traditional Mongolian dwellings, which are true mobile homes: big top–shaped tents made of yak skin that can be disassembled and transported from place to place. Lynne and Misha's yurt is twenty feet in diameter, with canvas walls stretched over a lattice frame and wooden supports for the pointed roof. It has hardwood floors, a kitchen area with sink and stove and a separate bathroom with a composting toilet. An old wood-burning stove in the middle provides heat and light.

I love my yurt home. I love its thin walls through which the calls of the owls and other night creatures enter. I love the shadows of the big maple trees swaying above the roof. The lightest rain shower sounds like a downpour on the canvas roof, and when it really storms it is impossible to carry on a conversation without yelling. I love the sound of the wind as it approaches like a wave, building up on the mountain, roaring toward the yurt, and then fading away down toward the creek.

I arrived here with only a carload of belongings, leaving the rest in Virginia until later in the season. I had a trunk full of clothes, a few books and photos, and one bowl, one mug, and two sets of silverware. It was only a fraction of what I owned, but I needed nothing else.

I remember a cross-stitch from my childhood that said, "Home is where the Army sends us." I wonder, in leaving my old life, whether I have run from something, or toward something. Perhaps it doesn't matter. By moving north, to Vermont, to Kroka, I have discovered my own true north and my home.

I was settling into my new life in Vermont, thinking that I had avoided, or experienced and worked through, an early midlife crisis, when, to my surprise, I learned that my midlife crisis might actually be late. The day after I drove the rest of my belongings from Virginia to Putney in a U-Haul, I was diagnosed with advanced cancer. I felt as though the rug had been pulled out from under me, just when I had finally fit all the pieces of my life together in a meaningful way. I had to return to Virginia for treatment, leaving behind Kroka and my new life—at least for a while.

Soon after my diagnosis, I received a package from all the students from the previous summer's Paddlers' Journey Up North. Lauren had made sketches of all of the paddlers, and wrote me a letter that read in part, "This Earth has been so much better since you lived in its woods and paddled its waters, and we all love you for that, but we also love you for all the smiles and laughs, caring and teasing, fun and games, and all that makes you you. That is what we love now and will always love because we know we will live it again."

✦ ✦ ✦ ✦ ✦

*Snap, clap-clap-clap . . . swish.* We go on like that for a long time, each of us quietly keeping rhythm in our own way, illuminated by the flickering reds and oranges of the campfire. As the fiery embers begin to cool in the night air, our music slowly fades out. We quietly file into the old round canvas tent, where our damp socks and long johns will steam on a line overhead as we sleep tightly, bicycle-spoked, around the woodstove.

# Acknowledgments

I would like to thank everyone who helped get the word out to the wonderful writers who submitted essays for this book, including Alev Croutier. Thanks, too, to my daughter Christina Henry de Tessan for coming up with the perfect title. My especial gratitude goes to Ingrid Emerick, whose ideas for the book, from conception to final editing, were constructive and inspiring—and all expressed in emails as brief and incisive as haiku. Finally, a paean of thanks to Pamela de Villaine, who made my own transformation into *une vraie parisienne* possible.

# About the Contributors

**B. Susan Bauer** was born in England and grew up in Ohio. She studied English at Smith College and the University of Tennessee. She is married to a clergyman and is the mother of two adult children. For eleven years she was administrator of the research ethics board at the University of North Carolina School of Medicine in Chapel Hill. From 1997 to 2003, she taught English in Namibia and Ghana, where she and her husband served as Lutheran missionaries. She lives in North Carolina and is writing a collection of essays about her experiences in Africa.

**Bonnie Lee Black**, an honors graduate of Columbia University's writing program, was a writer/editor and caterer in New York City before joining the Peace Corps at fifty and serving in Gabon, central Africa, for two years (1996–1998). She now lives in northern New Mexico, teaches English at UNM-Taos, and is working on a book of essays (with recipes) titled "How to Cook a Crocodile," about her experience in Gabon.

Born in Chicago, **Susanne Holly Brent** earned a journalism degree from Metropolitan State College in Denver. She has worked as a newspaper reporter and freelance writer and taught adult refugees English. She lives in Phoenix with her husband. While working on her novel, she works part-time as a waitress. Recent publishing credits include a short story in *Cup of Comfort for Christmas* and another in the *Cooweescoowee*, a literary journal from Rogers State University in Oklahoma. An inspirational piece for writers will be included in the *Writer's Byline Calendar of 2005*.

A native of northern Germany, **Dorothee Danzmann** lived and worked as an independent bookseller in Hamburg for most of her adult life before moving south three years ago to a cottage high on Mount Pelion in Greece. She works as a translator and finds the time and inspiration to write.

**Gunter David** was a reporter on major city newspapers for twenty-five years. He was nominated for a Pulitzer Prize by the *Evening Bulletin* in Philadelphia. Following the demise of the *Bulletin* he changed careers and obtained a master's degree in family therapy from Hahnemann University. Shortly after graduation, Ivan Boszormenyi-Nagy, M.D., head of the program and a key figure in the family therapy movement, took Gunter into his practice. Additionally, Gunter became a senior administrator in the Employee Assistance Program of Johnson & Johnson, where he provides therapy and addiction counseling to employees and their families.

**Penelope S. Duffy**, Ph.D., lives in Rochester, Minnesota. Under the last name Myers, she had a twenty-five-year career in neurologically based communication disorders. In 2001, on the publication of *A Stockbridge Homecoming* (Bright Sky Press), she took up creative writing full time, and has since published essays and stories. Her story about surviving a storm at sea is in *Steady as She Goes* (Seal Press, 2003). She has a forthcoming book titled *Lost and Found: A Journey Through Grief*, and is working on a novel that takes place in Nova Scotia against the backdrop of schooner fishing and World War I.

**Juliet Eastland** lives in New York City, where she writes in her office and plays the piano in her living room. Her writing has appeared on indiebride.com, blacktable.com, and knotmag.com. She recently composed the music for *Andromania: Men/ Sex/ Madness*, presented at New York's HERE Theater.

**Marie Campagna Franklin** is a writer and editor with the *Boston Globe* whose articles on education, travel, home, and garden have appeared for twenty years. A former college professor of journalism and communication, Campagna Franklin lives in Newton and Chatham, Massachusetts, with her husband and two teenage daughters. Her passions include travel, cooking, and home restoration.

**Rita Golden Gelman** is the author of more than seventy children's books, including *Inside Nicaragua*, which was one of the ALA's Best Young Adult Books of 1988, and *More Spaghetti, I Say!*, a staple in every first-grade classroom. She is also the author of *Tales of a Female Nomad: Living at Large in the World* (Crown, 2001). As a nomad, Rita has no permanent address. Her most recent encampments have been in Mexico and New York City.

**Paola Gianturco** is author/photographer of *Celebrating Women* (powerHouse, 2004) and co-author/photographer of *In Her Hands: Craftswomen Changing the World*. Her photographs have been exhibited at the United Nations, the U.S. Senate, the Field Museum in Chicago, and the International Museum of Women in San Francisco. She has chaired the Board of the Crafts Center. In an earlier life, she founded the Gianturco Company, which consulted about glass ceiling issues, marketing, and corporate communications; she was previously executive vice president of Saatchi and Saatchi's Corporate Communications Group; senior vice president of Hall and Levine Advertising; and public relations director for Joseph Magnin.

**Geoff Griffin** is a graduate of Pomona College and received his law degree from the University of Southern California. He is a sportswriter for the *Spectrum*, a daily newspaper in St. George, Utah. He lives with his wife, Lisa, and their two children in a small rural town where Lisa runs the health care clinic.

Ken Hruby came to the arts late, after a twenty-one-year career as an infantry officer. Upon completion of his military service, he attended the School of the Museum of Fine Arts, Boston, where he focused on sculpture. His critically acclaimed work has been widely shown and is included in several private and public collections, including the National Vietnam Veterans Art Museum in Chicago. He was the recipient of grants from the New England Foundation for the Arts and the Massachusetts Cultural Council. He works in a variety of materials, including installation, kinetics, video, and photography. Ken teaches at the Museum School and maintains a studio in Boston.

Gina Hyams lived in Mexico with her husband and young daughter from January 17, 1997, to January 19, 2001. There she worked as a correspondent for Fodor's travel publications and contributed articles to Salon.com and *Newsweek*. Now based in Oakland, California, she is the author of *Day of the Dead Box*; *Mexicasa: The Enchanting Inns and Haciendas of Mexico*; *Incense: Mystery, Rituals, Lore*; and the forthcoming *In a Mexican Garden* and *Paific Spas* (all published by Chronicle Books).

Phyllis Johnston has been a public affairs consultant for more than twenty-five years, writing radio and television ad scripts, position papers, and articles on a range of public policy issues. Her freelance writing has been published in the *Boston Globe*, *Campaigns & Elections*, and a number of technical journals. She lives in Sarasota, Florida.

**Li Miao Lovett** stopped being a good Chinese daughter in her twenties. She gave up well-paying jobs to work with at-risk youth, pursue writing, and advocate for the environment. A lover of mountains and deserts, she has hiked six hundred miles of the Appalachian Trail, and has backpacked in the deserts of California, Nevada, and Utah. As a writer and journalist, she tells stories of people who want to preserve the environment, their communities, and their ethnic heritage. Her work has been published in the *San Francisco Chronicle*, *Sierra Club Planet*, and *Taiwan News*, and broadcast on KQED public radio. She has begun working on a book about the experiences of refugees who return to their homelands.

**Edith Pearlman** has published more than 150 stories in national magazines, literary journals, anthologies, and online publications. Her work has appeared in *Best American Short Stories*, the *O. Henry Prize Collection*, *Best Short Stories from the South*, and *The Pushcart Collection*. Her first collection of stories, *Vaquita*, won the Drue Heinz Prize; her second, *Love Among the Greats*, won the Spokane Prize. Her third, *How to Fall*, will be published by Sarabande Press in February 2005. It won the Mary McCarthy Prize. Pearlman's short essays have appeared in the *Atlantic Monthly*, *Smithsonian*, *Preservation*, Salon.com, and *Yankee*.

**Melissa Peterson** participated in her high school's literary magazine and wrote articles for the school newspaper. She attended a literary conference in Atlanta, Georgia, and was selected to write updates for a national service organization's monthly newsletter. She finished her term of service at the program mentioned in the essay and received her scholarship. She recently made the Dean's List at Olympic College and ran for A.S.O.C. vice president. She is working on two book-length manuscripts.

**Maria Antonieta Osornio Ramirez**, known as Tony, was a parachutist in the Mexican army when, due to high winds, her parachute collapsed and she fell sixty feet to the ground, pulverizing the vertebrae in her neck. After three years in a military hospital, with the help of two female therapists, she regained some movement in her body. Today, she is able to dress, eat, write, and walk short distances on crutches. In 1997 she and Dr. Martha Babb founded Fundacion Humanista de Ayuda a Discapacitados (Humanist Foundation to Help the Disabled), to give hope and psychological help to others suffering from physical incapacity.

Until 2003, **Claudia Rowe**, an East Coast native, had never spent more than a few weeks west of the Hudson River. A journalist and longtime contributor to the *New York Times*, she had also written for *Cooking Light*, A&E's *Biography*, and other magazines. But a summer spent in Washington State convinced Rowe to put her belongings in storage and drive across the country to see what life, and writing, might be like on the Left Coast. She lives in Seattle now and has no regrets.

**Jennifer Karuza Schile** is a regular correspondent for *National Fisherman*, and has also been published in *Pacific Fishing* and *Alaska Fisherman's Journal*. In 2002, she was awarded an honorable mention in the memoir category of the Writer's Digest Writing Competition. She graduated from Western Washington University in 1997 with an English degree. Originally from Bellingham, Washington, she now lives in Seattle with her infinitely patient and kind husband, George, and their two much-loved dogs.

**Julie Seiler** left her law career to pursue her love of whitewater paddling and to share her passion for the outdoors with children. She divides her time between writing in Virginia and guiding wilderness expeditions in Vermont. Her work has appeared in *The Potomac Review*.

At age fifty-three, **Liz Seymour**, a Smith College graduate and freelance writer with credits in *Better Homes & Gardens*, *Traditional Home*, and the *New York Times*, exchanged a settled, nuclear-family existence for life in a six-person anarchist collective in Greensboro, North Carolina. Liz continues to write for travel and decorating magazines, but spends a greater part of her time working on community projects, writing an account of her recent life, and enjoying the company of her two adult daughters, who have patiently seen her through a series of sometimes baffling life changes. Her younger daughter is taking her train-hopping for her fifty-fifth birthday.

**Elizabeth Simpson** has published three nonfiction books: *The Perfection of Hope: Journey Back to Health* (M&S, 1997), *One Man at a Time: Confessions of a Serial Monogamist* (M&S, 2000), and *From Forest to Plains* (Guinness, 1975). She has written biographical entries on Canadian authors for *The Literary Atlas* (Greenwood Press) and has had two stories aired on CBC radio's "First Person Singular": *Dressed for Suicide* (2002) and *Puppy Love* (2003). She lives in Victoria, reviews for *Monday Magazine* and the *Globe and Mail*, and has recently completed a draft of her novel, "Under the Joker's Wing."

**Alice Steinbach**, whose work at the *Baltimore Sun* was awarded a Pulitzer Prize for feature writing, has been a freelance writer since 1999. Currently a Woodrow Wilson Visiting Fellow, she has taught journalism and writing at Princeton University, Washington and Lee University, and Loyola College. She is the author of *Without Reservations: The Travels of an Independent Woman* (Random House, 2000) and, most recently, *Educating Alice: Adventures of a Curious Woman* (Random House, 2004). She lives in Baltimore.

**Sachin V. Waikar** masqueraded (legally) as a psychologist and business-strategy consultant before becoming a write-at-home dad. His work appears in *Toddler* (Seal Press, 2003) and *Esquire* (okay, so it was just a letter) and has won the Mona Schreiber Prize for Humorous Non-Fiction. Sachin's novel-in-stories of East Indians and Indo-Americans is under review by several publishers. He lives with his family in the western suburbs of Chicago.

# About the Editor

Joan Chatfield-Taylor began her writing career at the *San Francisco Chronicle*, where she was a fashion editor and feature writer. As a freelance writer she has contributed to magazines ranging from *Allure* and *Architectural Digest* to *Food & Wine* and *Town and Country*. She has written several books, including a cookbook, a garden guide, and two books on the opera. She lives in San Francisco.

# Selected Titles from Seal Press

*Far From Home: Father-Daughter Travel Adventures* edited by Wendy Knight. $15.95, 1-58005-105-7. Honest essays by both fathers and daughters offer inspiration and insight into how travel can affect this tender and complex relationship.

*Making Connections: Mother-Daughter Travel Adventures* edited by Wendy Knight. $16.95, 1-58005-087-5. What happens when mother and daughter step out of the complacent familiarity of routine into uncharted territory? This collection offers ample inspiration and insight into how travel affects this most complex and intimate of relationships.

*Going Alone: Women's Adventures in the Wild* edited by Susan Fox Rogers. $15.95, 1-58005-106-5. Explores the many ways women find fulfillment, solace, and joy when they head out alone into the great outdoors.

*Expat: Women's True Tales of Life Abroad* edited by Christina Henry de Tessan. $16.95, 1-58005-070-0. An illuminating collection of women's writing that answers the question travelers so often ask: What would it be like to live here?

*France, A Love Story: Women Write about the French Experience* edited by Camille Cusumano. $15.95, 1-58005-115-4. Two dozen women describe the country they love and why they fell under its spell.

*A Woman Alone: Travel Tales from Around the Globe* edited by Faith Conlon, Ingrid Emerick and Christina Henry de Tessan. $15.95, 1-58005-059-X. A collection of rousing stories by women who travel solo.

Seal Press publishes a variety of fiction and nonfiction by women writers. Please visit our website at www.sealpress.com.